CONTENTS

ACKNOWLEDGMENTS

Acknowledgment is due to Methuen & Co. for permission to reproduce the home reading card from A. Griffiths and D. Hamilton *Parent, Teacher, Child: Working Together in Children's Learning* (Methuen, 1984); and to Ruth Merttens and Jeffrey Vass of The Polytechnic of North London for permission to reproduce examples of IMPACT materials.

Many have contributed towards the preparation of this book. I wish to thank the following for their personal communications on particular topics discussed in the text: Liz Allen of the Advisory Centre for Education; Diana Daly of Education Alert; Sue Hodgson of the Campaign for the Advancement of State Education; Martyn Long, Educational Psychologist for Norfolk County Council; Ruth Merttens of The Polytechnic of North London; Fred Naylor of The Parental Alliance for Choice in Education; Chris Miles of Laycock Primary School, Islington; and Sue Traverso of Sutton CASE.

My thinking on aspects of parental involvement in schools has been clarified by the many discussions I have had with heads and teachers on BEd in-service and MA courses at the Roehampton Institute, and I would like to mention especially Diane Norman who made such helpful comments on parts of an early draft. I owe a very special thanks to Paul Brannan, my wife Anne and elder son Peter, who read the whole text, provided important corrections, and made such helpful criticisms.

INTRODUCTION AND OVERVIEW

During the last decade or so, parents, teachers, politicians and the general public have shown a growing awareness of the importance of parental involvement in schools. Parents now matter! Of course, parents have always played an important part in their children's education: but their potential to do so is now more generally recognised and welcomed by shools, while their right to participate in schools' decision-making processes has assumed unprecedented political significance.

The purpose of this book is to explore a range of issues – ideological, political, professional, practical – which currently affect the relationships between primary schools and parents, and to examine these from the perspectives of parents, teachers and politicians. The general line of argument is that children's educational development is more likely to be enhanced not through 'parent power', which ignores professional perspectives, but by greater openness and trust in parent–teacher relationships and a willingness by both parties to engage in an honest dialogue.

The chapters are arranged around three broad themes. The theme of the two chapters which make up Part I is the significance of perceptions which parents hold of primary schools and which teachers and politicians hold of parents and their involvement in school affairs. In Part II five chapters focus on the duties, rights, influence and power of parents, teachers and local education authorities in their relations with each other. The six chapters which make up Part III are about communication and dialogue: how should and do primary schools keep parents informed, engage them in discussions, elicit their participation in children's learning, and initiate collaborative approaches to problems of pupil behaviour?

To begin with, however, a brief outline is given of the principal recent developments discussed in this book, and this is followed by an examination of the rationale for encouraging greater parental involvement in schooling.

RECENT DEVELOPMENTS AND CURRENT TRENDS

It is possible to identify two main strands in developments since the late 1970s. One has been the related concerns of enhancing parental rights and enforcing teacher accountability, notions which have come to occupy a central position in the programmes of the main political parties and the pursuits of parent organisations. The other has been the concern of many schools and the main parent organisations to engage parents in a more collaborative role in their children's education and school affairs.

Parental rights and power

Prompted by concerns about cost-effectiveness, the desire to raise standards and to make schools more responsive to the needs of industry and the economy, one of the main intentions behind the Conservative Government's Education Acts of 1980, 1981, 1986 and 1988 was to make schools more publicly accountable by providing parents with more statutory rights and political power, both as regards the education of their own children and in educational decision-making. Although Scotland has a separate system of education, a series of Scottish Education Acts during the same period reflected similar purposes though the provisions were not exactly the same. (Statements about the law in this book relate chiefly to the position in England and Wales, but brief reference is made to parallel legislation in Scotland.)

The principal *individual* or 'customer' rights which have been given to parents in England and Wales as a result of recent legislation (with references to relevant chapters shown in parentheses) can be summarised as follows:

1 *Special educational needs:* the rights to participate in assessment, to have access to information and advice, to attend the child's examination, and to appeal against decisions made (Chapter 3).
2 *Curriculum:* the right to complain if a school fails to honour its legal responsibilities with respect to the National Curriculum, religious education and worship, sex education and political education (Chapter 3).
3 *Free education:* no requirement to pay for activities which a school arranges within school hours (except for instrumental tuition and board and lodging on excursions) (Chapter 3).
4 *School choice:* the right of parents to send their child to the school of their choice, subject only to the limits imposed by the school's physical capacity, and for local authorities and schools to publish information to facilitate this choice (Chapter 4).
5 *Information:* the right to have detailed information about the school's curriculum and budget; to receive a school prospectus which must contain certain items of information; to be given access to key educational documents and their child's school records; and to see and discuss their child's National Assessments and to know the aggregated results of schools in the area (Chapter 7).
6 *Punishment:* the right to take civil proceedings on grounds of battery against teachers who inflict corporal punishment on their children (Chapter 12).
7 *Exclusion from school:* the right to be immediately informed if their child is excluded from school, why and for how long, plus rights of appeal not only to governors but also, in cases of permanent exclusion, to local independent appeal committees (Chapter 12).

Parents have also been given important *collective* rights:

1 *School government:* (*a*) the right to elect parent representatives to the governing body of their child's school, and to participate fully in all discussions including staff appointments; and (*b*) the right to receive an annual report from the governors and to attend an annual meeting at which, subject to a quorum being obtained, resolutions can be passed which governors and the LEA must consider (Chapter 5).
2 *Control of schools:* the right, through a ballot of parents, to allow or prevent the governors of their child's school applying for grant-maintained status and so opt out of local authority control, and the right to activate the application in the first place (Chapter 5).

Parental rights are also a feature of the 1989 Labour Party policy review statement. A Labour government would extend parental rights by including parent organisations in a general consultation exercise to establish an agreed national core curriculum; by establishing a home-school partnership agreement, setting out the respective rights of parents and schools; by improving the arrangements for disseminating information about schools, requiring each LEA to issue a guide to its schools and to set up a high street education advice centre. Labour has also promised to support, under certain conditions, applications from Muslims and those of other faiths to set up their own voluntary-aided schools within the maintained system, thus extending the scope for free education in religious schools. However, grant-maintained schools would be returned to local authorities, thus ending the rights of parents to play a pivotal role in taking schools out of LEA control.

The fact that a series of parental rights in education have been enshrined in legislation does not mean that all have been effectively realised in practice, as the main parent organisations have repeatedly pointed out. The House of Commons Select Committee on Education and several research reports have revealed glaring shortcomings in the way the rights of parents have been ignored or abused with respect to special educational needs. Another particular area of complaint has been the conduct of elections for parent governors and attempts to restrict the role of parents once elected. Nor do parents necessarily value some of their new collective rights: parents' annual meetings have frequently been poorly attended and inquorate, while parent ballots have shown divisions about schools 'opting out' of local control.

Home and school working together

The other main development in parental involvement, particularly in primary schools, has been concerned with day-to-day home–school relationships. The buzz words are 'participation', 'collaboration' and 'partnership', which recognise the interdependence of parents and teachers. When the Hadow Report on the primary school was published in 1931, the section on relationships between school and home was given just one paragraph. By contrast, the Plowden Report on primary education, published in 1967, contained a full chapter entitled 'Participation by Parents', while the Warnock Report on special educational needs in 1978 suggested a deeper relationship in its chapter on 'Parents as Partners'. It is significant that the Hargreaves Report on improving London secondary schools (ILEA, 1984) *began* with a section called 'The Teacher/Parent Partnership'. In the same vein, the Thomas Report on primary education in London (ILEA, 1985a) contained a section called 'Parents as Collaborators', concurring with the view that parents should share in the activities of the school. The Government itself acknowledged, in its White Paper *Better Schools* (DES, 1985a), that once the age of compulsory education is reached, 'parents and school become partners in the shared task for the benefit of the child' (para. 197).

Recent reports by some of the teacher unions, whilst punctuated with caveats and cautionary notes, also acknowledge the need for a more close and constructive two-way relationship between home and school, with an emphasis on *shared objectives* and *complementary roles* for teachers and parents. The National Union of Teachers' pamphlet on parents (1987) devotes substantial space to 'establishing a partnership' in a range of curriculum activities; the Assistant Masters and Mistresses Association (1988) has strongly supported the idea of parental involvement in reading programmes; the Professional Association of Teachers (1987) has noted how 'professionally handled . . . parental involvement becomes an additional tool which serves to enrich or improve the quality of the educational situation for all those involved'; while the National Assocation of Head Teachers (1988) has proposed a home–school 'contract of partnership' which would, amongst other things, 'seek to . . . create an ethos of understanding and openness in home–school relationships'.

Primary schools and LEAs have certainly varied in the extent to which they have embraced the general trend towards more positive initiatives for strengthening home–school links and developing partnership schemes, but the range of developments (discussed in Chapters 8–12) has included the following:

1 *More effective communication* by means such as home-visiting, curriculum workshops and support for minority parents.
2 *Appointments of home–school liaison officers* e.g. home–school liaison teachers, teacher–social workers, educational home visitors and other professionals whose role is to improve the quality of communication between parents and teachers.
3 *Home–school curriculum projects*, principally in reading, but also in other areas such as mathematics and writing.
4 *Involvement in school curriculum activities*, including classroom lessons.
5 *School discipline projects*, by which parents and teachers jointly monitor children's behaviour in school.
6 *Decision-making* which involves extensive consultation with parents in aspects of curriculum planning and behaviour policy.
7 *Community initiatives*, utilising the skills and resources of parents and others in community projects, schools and centres.

Legislation has played no part in these aspects of parental involvement. When on 20 November, 1987 Kenneth Baker, the then Secretary of State for Education, explained to the House of Commons that the Government's purpose in introducing the Education Reform Bill was to 'galvanise parental involvement in school', he was thinking in terms of 'parent power' and overlooking the many ways in which the interest and participation of parents was already being successfully enlisted in schemes generated by the energies of individual schools and teachers, educational researchers, LEAs and community project organisers.

DEVELOPING HOME–SCHOOL RELATIONSHIPS: WHY BOTHER?

Developing effective relationships between teachers and parents is demanding, both in terms of time and energy. There needs to be, therefore, a clear rationale for such activities to persuade teachers that the effort is all worth while. On what grounds, then, can policies for better communication with parents and their involvement in the curriculum and school affairs be justified?

There are three main reasons. The first is based on the concept of parental rights. The other two are based on the research evidence relating to parental influences and the impact of home–school policies.

1 The right of parents to have influence in schooling

This argument is based on the principle that parents cannot adequately care for their children unless they are given opportunities to understand what their children are doing in school and learn how they are progressing. In so far as parents are responsible for their children's educational development and are the school's clients, schools have a reciprocal duty to help parents fulfil these obligations. Parents should, at the very least, have the right of access to comprehensive information about their children's work and opportunities to discuss their children's progress and the school's approach to the curriculum. It can be further argued that parents need to be able to engage in a participatory role, complementing the work of teachers and other professionals, on the grounds that this allows them to support their children's education more directly and constructively as well as deepening their understanding of educational processes. For similar reasons, parents are entitled to play a part in the formulation of school policy since this too allows them to take a more active part in their children's educational development, as well as giving the school authorities and teachers the advantage of their perceptions and insights.

2 Parental influences on children's attainment and progress

The Plowden Report (CACE, 1967) has frequently been cited for its emphasis on the importance of parental attitudes to education. Research undertaken for the Committee assessed the relative contributions made by 'parent attitudes' (e.g.

initiatives shown by parents in liaising with teachers, time spent in helping their children with schoolwork, and access to books in the home), 'home circumstances' (e.g. physical amenities, father's occupation, and parents' own education) and the 'state of the school' (e.g. features of its organisation, staff experiences and HMI judgements). It was concluded that of these, parent attitudes were the most important and state of school the least. However there were other, less-publicised findings. Variations in parents' attitudes were only moderately associated with occupational group and material circumstances. Furthermore, although liaison with school was more frequent in the higher socio-economic groups, little distinction was found between the proportion of parents in each occupational group who wanted the schools to give their children work to do at home: yet in this respect, schools were responding far less favourably towards the children of manual workers.

Longitudinal studies which have followed the progress of children throughout their primary and secondary schooling do not deny the significant relationship between parental support and success at school. However, evidence from more recent studies have modified our view about the significance of parental influences in at least three important respects.

First of all, it is wrong to assume that working-class parents have neither the inclination nor the application to become involved in their children's schooling and educational development. Recent evidence based on in-depth interviews suggests that the vast majority of working-class parents *do* take a deep interest in their children's schooling, hold high aspirations for them, and spend time helping them with schoolwork such as reading–though, consistent with the Plowden findings, teachers are frequently unaware of this (Tizard *et al.*, 1988). Secondly, recent studies which have analysed interactions between young children and their mothers have challenged conventional wisdom by showing that, *across* the social spectrum, the home itself provides a stimulating learning environment, not least in the richness of everyday conversations (Davie *et al.*, 1984; Tizard and Hughes, 1984; Wells, 1984; Hughes, 1986).

The third point is that parental interest and involvement in schooling does not exist independently of what the school does. At both infant (Tizard *et al.*, 1988) and junior (Mortimore *et al.*, 1988) levels, it is clear that some inner-city schools are markedly more successful than others in establishing effective home–school liaison and in giving parents a sense of belonging to the school community, regardless of their social class or ethnic group. As Dowling (1985) has argued, families and schools are interrelated in a dynamic reciprocal relationship so that 'the definition of a school as *good* is highly dependent on the perceptions of parents who in turn are constantly being influenced by the school's attitudes towards them' (p.12).

In short, the home as well as the school is part of the child's educational environment. Given that most parents (including those in so-called 'disadvantaged' areas) want to facilitate their children's learning, are already making efforts to do so, and have much of value to contribute, it is part of the school's professional responsibility to bring families into a closer working relationship.

3 The impact of home–school policies on children's progress

Recent research also provides direct evidence of the impact of parental involvement on children's progress at school. Evaluations of home–school reading projects, discussed in Chapter 9, certainly point to the benefits of such collaboration. Some schemes have produced significant gains in reading scores; but even when this has not happened, there has been a noticeable improvement in attitudes, both to reading and schoolwork in general, and to relationships between child, parent and teacher. A recent research project (Dye, 1989) concerning parental involvement in the reception classes of four outer London infant schools has also produced encouraging results. In the experimental group, parents from various ethnic and social backgrounds participated in a special programme of activities in school and at home. Children from this group demonstrated significant improvement in twenty-two of the forty-four areas tested; by contrast, those in the control group with normal but not enhanced parental involvement showed gains in only three areas.

Further evidence comes from the Junior School Project (Mortimore *et al.*, 1988), a longitudinal study which followed the progress of 2000 children in fifty London schools and utilised a more comprehensive range of home and school variables than those of earlier investigations. An important finding was that school factors, compared with home circumstances, were shown to have a stronger relationship with children's educational progress. It seemed that the more successful schools were not only engendering a stronger sense of purposefulness through their leadership styles, teaching arrangements and school climate, but were also developing pro-active policies for parental involvement. Pupil achievement and motivation was better in schools which, among other things, involved parents in the classroom and on educational visits, allowed parents easy access to the head and class teachers, and encouraged parents to take an active part in their children's education at home. Somewhat surprisingly, no relation was found between effective schooling and the existence of a parent–teacher association. As the researchers hypothesise, this could be because the formal structure of some PTAs intimidates some parents.

That children should benefit from the efforts of schools to work with parents is not surprising for three main reasons. First, in so far as effective teaching demands an understanding of the learner, liaison with parents is essential in order to gain a more complete picture of the child. This means using the parents' knowledge and experience, and understanding their beliefs and attitudes about their child and about education. Secondly, parents are an invaluable resource for schools – not just for fund-raising and 'support' activities, but in an educational capacity. This does not mean acting as unpaid teacher-substitutes, but rather acting as complementary educators at home and in the classroom. Involving parents is also of crucial importance in constructing programmes of work in sensitive areas such as multicultural education, sex education and drug, solvent and alcohol abuse. Thirdly, there are important psychological benefits which all three parties can gain from home–school collaboration. *Parents* gain insight into the school's purposes and approaches and find mutual support in discussion groups with other parents. *Teachers* benefit from parents' cooperation and a knowledge of their perceptions of problems. *Pupils* are less likely to become frustrated through inconsistent strategies and misunderstandings between home and school, and they are more likely to feel reassured in the knowledge that parents and teachers are trying to work in the same direction.

Nothing that is said in this book, however, should be taken to suggest that parent–teacher collaboration is devoid of problems for teachers. Some of these are *ideological*–traditions about professional boundaries and who possesses the relevant expertise in educational matters; some are *psychological*–feelings of being threatened through having one's work exposed to public scrutiny and one's perceptions and beliefs challenged by counter-perceptions and counter-beliefs; some are *political*–the lack of adequate resources and teaching personnel; some are *professional*–the lack of training in communicating with parents and in working with them collaboratively; and some are *practical*–the lack of time to think about and implement constructive liaison strategies. The DES 1988 survey of primary school staffing showed that teachers, on average, have only about forty minutes of non-contact time a week; and the situation will not improve as initiatives under the Education Reform Act begin to make their demands on teachers' time and energy. What fortunately remains the case, is that those schools which have succeeded in developing two-way working relationships with parents have usually found their efforts amply rewarded–and so have the children!

PART I

PERCEPTIONS AND PERSPECTIVES

1 | PARENTS' PERCEPTIONS OF SCHOOLS AND SCHOOLING

An important factor which determines the quality of home–school liaison is the degree to which teachers are sensitive to the feelings and aspirations of the parents. This should not be taken to imply that parents hold a common view about schooling or that their beliefs are necessarily at variance with those expressed by teachers: but unless the school listens to what its parents have to say and values their perspective, it lacks the knowledge on which to base any debate and develop constructive relationships. This first chapter, therefore, examines some recent evidence about parents' opinions of schools, particularly those in the primary sector. Of course, knowledge of these general findings is no substitute for eliciting the views held by particular groups of parents with whom the school is working, a theme which will be taken up in Part III of this book.

THE QUALITY OF SCHOOLING

A MORI opinion poll carried out for *The Independent* and the BBC in May 1989 suggested that the public, in general, has a high regard for teachers. A sample of 1200 adults were asked to select the two or three groups in society which they respected most: teachers came third with a score of 40 per cent, outstripped only by doctors (79 per cent) and the police (58 per cent). Unfortunately, when the respondents were asked which groups they thought were most respected by the Government, teachers came bottom with a score of only 4 per cent (*Times Educational Supplement*, 12.5.89)! As regards the views of parents in particular, recent polls suggest that the great majority have a favourable view of teachers and teaching practices, though a sizeable minority do not. In a survey of almost 2000 parents, carried out by MAS Research for the National Union of Teachers, 81 per cent expressed satisfaction with their children's schooling (*Times Educational Supplement*, 29.1.88).

This high level of general satisfaction seems particularly apparent in primary schools. In a MORI poll conducted for *The Sunday Times* (17.1.88), the proportion of primary and secondary school parents who rated their child's education as 'good' or 'very good' was the same (61 per cent); but more primary than secondary parents considered the quality of education to be 'excellent' (17 v. 9 per cent) and more secondary than primary school parents thought it 'poor' or 'very poor'

(10 v. 5 per cent). These figures were almost the same as in a similar poll two years previously. As regards parental involvement in school affairs, the position again seems better in primary schools. The same MORI poll found that only half of secondary school parents seemed satisfied with opportunities for participation, with one in three wanting more influence; by contrast, three-quarters of primary parents said they were happy with their level of involvement, though one in five did want more say.

Although these figures of general satisfaction are reassuring for primary school teachers, other evidence suggests that parents express more disquiet when they are questioned about *specific* practices. In their longitudinal study of 700 children in the east Midlands, the Newsons (1984) found that teachers shouting was the major complaint which mothers made on behalf of their eleven-year-old children. Their personal major concerns were lack of regular homework for top juniors and ineffective teaching. Among the parents of 222 children interviewed for the London Junior School Project, four out of five said they were satisfied with their child's school, and two out of five could cite no particular dislikes: but over one-third of parents complained about bad discipline and the same proportion about their child not being 'stretched' (Mortimore *et al.*, 1988). Again, in recent interviews with a sample of London infant school parents, 91 per cent could mention at least one aspect of the school with which they were satisfied, but one in five parents were unhappy about some aspect of the teaching methods, and many parents felt that they lacked adequate information about their child's progress (Tizard *et al.*, 1988).

This latter criticism also came through strongly in a Gallop Poll among 1028 parents in 1987, 40 per cent saying that they did not receive enough information about their child's work at school. Moreover, if primary schools are like their secondary counterparts, parents feel that schools are providing information less effectively than the teachers themselves believe (National Consumer Council, 1986; Woods, 1984).

THE PURPOSES OF SCHOOLING

A tension is sometimes held to exist between the purposes of schooling as expressed by parents and teachers. For instance, the fact that an increasing number of parents of young children are opting for education in private preparatory schools might suggest that many are looking for a more traditional ethos than schools in the maintained sector often provide. Some research evidence suggests that parents think of education in more functional terms than teachers, who are said to adopt a more fluid perspective. In extended interviews with more than forty parents from various backgrounds and teachers in primary and middle schools, Cullingford (1984) found that the parents' strongest expectation was that their children should be helped to obtain jobs; teachers, in contrast, consistently spoke of education as the means by which children were given autonomy and self-reliance. The parents also wanted schools to teach their children right and wrong and good manners, whereas the teachers saw this as essentially the parents' role, viewing their own task as less impositional and more in terms of teaching the skills that facilitate social education.

A mismatch of expectations is also sometimes evident between minority parents and schools. According to Tomlinson (1984), Caribbean parents often want a greater emphasis on basic skills, discipline and equal opportunities to pass public examinations, while Muslim parents often criticise the unresponsiveness of schools towards recognising their cultural religious values. To get over this problem, groups of minority parents have set up Saturday morning supplementary schools, and Muslim parents frequently arrange for their children to receive separate religious instruction.

Other evidence, however, points to the dangers of stereotyping parents' perceptions on the role of schools. Atkin and Bastiani (1986), for instance, argue from their findings, based on loosely-structured interviews with parents from all social classes, that 'rather than parents and teachers having *different* understandings there is as much variety among parents in relation to concepts of teaching as there is among the teaching profession' (p.19). This view is borne out in Johnson and Ransom's (1980) interviews with parents from public housing estates. A wide range of expectations were found—social, educational, vocational, skill-based, concerned with individual needs—with no one category predominating:

> Talking with mothers and fathers in the privacy and individuality of their family homes is an experience which reveals the inadequacy of stereotyping. Expectations and attitudes vary widely among families in roughly equivalent economic circumstances. (p.185)

That parents are not a homogeneous group in their beliefs about education is suggested also by Skelton (1987), who asks: 'Where . . . is the consensus about sex education, the role of grammar in the language curriculum, the importance of practical work in mathematics, or the place of religious education in state schooling?'

Some evidence also questions the claims we saw earlier, that parents in general adopt an essentially instrumental view of education. In a study concerned with choice of primary schools in three Scottish education authorites, parents did not appear to be motivated by the school's performance in basic skills but rather the child's happiness (Petch, 1986). Of course, this criterion might be bound up with beliefs about the three Rs, but it was expressed more in social terms such as the child's wish to be with friends or a desire to avoid rough and rowdy children. Another example comes from the Cambridge Accountability Project, in which Elliot (1981) examined the criteria by which parents choose and judge a secondary school in a situation of free parental choice and falling rolls. The main reasons which emerged were not so much to do with discipline, basic skills and examination results as with the provision of a balanced all-round education, the child wanting to go to the school, and a curriculum which catered for personal and social as well as academic development. Again, a study of secondary school preferences by London primary school parents showed that 'the child's choice was regarded as of the same importance as "good discipline", and more so than "good exam results" ' (ILEA, 1985b).

The notion that parents' perceptions of the purpose of schooling are at variance with those held by teachers is therefore by no means supported in all the research findings. Much of the evidence suggests a greater variety of views, and a greater recognition that there is more to education than the 'basics', than is sometimes supposed. It also seems the case that although some LEAs assume that examination results are the key criterion by which parents choose a secondary school, others, in contrast, are enlisting parental support through partnership schemes which aim at reaching agreement with parents about values, purposes, and the conditions of effective learning (Ranson *et al.*, 1987).

SUMMARY AND CONCLUSIONS

Although the great majority of parents express favourable views of schools, particularly in the primary sector, they often have criticisms to make of certain aspects. The most important causes for concern relate to communication about their child's progress, information about school policies and practices, and teaching methods.

Some studies suggest that parents have a predominantly instrumental view of education, whereas teachers are more concerned with 'all-round' development. Other investigations, however, reveal a variety of understandings and perceptions among parents, even within particular socio-economic groups. It may be that different ways of sampling parental opinion and in structuring and conducting interviews elicit different kinds of responses.

What practical implications do these findings have for primary heads and teachers? Certainly they can be reassured by the high level of general respect which they command from parents. Further, a number of studies demonstrate that there is no impregnable divide between parents and teachers about the purposes of education, though there may be differences of emphasis. At the same time, as the National Association of Head Teachers (1988) has recognised, it is clear that schools need to work for a greater consensus about the purposes and practices of schooling and to respond constructively to a number of specific concerns which parents are expressing. A spirit of partnership cannot exist if one of the partners feels ineffectual or confused through lack of information and understanding about the school's practices.

Whilst there is much willingness among parents to develop common understandings with teachers, the development of constructive home–school relations depends upon schools working to improve the quality of communication and to develop opportunities for genuine dialogue. As we shall see in Part III of this book, parents may steer clear of general meetings which have no obvious bearing upon what their children are now doing; but most will readily participate in discussion and activities, individually or in small groups, when these are centred around issues which are seen to have immediate implications for their children's progress, when they know that their perspective will be valued, and when they are given relevant guidance and support.

Further Reading

Parents' perceptions about schools are explored by Tony Becher *et al*. in Chapter 3 of *Policies for Educational Accountability* (Heinemann, 1981) and, more recently, by Barbara Tizard and her colleagues in Chapter 9 of *Young Children at School in the Inner City* (Lawrence Erlbaum, 1988).

2 | PERSPECTIVES ON PARENTAL PARTICIPATION IN SCHOOLING

In spite of increasing public interest in parental rights and involvement in education, there remains a wide spectrum of views among both the professionals and the politicians about the kind of role which parents should play in schooling and the degree to which they want and are able to play a major part. It is possible, however, to identify three broad positions. In the first, the bulk of parents are regarded, overtly or covertly, as problems: either they are assumed to be disinterested in their children's education and unreceptive to requests for involvement, or they are seen as having too much to say and would try to take over if given the chance. A second view regards parents essentially as customers or clients, and sees the role of schools as one of responding to parents' consumer needs. The third position is that parents do and should desire influence but not control: it is right that they should assume a participatory but not dominating role in education, and schools should encourage them to do so. This chapter consists of an examination of each of these perceptions.

PARENTS AS PROBLEMS

Some schools regard parental involvement as an intrusion into their relationships with pupils. They believe that parents lack the necessary knowledge, skills and insight to determine what is in the best educational interests of their children, and that this responsibility should lie with the professionals. As Sharpe (1980) has noted, parents have always been regarded as problems but the kind of problem which they present has changed. The early Church schools saw themselves as rescuing children from parental moral decadence, while the later Board schools saw themselves as rescuing children from parental exploitation. More recently schools have seen their role as one of compensating for educational deprivation in the home environment, while some schools today, faced with universal access to the public examination system, are concerned to restrain unrealistic parental expectations.

Certainly in the past, schools have often made no bones about their distaste for parental involvement. Acknowledging that both parents and teachers wish the child well, Willard Waller (1932), one of the early educational sociologists, added:

> . . . but it is such a different kind of well that conflict must inevitably arrive over it . . . The fact seems to be that parents and teachers are natural enemies, predestined each for the discomfiture of the other. (Waller, 1932, p.68)

Waller did not leave the matter there, however, since he went on to suggest that, if only parents and teachers were to meet more often and have their say unreservedly, school practices might become so changed as to amount to a revolution. However, when Patrick McGeeney wrote his celebrated book *Parents are Welcome* in 1969, he was able to quote numerous examples of policy statements hostile to parental involvement and notices at school gates with statements such as 'No Parents Beyond this Point'.

Whilst the signs forbidding entry have virtually disappeared, parents can still be discouraged from visiting the school. They may be kept at arm's length by the infrequency of meetings, by having to make formal appointments before seeing the head, or by being deprived of free access to classroom teachers. They may also be put off by the reception they receive when they come into school. Some schools may keep parents at a distance because they harbour beliefs that those in manual occupations are uninterested in their children's education and that their presumed poor attitudes to schooling are responsible for their children's educational failings.

The feelings that parents are problems is not confined to the public sector or to working-class homes, as Baroness Mary Warnock admitted in her 1985 Richard Dimbleby lecture. Recalling her days as a headmistress of a selective Oxford school, this is what she said:

> Of course, a lot of the trouble lies with the parents . . . We at school divided parents roughly into two categories: the pushy and the indifferent. The pushy parent is always certain that he is right, both in his estimation of his child's ability, and in his views about what should be taught in school, and by what method . . . The pushy parent is generally, though not exclusively, middle-class. His guiding principle is that his child is superior to others . . . The indifferent parent is, obviously, less trouble . . . He is never seen at school; he does not answer letters . . . For the indifferent parent, school is a tiresome necessity, the teachers intruders no more welcome than tax-collectors. Though generally not available if attempts are made to contact him, if roused, the indifferent parent is capable of violent invective against the failure of the school to keep his daughter out of trouble or get her through her CSEs.

On this view, then, all parents are problems because they are either unduly demanding or lack interest. These admissions, it may be noted, come from the author of a government-commissioned report (DES, 1978) which advocated that schools should work with parents as partners!

As will be seen in later chapters, various pieces of legislation have made schools and local authorities more accountable to parents and have set limits to the distance at which they can be held. Yet while fewer schools today are *overtly* holding parents at a distance, there is still a common belief that parents are usually the source of the problem in the case of disaffected pupils or those with learning difficulties. In short, although the 'no entry' signs have been taken down, parents are still frequently regarded *covertly* as problems.

Widlake (1986) has argued that the concept of compensatory education in the 1960s unintentionally added to communication difficulties with working-class parents by defining them as inherently inferior and attributing to schools the role of compensating for the educational deficiencies of 'disadvantaged' homes. A similar view is contained in the work of Reeves and Chevanne (1983), who point to the pervasive but unfortunate consequences of explanatory theories based on educational 'deprivation' and 'disadvantage'. The Plowden Report (CACE, 1967) was particularly influential in perpetrating the belief that schools could and should compensate children for the cultural deprivation of their home life:

> Schools in deprived areas should be given priority in many respects . . . The justification is that the homes and neighbourhoods from which many of their children come provide little support and stimulus for learning. The schools must supply a compensating environment. (para.151)

The 'myth of the deprived child' has been exposed by a number of writers. One of the earliest was Ginsburg (1972), who argued that there was no evidence to show that the home environment of poor children was marked by a deficiency in stimulation, preventing mature intellectual development. More recently, Barbara Tizard and Martin Hughes (1984) have suggested from their analyses of young children's talk at home that working-class children sometimes appear immature to teachers because they are more adversely affected by the demands which school makes upon them: for instance, they have to listen to the teacher for long periods of time when they are used at home to more of a balance in the proportion of adult talk to child talk. The same writers concluded that, although there was a difference in language *style* related to underlying values and attitudes, working-class children were as competent at conceptual and logical thinking as middle-class children.

Nonetheless, beliefs in parental deficits are hard to eradicate. For instance, in their interviews with fourteen inner-London nursery teachers, six told Barbara Tizard and her colleagues (1981) that the parents made no positive contribution to their child's education. Typical comments were: 'In an enabling middle-class home, yes, but not round here' and 'To be frank, the children are better off at school' (p.46). Apparently the staff did not know that between two-fifths and three-quarters of the parents, depending on the school, were trying to teach their children the three Rs. In a more recent study of London infant schools (Tizard *et al.*, 1988), almost a third of the teachers maintained that few or none of the parents provided adequate support for their children's reading; yet 97 per cent of the first-year parents said they regularly heard their child read. Again, in a recent study of views held by 428 junior school heads and teachers, Croll and Moses (1985) found that the child's parents or home circumstances were used to explain about 30 per cent of children who were slow learners or poor readers and about 66 per cent of children who had bad behaviour, emotional or discipline problems.

Professionals in the social services as well as teachers are also apt to explain poor pupils' problems in terms of the personal qualities of the parents. Reid (1987), for instance, has suggested that too often only lip service is paid to the psychological effects which poverty, poor housing and a dependency on social services can have on family life and bringing up children. She asks:

> If a note is made about familial or parental characteristics, behaviour or crises, what yardsticks of pathology or normality are being used explicitly or implicitly? . . . If it is noted that a child is from a single-parent family, is this because, for example, the practitioner acknowledges the material hardship that often goes along with this status and the consequent spin-offs for the children and adult concerned, or could it be that they uncritically hold the view that the normal well-adjusted family has two parents and that any deviation from that offers an inferior context, *per se*, for the socialization of the child? If it is recorded that the mother goes out to work, is this based, even partially, on the assumption that caring and loving mothers don't? (p.193)

In fact, Milne *et al.* (1986) found that an apparent statistical relationship between achievement at school and living in a one-parent family could be explained almost entirely in terms of the lower income levels of single parents. Heyns and Catsambis (1986) have also shown that reported relationships between mothers working and lower school achievement are substantially reduced when a range of other domestic and personal factors are taken into account.

Stereotypic beliefs about deficits in children's home background are also sometimes held about minority families. In one study, primary heads were prone to label Afro-Caribbean and Asian parents as 'disadvantaged' and to see the school's goal as one of 'overcoming disadvantage' (Rex and Tomlinson, 1979). Further, explanations about the 'underachievement' by Afro-Caribbean children has sometimes been accounted for in terms of linguistic inadequacies in the family's culture. The Rampton Committee (1981) reiterated 'the particular linguistic difficulties of West Indian children' (p.11) and bemoaned a state of affairs whereby 'many West Indian parents . . . may not recognise the importance to a child of an unstrained, patient and quiet individual dialogue with an adult' (p.16). Evidence subsequently presented to the Swann Committee (1985) tried to correct this perception by demonstrating that black parents have high aspirations for their children and devote much time to helping them in school-related activities such as reading; and recent evidence from a sample of thirty-three London infant schools suggests that differences at entry in literacy and numerical skills cannot be attributed to the ethnic origins of the parents, and that black parents are deeply committed to helping their children with school work, typically giving them more help than white parents (Tizard *et al.*, 1988).

Of course home influences are significant and powerful, and of course there are individual cases where parents seem largely to blame for their children's poor attainment, behaviour or attendance. But by locating the source of the trouble in parents' personal qualities as if these existed independently from their material circumstances, and by stereotyping certain social classes or cultural groups as 'the problem' in education, the role of the school in enhancing children's learning opportunities is thereby underestimated or even ignored. Recent studies in school effectiveness have pointed to the significance of the school's role in children's progress over and above that of the home. For instance, in the London Junior School Project, a longitudinal study which monitored changes in attainment, attitudes and behaviour from the ages of seven to eleven years, educational outcomes were found to be related to background factors such as social class and race: but when account was taken of pupil attainment at entry to junior school, the school was found to have made a much larger impact upon progress than background factors (Sammons and Mortimore, 1989).

Beliefs in cultural deprivation, with its associated assumption that 'problem children' are that way because they come from 'problem homes', have unfortunate consequences for children. Apart from absolving the school of responsibility, they encourage teachers to hold low expectations of these pupils and to underestimate the importance of changing teaching styles and curriculum provision. Moreover the benefits to be gained from working *with* parents rather than without them are not considered. On these grounds, a policy which is based on assumptions that certain parent cultures constitute a problem is not only grossly misleading but is positively unhelpful.

PARENTS AS CUSTOMERS

Parents are sometimes described as clients, customers or consumers. The latter term is misleading since it is the child who is the consumer. The parent can more intelligibly be perceived as a client or customer who chooses a particular school on behalf of the child and wishes the child to realise the benefits of that choice. Undoubtedly parents do have customer-needs. In particular they are entitled to information about their children's progress at school, to explanations about teaching methods and curriculum content, and to advice about how they can help their children.

There are two main senses in which parents can be regarded essentially as customers. On the one hand parents may be encouraged to assent unquestioningly to the judgements of teachers and other professionals, who are said to possess special expertise. The school 'knows best'. On the other hand, the school may believe that parents have the 'right' to secure the kind of education which they want for their children, and that the school should allow its policies and practices to be determined accordingly. The parent 'knows best'. The distinction is thus between perceptions of parents as customers who depend upon professional expertise and as customers who have the right to shape the ethos of the school. Most schools operate somewhere between these two extremes, which can be regarded as poles of a continuum.

Some research suggests that school staff who see parents in the first sense, as clients needing expert advice, are responding to the way many parents in fact think about teachers. For instance Nias (1981) recorded how, in all the schools involved in the Cambridge Accountability Project, parents were ready to accede to the claims of teachers who defended their right to autonomy based on expert knowledge. A comparable problem exists in special education, where, apart from teachers, many other professionals can be involved – psychologists, therapists, inspectors and advisers, counsellors, social workers, psychiatrists, medical officers, paediatricians, health visitors. Because parents of handicapped children need special help and resources, they can easily become unduly dependent upon professionals for defining their children's needs and prescribing courses of action. As Gliedman and Roth (1981) have noted, some professionals, wanting to demonstrate their authority and influence, prefer parents to be passive and ignorant. Fortunately, the alternative view that professionals should give the parents a more constructive and collaborative role has recently gained more general recognition in special education.

A school which perceives parents as customers may welcome parental support, but on matters which are peripheral to its decision-making. It recognises that it can become a more flourishing and efficient institution if parents are encouraged to assist with the school fête, to make costumes and scenery for the school production, to raise money for new equipment, to lend a hand on educational trips, and to help catalogue library books. ·Yet for all their loyalty, cooperation and interest the parents are fundamentally occupying a passive role since any involvement is strictly on the professionals' terms. Anything which questions curriculum practices or school policy is seen as 'interference', since parents should accede to the school's superior judgement. As the head of a community school has suggested, 'Some teachers see the extension of a school's relationship with parents as no more than an opportunity to impress on them the school's point of view on aspects of the curriculum (Marland, 1984).

The alternative sense in which parents are perceived as customers entails the surrender, in part at least, of the school's right to make decisions on the basis of its inherent authority. The argument is based on the belief that educational standards have fallen, about which there is much controversy. The solution is seen partly in terms of giving parents a greater choice in education and partly in terms of giving them the power to manipulate school policy. These twin ideas have been prominent in recent writings and speeches from members of the various 'New Right' groups, such as the Adam Smith Institute (1984), the Institute of Economic Affairs (Sexton, 1987) and the Hillgate Group (1986). Teachers are held to have abused their position of authority by neglecting traditional standards and by adopting biased stances in the presentation of controversial issues. They are therefore urged to be less possessive about their professional territory and to be more prepared to offer the kind of education which the parents say they want.

An example of this style of thinking can be found in the radical manifesto *Whose Schools?* by the Hillgate Group (1986). This body of five (Caroline Cox, Jessica Douglas-Home, John Marks, Roger Scruton and Laurence Norcross) argue that teachers have allowed the curriculum to become politicised and illiberal. Schools, they say, should be self-governing institutions, owned by individual trusts rather than LEAs, and subject to populist appeal:

> Their survival should depend on their ability to satisfy their customers. And their principal customers are parents, who should therefore be free to place their custom where they wish, in order that educational institutions should be shaped, controlled and nourished by their demand. (p.7)

The effects of this policy on maintained schools is claimed to be beneficial, the assumption being that a school's success is essentially a function of the teacher's efforts and has little to do with the socio-economic status of its intake:

> Schools will have to work in order to stay in business, and the worse their results, the more likely they will be to go to the wall. (p.16)

Comparable suggestions are contained in a book called *Power to Parents: Reversing Educational Decline* by Antony Flew (1987). Arguing in favour of an expansion of independent schools and the adoption of education vouchers to give parents a greater choice of school, Flew believes that schools should see themselves as 'educational firms', subjected to 'the incentives and disciplines of the market'.

One of the most throughgoing statements of this position is set out in a paper by the Director of the Institute of Economic Affairs, Stewart Sexton (1987), who maps out a plan 'to "privatise" the State education system'. Aware of the political sensitivity in this suggestion, he outlines a series of stages for implementation over some years. Parents would be credited with a sum which represented the average annual cost of school education (varied according to the child's age), and would be able to 'top up' the value of this credit if they wished to send their child to a maintained or independent school which had a higher annual cost. LEAs would provide schools where no supplementary payment was required, but it is envisaged that eventually almost all schools would become independent charitable trusts with local authorities reduced to a supporting role.

(Foreshadowing his Education Reform Bill of 1987, Kenneth Baker gave official Government backing to the spirit and language of the market place. In a speech to the 1986 Conservative Party Conference, he argued that parents rather than the 'producers' were better able to discern what was educationally good for children:

> Education can no longer be led by the producers—the academic theorists, the administrators and even the teachers' unions. Education must be shaped by the users—by what is good for the individual child and what hopes are held by parents.

Consistent with this free market ideology, Baker's 1988 Education Reform Act gave greater powers to parents making it more possible for them to secure a place for their children in the school of first choice and by empowering them to persuade the governors of a school to opt out of local authority control and enjoy a measure of independence with maintenance costs met from central funds. The arguments surrounding these and similar developments will be discussed in Chapters 4 and 5.

Even before the pressures generated by the 1988 Act, however, many local authority schools, faced with the threat of closure brought about by falling rolls and stiff competition from neighbouring institutions, were feeling the pressure to indulge in salesmanship and the promotion of 'image' in the process of competing for custom. In an analysis of marketing strategies in primary education, Brunt (1987) argued that teachers should apply some of the lessons learned from studies in industrial selling practices:

> . . . a school should face outward towards the wants and needs of the users and not

inwards towards what it likes doing or what it is experienced in doing. (Brunt, 1987, pp.217–18)

On this view the aspirations of the 'users' are all-important and must supersede those of experienced teachers.

It may be that a climate of discontent will be fuelled by the New Right argument which alleges that many of Britain's schools are in a state of crisis; and this, together with the publication of test results required under the 1988 Act may encourage more parents to judge schools in simple 'benchmark' terms. Whatever may be the educational aspirations of parents and teachers, however, a philosophy which puts user-orientation first and last is unlikely to be in the long-term interests of parents, teachers and pupils. For instead of trying to develop greater understanding by both parties and to determine agreed ends of education, it fosters a combative atmosphere and undermines public confidence in teachers' competence (Munn, 1985). As Ranson *et al.* (1987) have suggested, 'Consumerism isolates people and, importantly, eschews the practice of reason between groups: the market does not conceive of accountable discourse'.

PARENTS AS PARTNERS

An alternative to the 'customer' perspective is one in which parents are regarded as participants in the mainstream events of the school's life. The most thoroughgoing version of the participatory model involves a 'partnership' between parents and teachers. It suggests a two-way relationship, each partner recognising the unique contribution which the other can make to the child's development and to educational decision-making. Teachers who seek to develop a partnership with parents try to shed their impregnable cloak of 'expertise' by demystifying their professional understandings and accepting the parents' perspective as valid and valuable. This kind of relationship is sometimes said to be based on a principle of 'equal' partnership: this certainly does not mean that teachers have no special skills or experience, but rather, as Pugh (1985) has argued, that each partner recognises the other's skills and experience to be of equal *value*. In response to the 'New Right' onslought, the Labour Party (1988) has taken the 'partnership' philosophy under its wing in a policy document outlining specific ways in which schools should improve communication with parents and develop closer involvement, but the concept of partnership was also espoused by the Conservative Government in its policy paper *Better Schools* (DES, 1985a).

The term 'partnership' is used in two main senses:

(i) parents may be invited to participate directly in the education of their own children;

(ii) parents may be invited to participate in policy-making and curriculum development.

Each of these notions will now be examined.

Parents as partners in the education of their own children

· The first sense of the term 'partnership' involves the principle that schools should recognise the family and community as a major educational resource and engage parents as complementary educators. This contrasts with the 'consumer' view that the role of parents in education is to pick and choose from a range of professional offerings.

One of the main ways in which primary school parents are invited to act as complementary educators is through home–school learning projects, principally in reading and language, mathematics and writing (see Chapters 9 and 10). As Meighan (1981) has put it, parents who were once seen as part of the problem in education are now seen as part of the solution. They no longer need to engage in surreptitious teaching at home to avoid the label 'interfering'; they can now do so openly and with the school's encouragement and support.

Community partnership projects and parent centres have been set up in some local authorities to help teachers, parents and other members of the community to work together more effectively. Examples can be found in Coventry, Glasgow, Liverpool and the London Borough of Newham (see pp.134–6). The participatory philosophy underlying these schemes has been described by Paul Widlake (1986) as a move away from the paternalistic approach, in which teachers 'explain' to parents, to one which starts with the community and gives a central role to home–school liaison workers:

> Parents are viewed . . . as people exercising some control over their own lives, with more than marginal responsibility for the devlopment and education of their children. They are seen as capable of personal development, initiating, organizing and sustaining activities. The very thought of these people being verbally destitute is enough to reduce one to helpless laughter, in view of their linguistic vigour and inventiveness. (Widlake, 1986, p.16)

The theme of partnership between parents and professionals has been especially prominent in recent thinking about children with special needs. The Court Committee on Child Health Services (1976) argued that professionals in child care:

> . . . should see themselves as partners with parents . . . Parents' understanding of children's development and illness varies widely and this is due in part to the poverty of professional communication. (para.5.6)

A similar and major thesis of the Warnock Report (DES, 1978) on special educational needs was that:

> . . . professional help cannot be wholly effective – if at all so – unless it builds upon the parents' own understanding of their children's needs and upon the parent's capacity to be involved . . . Parents can be effective partners only if professionals take notice of what they say and of how they express their needs, and treat their contributions as intrinsically important. (para.9.6)

By emphasising the particpatory role of parents, the dangers of undermining parents' feelings of adequacy are reduced: the focus is not on parents as clients but on parents as *agents*, not on parent power but on parent *empowerment*.

Another key area in which partnership models have been developed is pre-school education. Parents may collaborate with professionals in assessing the child's needs, implementing a course of action, visiting homes, helping in home-based intervention schemes, running playgroups and parent education groups, and helping in nurseries. Through its partnership conferences and papers, the National Children's Bureau has been instrumental in developing good partnership practice at this age-phase. For as Pugh (1985) has emphasised, pre-school workers need to consult with parents and listen to their concerns if the child's nursery or other group experience is to be maximally beneficial, relating to and complementing experiences in the home.

Of course, there is often a mismatch between the practice and the rhetoric. 'Involving' parents sometimes amounts to subjecting them to what Cunningham (1983) has called 'expertosis'. In this situation, the parents are encouraged to help their child but feel confused and overwhelmed and effectively disabled by the professional's expertise. By contrast, a commitment to genuine partnership 'involves a full *sharing* of knowledge, skills and experience', and 'rests on the assumption that children will develop and learn better if parents and professionals are working together on the basis of equality than if either is working in isolation.' (Mittler and McConachie, 1983, p.10, emphasis added)

Teachers who resist the prospect of operating in partnership with parents fear that their professional status will be eroded. This view, however, is based on an unnecessarily restricted view of professionalism in education. A school teacher's expertise is not like that of a brain surgeon whose skills are exceptional and whose authority it would be dangerous for lay people to challenge. Darling (1986) suggests that teaching is more like gardening – it is something that most people can do at some level even though training provides special skills and knowledge. For a teacher, 'being professional' should not therefore imply that all teaching tasks can be performed legitimately only by specially trained employees. An alternative view is that the teacher or other professional, by virtue of special training, possesses the necessary criteria to determine what is needed in order to provide the most suitable learning environment for the pupils – and this should mean acknowledging the special role which parents can play. As Mittler and Beasley (1982) have put it, 'learning to give away our skills is one of the most difficult skills that we ourselves have to learn and that we shall have to teach future generations of our students to learn' (p.16).

Parents as partners in policy-making and curriculum development

Schools are often better at providing information than at acknowledging the validity of criticism; while they welcome parents asking questions, they are less enthusiastic when parents question school practices – though individual teachers can sometimes use parents as allies to voice their own concerns in matters such as shortage of resources. The Taylor Committee (DES, 1977) broke new ground in recommending not only that parents should have legal representation on school governing bodies but also that they enjoy equal status with other members. Parents would thus not only be partners in the education of their own children but also in the life of the school generally.

Whereas the market place ideology creates a tension between parents and professionals, the participatory model sees them as one in the decision-making process. Joan Sallis, a parent member of the Taylor Committee, has argued that in this partnership model accountability is mutual. This means that parents should be answerable to the school as well as vice versa:

> We *share* responsibility with the school for the education of our children . . . School and parents must be accountable *to each other* for their contributions to a shared task. (Sallis, 1982, p.16, emphasis added)

Although the 1980 Education Act gave parents legal representation on governing bodies, the Conservative Government Green Paper *Parental Influence in Schools* (DES, 1984), went further in advocating that the proportion of parents should be so increased as to give them a position of *control*. To have implemented this policy would have emphasised the separateness of parents and teachers in decision-making rather than a sharing of responsibility. Yet as Sallis (1982, p.15) had earlier put it on behalf of parents, 'It is insight we need, not oversight'. Such was the overwhelming opposition to the Green Paper recommendation, not least from parents themselves, that in the 1986 Education Act parents were given increased representation on school governing bodies, but not a majority. The impetus for this development, which abolished the position of dominance previously enjoyed by the LEA representatives, was no doubt the Government's wish to broaden the base of its political authority and give legitimacy to its policies. Nonetheless the opportunity for parents to influence decision-making over a range of important matters is there for parents to use as they wish.

However, although parental representation on governing bodies is very important, by itself it constitutes a limited view of parental participation in decision-making since so few parents are directly involved. In theory, all can participate in the governors' annual meeting with parents, now obligatory under the 1986 Act, but in practice few seem willing to take advantage of this opportunity (see p.112). Some schools have therefore encouraged a larger number of parents to collaborate in policy-making by involving them in consultative committees set up to consider particular issues. Examples are the development of policies concerning sex education, drug abuse, multicultural education, equal opportunities for boys and girls, special educational needs, or new procedures for assessment. Some schools also invite parents to consultative open meetings to explain curriculum developments and to thrash out proposed school policies before they are finalised. These give teachers the opportunity to see the school through the eyes of parents and to ensure that new ideas are developed with the benefit of parents' insight and support.

SUMMARY AND CONCLUSIONS

This chapter has outlined contrasting perceptions of parents and their role in schooling – as problems, as customers and as partners. At the same time, it was suggested that each of these perceptions can be realised in different ways. Thus parents may be regarded as problems overtly, by, for instance, restrictions on their right to see class teachers or to be involved in school matters, or covertly in the sense that they are assumed to be the cause of learning and behavioural failings in their children. Parents may also be seen as customers in different senses. At one extreme, they are regarded as clients who need expertise to decide what is in their children's best interest; at the other, they are viewed as consumers who, on their children's behalf, have a right to determine the school's curriculum policy and ethos. Lastly, parents may be seen as participants or partners in more than one respect – as complementary educators of their own children and perhaps of others, and as partners in the development of school policy.

Of the three broad perceptions outlined, the partnership model of parent–teacher relationships is the one which seems the most educationally productive. This is because, in contrast to the customer/market-forces persepctive, it does not assume a tension between parents and teachers but strives to dissolve their separateness, emphasising the need for mutual understanding, mutually agreed goals and complementary educative roles. Children's learning is more likely to be enhanced if all the significant adults in the child's life regard each other's views as important. The experience of home-reading projects and other evidence demonstrates convincingly how fallacious it is to believe that whole groups of parents (as distinct from certain individual ones) are inherently disinterested in, or hostile to, their children's schooling. The view that parents are no more than customers is also unsatisfactory since it encourages an unnecessary one-way relationship, with its emphasis either on teachers' unique expertise or on populist appeal. It is difficult to agree about effective ways of enhancing children's development if one side or the other is inordinately preoccupied with 'rights'.

Of course, complete harmony will never be obtained. Certain issues such as approaches to the teaching of reading and mathematics, sex education and religious education are bound to remain controversial, as will issues over the control of education. Some parents will also resist working collaboratively: they may not have the time or want to give it; they may find the school atmosphere off-putting; they may associate school involvement with their unhappy memories as a pupil; or they may believe that education is best left to the professionals. Some parents may therefore need to be persuaded that collaboration is desirable and they will need help to participate constructively. Recent evidence also shows that teachers are apprehensive about working closely with parents (Jowett and Baginsky, 1988). Initial and in-service training must therefore make provision in this area, for example in helping teachers to communicate effectively with parents about their children's progress, to use them effectively in the classroom and in home–school projects, and to run workshops and consultative meetings. The effort should be worthwhile since parental participation must maximise the chances of children developing within a framework of consistent goals which both parties have discussed and understood, even if commitment is variable. In this way the influences of home and school are more likely to work in the same planned direction.

If we value the idea of a society in which the interests of the individual and the community are seen as one and not in conflict or competition, then it must be incumbent upon teachers and parents to work together towards mutually agreed ends. This will not come about if schools operate in the belief that parents are problems or that they are just customers. Nor, of course, will it come about if schools believe that partnership has been achieved once parents are encouraged to tick a card saying that they have heard their children read. Partnership above all is about dialogue and mutual respect, each side recognising the contribution which both partners can make to the enterprise of education.

This general argument, however, needs to be qualified in two important respects. The first concerns the limitation of involving only parents in the partnership. Teachers and parents can work together to help pupils learn more successfully, but the determination of the general educational policies of a school are in the interests of the whole community and not only those who, at the moment, are parents of pupils or who are employed as teachers. This is why it is important for school governing bodies to be representative of the local community in general, and not just one part of it.

Secondly, the participatory model will only succeed if it also embraces relations between teachers and pupils. Clearly the role of pupils, particularly in the primary school, will be limited in scale and scope, but it will be nonetheless significant. If we wish to avoid feelings of alienation among pupils, then there must be some sense in which they too are enabled to feel like participants by being incorporated into the decision-making processes of the school. The argument here rests on the assumption that if teachers wish their pupils to develop into responsible agents then they need to involve them in taking real responsibilities at levels appropriate to their development, for instance in discussing learning goals, planning programmes of work, helping to formulate school rules, and running school clubs.

We end this chapter, then, by suggesting that the model of parent–teacher relationships which is the most educationally viable is a participatory one in which parents and teachers work toward mutually agreed goals and practices. We have also argued that this does not entail a devaluing of teachers' professionalism: on the contrary, it provides the means by which successful teaching can be more fully realised.

Further reading

A useful collection of readings which deals with a range of issues is *Parents and Teachers* 1: Perspectives on Home–School Relations, edited by John Bastiani (NFER–Nelson, 1987).

An attack on assumptions about intellectual deprivation in working-class homes can be found in *The Myth of the Deprived Child* by H. Ginsburg (Prentice Hall, New Jersey, 1972) and in Chapter 6 of *Young Children's Learning* by B. Tizard and M. Hughes (Fontana, 1984). Comparable arguments with respect to black families can be found in an article by Frank Reeves and Mel Chevannes, 'The ideological construction of black underachievement' in *Multicultural Education*, **2**, 1 (1983).

For a discussion about professional 'expertise' in relation to parental 'rights', see the paper 'Parents and professionals' by J. Gliedman and W. Roth in W. Swann (ed.) *The Practice of Special Education* (Basil Blackwell/Open University Press, 1981). Although focusing on handicapped children, the arguments have general application.

The consumerist ideology is clearly represented in the Hillgate Group's manifesto *Whose Schools?* (1986) and the group's assessment of the Conservative Government's policies in *The Reform of British Education* (Claridge Press, 1987); in Antony Flew's *Power to Parents: Reversing Educational Practice* (Sherwood Press, 1987); and in Stewart Sexton's *Our Schools – A Radical Policy* (Institute of Economic Affairs Education Unit, 1987).

For a brief critique of the consumerist view, see Ted Wragg's *Education in the Market Place: The Ideology Behind the 1988 Bill* (NUT, 1988) and Pamela Munn's article 'Accountability and Parent–Teacher Communication' in *British Education Research Journal*, **11**, 105–10, reprinted in A. Cohen (ed.) *Early Education: The Parents' Role* (Paul Chapman, 1988). The market place philosophy is also criticised in *Schools, Parents and Governors: A New Approach to Accountability* (Routledge, 1988), in which Joan Sallis convincingly presents an argument in favour of partnership. The place of this concept in special education is discussed in Chapter 9 of the Warnock Report *Special Educational Needs* (DES, 1978) and in *Partnership with Parents* by P. Mittler and H. Mittler (National Council for Special Education, 1982). For readers interested in the pre-school context, see the series of Partnership Papers edited by Erica De'Ath and Gillian Pugh and published by the National Children's Bureau, and the set of case-studies in *Partnership in Action: Working with Parents in Pre-School Centres* by Gillian Pugh *et al.* (National Children's Bureau, 1987).

The arguments supporting the partnership model in relation to management policy making are set out in Chapter 4 of the Taylor Report *A New Partnership for Our Schools* (DES, 1977).

For a challenging thesis on possible ways forward, see Phil Woods' article 'A strategic view of parent participation' in *Journal of Education Policy*, **3**, 4, (1988).

PART II

DUTIES, RIGHTS AND POWER

3 | BASIC RIGHTS AND DUTIES

Much of the material in Part II of this book is concerned with the enhancement of parents' educational rights as a result of Acts of Parliament. In order to evaluate these statutory provisions, however, we need first to consider the moral basis for parental rights. By 'parent' here is meant not just a biological parent but 'a guardian and every person who has actual custody of the child' (Education Act 1944, Sect. 114).

THE MORAL BASIS FOR PARENTAL RIGHTS IN EDUCATION

A moral right is not the same as a legal right. For one thing individuals may believe they have moral rights which are not recognised in law; for another, they may consider that some legal rights are morally ill-founded. Broadly speaking, parental moral rights in education are about justified claims which parents have about educational provision, particularly, but not exclusively, with regard to their own children. However, such rights cannot be considered in isolation from the rights of children and the rights of teachers, each of which in turn may need to be constrained by considerations about the general interests of the community.

Parents' rights and children's rights

Everyone acknowledges that it would be inappropriate for children of primary school age to have full control over major decisions which affect their educational opportunities. Certainly (as is argued below) children have the right to be involved in such decision-making, but their level of experience, knowledge and intellectual maturity make it inappropriate for them to have the final say. Even though adults do not always use the most appropriate criteria when making educational decisions for their children, in general they are more likely than children to put long-term interests before immediate wants. What, then, in a society where children are typically brought up in families, are the moral arguments to which parents might appeal if they wish to exercise a 'right' to make decisions about their child's education?

There is one sort of argument which most people in our society would today regard as abhorrent. This is that children should be seen as the property of the parent, who therefore has absolute right over the child's upbringing. For children are not objects but developing persons. As Olafson (1973) has argued, parents 'expose themselves by the decisions they make to an eventual judgement by those in whose behalf they act' (p. 180). The exercise of unlimited rights would be to treat children not as individuals with unique centres of consciousness but simply as means to parents' gratification. For this reason it is now a criminal offence for parents to neglect or exploit their children, to subject them to physical or sexual abuse, or to send them to work and deprive them of full-time education. The law thus recognises that parents can be deprived of their normal right to bring up their own children, and a court may issue an order requiring a child to be taken away from the biological parents and put in care. As the Children's Bill of 1989 makes clear, it is the welfare of the child that must be paramount in the court's decision about his or her upbringing.

The main argument in favour of parents' rights in their children's education derives from the notion that parents must be given those rights which allow them to discharge their responsibilities to care for their children. The link between parental rights and responsibilities in education has been illustrated by Pat White (1983). Parents' educational responsibilities, she suggests, include language development and social training in the early years, mediating between the child and the school to ensure that progress is being made, and generally helping to develop the child's interests and talents. The rights which parents need to discharge these duties include, for instance, the right to impress upon the child certain moral values such as honesty and treating others with respect, the right to have access to teachers and school reports affecting the child, and the right to insist that the child engages in certain sorts of enriching experiences.

Importantly, the argument that parental rights in education spring from parental responsibilities also sets *limits* to the rights which parents can justifiably claim. Thus in placing responsibility for a child's education in the hands of the parents, Principle 7 of the United Nations *Declaration of the Rights of the Child* not only declares that the guiding principle shall be 'the best interests of the child' but points in general terms to what these 'best interests' are:

> He shall be given an education which will promote his general culture, and enable him, on a basis of equal opportunity, to develop his abilities, his individual judgement, and his sense of moral and social responsibility, and to become a useful member of society.

Two points need to be noted about this clause. First, the inclusion of the words 'individual judgement' here suggests that parental duties should have regard to the child's developing rationality and autonomy. This implies that the child's perspective should be taken progressively into account as soon as his or her intellectual development permits, and that this perspective should relate to, among other things, the child's educational opportunities. As John White (1982) has put it, 'Parents . . . have obligations as educators, not independent rights as progenitors' (p. 167). It is also important for children's personal dignity to *feel* that their persepctive is being taken seriously, and this is most likely when their parents include them in decision-making at an appropriate level as soon as possible. The second point to note about the UN declaration is that the child should be educated in 'social responsibility' and become 'a useful member of society'. In short, the educational rights which parents claim must be commensurate both with the right of children to develop as persons and with the general interests of the community.

Of course, the child's need to have educational decisions made on his or her behalf does not in itself imply that such decisions for children should be made exclusively (or at all) by the child's parents. Other adults – perhaps grandparents or other relations, godparents, friends of the family, teachers, educational social workers or educational psychologists – may in some cases be as well or better placed to understand what is in the best educational interests of the child. There is also an argument, though beyond the scope of this book, that children might be better off if they were brought up in other kinds of social units where they were subjected to the collective rights of adults in the community. However, debate about the particular arrangements in which children are brought up does not affect the basic argument that those who make decisions about a child's educational opportunities must respect the child's developing personhood.

Parents' rights and teachers' rights

We have seen that parents' rights in education should be constrained by considerations of children's rights as persons. We next consider the possibility that teachers' rights should be curtailed by the rights of parents. There are two main areas of concern here. The first concerns the content of the curriculum and the second, teacher accountability.

The curriculum

The establishment of a national curriculum is a reflection of the Government's view that *neither* parents *nor* teachers should be left to determine the content of education. This development in central direction may seem at variance with other recent educational legislation which has bequeathed greater managerial freedom to schools and more political power to parents. However, as Maclure (1988) points out, it is only possible to take the risks entailed in giving schools and parents greater autonomy if they exercise their powers within a clearly defined framework of curriculum policy.

John White (1976) has contended that what children are taught in schools helps to shape their developing sense of values, which in turn helps to determine what future generations will count as the Good Society: decisions about the general framework of the curriculum therefore have important implications not only for children's personal development but also for the general shape of society. From this standpoint, because neither teachers nor parents alone are the representatives of society, neither group alone is justified in determining the content of the curriculum, which is a political matter and therefore the responsibility of the State. However, as White (1988) also insists, a national curriculum should reflect the common wish 'to live in a free, democratic country in which ordinary people are not puppets of those in government and have each an equal right to participate in political decision-making' (p. 120). On this criterion, there are grounds for criticising the way in which the framework of the present National Curriculum, although agreed by Parliament, was determined by the Government in face of considerable opposition from professional and parent organisations (Haviland, 1988); by the same token, one can deplore the powers now vested in the Secretary of State, who appoints all members of the National Curriculum Council and who can vary the Council's recommendations for the content of study programmes. A national curriculum should be nationally agreed: because of its pervasive cultural implications, it is too important to be left to any one group, whether this is the politicians (and particularly when all the initiative comes from one part of the political spectrum), the professionals or the parents. It will obviously be difficult, if not impossible, to reach a societal consensus even on the basic structure; nonetheless there should be a real sense in which a national curriculum reflects the aspirations of all significant groups in society.

Teacher accountability

If parents as a constituency have no special claim to control the shape of the curriculum, do they have any special rights to call teachers to account with respect to school processes – the organisation of the curriculum, teaching methods, ways of grouping pupils, classroom management styles, forms of record-keeping and the disclosure of information?

Although there is general acceptance that teachers should be publicly accountable for their decisions and actions, there is much controversy about the form which this should take, particularly with respect to parents. One view is that adopted in the East Sussex Accountability Project (Becher *et al.*, 1979). This recognised the complexity of the matter by suggesting that distinctions need to be made between teachers' contractual obligations to their employers, their professional responsibilities to themselves and each other, and their moral duty to be answerable to the parents. The latter was seen to include explaining curricular aims and methods, reporting on children's progress and disclosing problems, and investigating parental complaints. However, there was no suggestion that parents should sit in judgement on teachers; on the contrary, the aim of the Sussex project was to devise a model of accountability which would facilitate feelings of trust between those involved, including teachers and parents.

Since the East Sussex project, much legislative water has flowed under the accountability bridge. Provisions in recent Education Acts (discussed in later chapters) place parents and schools in a new style of relationship which give parents a good deal more 'clout' (see summary in Introduction, pp. 2–3). Some teachers (and also some parents) fear that the balance of power has tilted too far in favour of parents, making it difficult for teachers to be loyal to their professional convictions. There is concern, for instance, that publication of national assessments and the need to promote school image in an era of open enrolment could have such backwash effects that teachers will no longer have the freedom to make judgements which they believe to be in the children's best educational interests. Instead they will be victims of lay pressure, compelled to adopt a pedagogic style which compromises their professional integrity.

The rightness of particular provisions can certainly be questioned and will be considered in appropriate sections in this book. In this section it is important to make three general points about the relationship between teacher accountability and professional responsibility. The first is that parents cannot exercise their duty to care for their children unless schools involve them in those issues which make the discharge of that responsibility possible. It is right, therefore, that schools and education authorities are now required not only to provide certain sorts of information but also to respond to challenges about their practices and to involve parents individually and collectively in decisions which affect their children's educational opportunities. The fact that some parents may handle these rights clumsily or use them as a means to try to exert control does not affect the basic issue, which is that they need to have statutory rights which enable them to care responsibly for their children.

The second point questions the ability of teachers to make sound professional judgements without liaison with parents. As professionals, schools need regularly to review their teaching arrangements, and individual teachers need to decide how to make their teaching maximally effective. It is therefore incumbent upon schools and teachers to draw on evidence which helps them to evaluate their work and to learn about their pupils' interests, abilities and attitudes, and some of that evidence emerges as a consequence of honest and open communication with parents. In this sense, teacher accountability to parents is not something which should be regarded as additional to their professional duties but something which is integral to them.

The third point relates to the form and manner in which teacher accountability is realised. Certainly the law is at fault if aspects of it make it necessary for teachers to adopt practices which they know are educationally wrong. Yet much depends on how schools choose to respond to the new challenges. As was argued in the last chapter, an approach by which schools work collaboratively with parents in their children's learning, each partner respecting the other's perspective, is the one which seems most likely to help bring about mutual understanding and thus be in the children's best interests. For accountability is not just about the apportionment of praise and blame and possibly the use of sanctions, but should involve:

> . . . a *search for agreement*, a *sharing of language* in which to talk about purpose and practice and performance. Accountability institutionalises a *discourse* about purpose. (Ranson *et al.*, 1987, p. 5, emphasis added)

The test, therefore, will be whether the new legislation turns out to be a stimulus for discourse or discord.

SCHOOL ATTENDANCE AND WELFARE SUPPORT

We now turn to certain basic educational rights and responsibilities which parents have in law. Although, as we shall see in the next chapter, parents are given some discretion in *how* their child is educated, they have a basic duty to ensure that he or she receives 'efficient full-time education, suitable to his age, ability and aptitude, and to any special educational needs he may have, either by regular attendance at school or otherwise' (1944 Education Act, Sect. 36, as amended by the 1981 Act, Sect. 17).

Provided these conditions are satisfied, children are not required by law to be educated in school. As the 1944 Act puts it, they may be educated 'otherwise', a term which gave its name to the organisation Education Otherwise, which exists to provide support and information for families whose children are educated outside school. Official numbers of children who are educated at home are not collected, but in 1987 estimates ranged from 5000 to 20 000 (Deutsch, 1987). Parents do not have to inform their LEA or seek any kind of official approval to educate their children outside school; nor do they need to possess any formal qualifications or teaching experience. However, LEAs have a duty to ensure that parents are fulfilling their legal duties when it appears that they are not or if their children leave school to be educated at home (1944 Act, Sect. 37). LEAs may also themselves provide education at home or in units outside school if the child cannot attend a suitable school (1944 Act, Sect. 56) or if the child's special needs cannot be met in a school (1981 Act, Sect. 3).

If an LEA is not convinced that a child of compulsory school age is being provided with a suitable education, it can serve a school attendance order on the parent requiring the child to be registered at a particular school (1944 Act, Sect. 37). Under the 1980 Education Act, however, the authority must first give written notice to enable the parent to choose an alternative school (Sect. 10), and it is under a duty to comply with the parent's preferences subject to the limitations set out in the 1988 Education Reform Act (see pp. 60–1). Parents who disobey an attendance order commit a criminal offence and can be prosecuted.

Criminal proceedings may also be taken against parents who fail to ensure that their child regularly attends the school at which he or she is registered (1944 Act, Sect. 39), though the school and educational welfare officer will have first done all they can to get the child back to school. Magistrates may impose a fine or (on a third conviction) imprisonment for up to a month (Sect. 40). Attendance is compulsory for pupils registered at a school, though absence is legally permitted for illness or any unavoidable cause, for a day set apart for religious observance by the religious body to which the parent belongs, for special occasions for which leave of absence has been given (e.g. a two-week annual holiday which can only be taken during term time) or in circumstances where the LEA has not arranged transport to a school which, although the nearest to the child's home, is beyond walking distance (see below).

Where a child is not receiving full-time education or is not attending school and also appears to be in need of help, the LEA can start proceedings for the child to be taken into care under the Children and Young Persons Act, 1969. This initiative may be taken as well as, or instead of, prosecution under the 1944 Act, and the court in any criminal case can direct the LEA to institute care proceedings. In Scotland, comparable provision exists to enforce school attendance and provide care under the Scottish Education Act 1962 and the Social Work Act 1968.

In order to help children take full advantage of schooling, certain welfare benefits are available. Briefly, they are these:

Transport   Under the 1944 Education Act, LEAs must provide free transport, or pay travelling expenses, to enable children to attend their nearest school if this is beyond walking distance from their home. This was defined as two miles for children under eight years and three miles for older children. The 1986 Education (No. 2) Act added that, in deciding whether it had a duty to provide transport, the authority should bear in mind the age of the pupil and the nature of the alternative routes. In 1988 the House of Lords ruled that Devon LEA did not act unreasonably in refusing a bus pass to a nine-year-old boy who lived 2.8 miles from school, and that the parent's legal duty to ensure attendance might involve accompanying the child if the route was dangerous (R. v. Devon County Council, ex parte George A.P.).

Clothing   Under the 1944, 1948 and 1980 Education Acts, LEAs can make grants for clothing, including school uniform and sports kit.

School meals and milk   LEAs have not been obliged to provide school meals or milk since the 1980 Education Act, and many no longer do so. By the Social Security Act of 1986, LEAs are allowed to provide free milk and meals only to children of low-income families whose parents are on Income Support; those on Family Credit can receive extra money to help them pay.

SPECIAL EDUCATIONAL NEEDS

The 1981 Act

One of the most important themes running through the Warnock Report (DES, 1978) was the insistence that 'the successful education of children with special educational needs is dependent upon the full involvement of their parents' (para. 9.1). The 1981 Education Act, which established a new framework for special educational provision, formalised this involvement by giving parents certain specific rights and responsibilities. Comparable provision north of the border was made in the same year in the Education (Scotland) Act.

The 1981 Act also widened the *scope* for parental involvement in decision-making processes. A school-age child with special educational needs was defined as one who 'has a significantly greater difficulty in learning that the majority of children of his age' or 'has a disability which either prevents or hinders him from making use of educational facilities of the kind generally provided in schools, within the area of the local authority concerned, for children of his age' (Sect. 1). This represented a fundamental change of outlook. The older concept, affecting about two per cent of children, was of special educational 'treatment' based on defined *categories* of handicap such as 'maladjusted' or 'educationally sub-normal' and thus making a clear division between non-handicapped and handicapped children. The new concept instead recognised a *continuum* of special needs affecting about one in five children. The 1981 Act envisaged a move towards a situation whereby most children with special educational needs would be taught in ordinary schools (where, given the wider, more-embracing definition, most of them would be in any case).

A local authority decides, through a process of *assessment*, whether a child has special educational needs which require special provision. For this purpose, the LEA is required to follow a set of rules which give the parents specific rights at each stage in the assessment procedures (1981 Act Sect. 5, sch. 1). After assessment the LEA decides whether the kind of help needed would not otherwise be available. In that case a *statement* is issued describing the child's needs and specifying the way they should be met in an ordinary or special school. It should be noted that most children with special educational needs are educated without recourse to 'statementing', which is needed only when provision is required beyond the normal school facilities.

During the course of the assessment procedure, the LEA is obliged to involve parents continuously as follows:

1 Whenever the LEA propose to make an assessment of a child's educational needs, it must:
   – inform the parents that it intends to make such an assessment;
   – supply the parents with information about the assessment procedure;
   – provide the parents with the name of an officer from whom they may obtain further information; and
   – inform the parents of their right to state their views ('make representations') to the authority within a period of not less than twenty-nine days.

   The Act also gives parents the right to initiate the process of assessment themselves, and the local authority must comply with their request unless they judge it to be 'unreasonable'.

2 After the period of twenty-nine days has elapsed, the LEA must write to the parents to say either: (*a*) that it intends to proceed with the assessment and why; or (*b*) that it has decided after all not to assess the child. Where the LEA refuses to assess, the parent can appeal to the Secretary of State for Education under the 1944 Act, but in 1986 only about one case in ten was decided in the parent's favour (Goacher *et al.*, 1988).

3 For the assessment itself, the comments which the parents have made must be taken into account along with the *advice* it receives from professionals (e.g. the head, teachers, educational psychologist, a doctor). The doctor or educational psychologist will need to carry out an *examination* on the child, at which the parents have a right to be present and submit their own information if they wish (perhaps evidence from an independent assessment). The LEA might also hold a case conference involving the professionals, and the parent might be able to attend this too. Parents have a duty to ensure that their child attends examinations for special needs unless they have a reasonable excuse, and they can be fined accordingly.

4   Once the assessment is completed the LEA makes one of two decisions: (*a*) If it believes that the LEA should make special provision in an ordinary school or place the child in a special school, it prepares a draft statement and sends this to the parents together with copies of all the reports and advice. The parents are also given a 'named person' from whom they can seek independent help and advice. Fifteen days are given in which the parents can comment on the draft statement and meet an LEA officer and professionals involved in the assessment. They can also ask for further meetings within another period of fifteen days, after which they have a further fifteen days to make further comments and submit additional evidence. The draft statement will indicate the type of school recommended for the child, and the parent has the right to visit any school named. (*b*) Alternatively, the LEA may decide that it does not need to make special provision, in which case it writes to the parents accordingly, informing them of their right to appeal against the decision to the Secretary of State.

5   After making any amendments to the draft, the LEA sends the parents a copy of the final statement and arranges for the special provision, telling the parents that they may appeal to the authority's appeal committee if they are dissatisfied. LEAs are not legally bound to conform to decisions of appeal committees, however, although they are obliged to reconsider the case in the light of the committee's observations; but the parents have a final right of appeal to the Secretary of State, who does have the authority to order the LEA to amend or withdraw the statement. During the first three years of the Act, local appeal committees upheld the LEA decision in almost three out of every four cases. In two-thirds of these parents accepted the outcome; the remainder appealed to the Secretary of State, who asked the LEA to amend the statement in over a quarter of the cases (Goacher *et al.*, 1988).

6   As part of a process of continuous assessment, a statement must be renewed annually with full re-assessment when the child is between twelve-and-a-half and fourteen-and-a-half years old, and the view of the child's parents should be included wherever possible.

7   Under the 1988 Act, an LEA wishing to amend a statement must inform the parents of their rights to make representations and to appeal.

The implementation of the 1981 Act

To what extent has the 1981 Act and its implementation really empowered parents and thereby given children with special educational needs a new deal?

The Act made the LEA accountable to the parents for the appropriateness of the assessment and any special provision. Moreover in extending the rights of parents beyond that given in the 1944 and 1980 Acts, the new legislation provided a framework in which the role of parents could become integral to the decision-making processes. As DES Circular 1/83 emphasised:

> Assessment should be seen as a partnership between the teacher, other professionals and the child's parents, in a joint endeavour to discover and understand the nature of the difficulties and needs of individual children. Close relations should be established and maintained with parents and can only be helped by frankness and openness on all sides.

In short, the potential was made for parents to be regarded as agents rather than clients (Russell, 1983).

Nonetheless, as Peter Newell (1983) noted when the new law was implemented, the 1981 Act is no parents' charter. Although parents have the important right to question the opinion of the professionals, who in turn are encouraged to regard the parent's view as valid, there is no genuine partnership since the distribution of power is weighted towards the local authority. Besides being able to compel assessments against the parents' wishes, the LEA, as already noted, can ignore the view of the appeal committee which takes the parent's side. This, of course, protects LEAs from incurring unwelcome expenditure.

Additionally, the challenge of the new roles given to parents, who could easily be intimidated by the whole porcess, presupposes a high level of personal communication between them and the professionals. But the 1981 Act made no provision for professionals to learn counselling skills, nor did it require local authorities to advise parents on how to prepare their submission. Parents need special help to gain the skills and confidence needed in cooperative decision-making, but a survey in the mid-1980s showed that only 11 per cent of LEAs were providing such training (Goacher *et al.*, 1988). Furthermore, the Act virtually ignored the needs of non-statemented children with special needs and the involvement of their parents. For those being formally assessed, however, guidelines have been produced by Sheila Wolfendale (1988). These help parents to compile 'profiles' of their child's health, coping skills, areas of competence, behaviour, relationships with peers and adults in different settings, and favourite activities. They also invite parents to express their own views and beliefs about the child's needs.

Procedures for assessment and statementing, however well formulated, cannot guarantee good practice. In a recent study of fourteen Asian parents whose children had been statemented, not one knew that their child had been through the procedure! (Rehal, 1989). As Dyson (1987) has illustrated through case studies, the avowed reasons for assessment are not necessarily the same as the real ones. Far from being a means of genuinely assessing a child's needs, assessment may be used for purposes which protect the LEA by, for instance, discounting the parent's view and validating the professionals', persuading parents to accept the LEA placement, or defusing the anger of parents who say nothing is being done. Certainly some LEAs have followed the spirit of the Act, but a large body of evidence shows wide variations in the extent to which this has been observed, not least with respect to parents' rights.

The crux of the matter appears to be a reluctance on the part of some LEAs to facilitate the means by which parents might challenge official recommendations and insist on the provision of new resources in ordinary schools. In their report on the implementation of the 1981 Act, the House of Commons Select Committee on Education (1987) argued that, despite their enhanced legal position, parents often felt that their role was not taken sufficiently seriously. Specifically, they often complained about the inadequacy of information and advice about the assessment procedures and choice of special provision, maintaining too that their views were often not properly taken into account. They also had to wait an inordinate length of time (over a year in some cases) before they received a statement, the language of which was often complex and bewildering, particularly for ethnic minority parents. The Committee (who themselves had trouble finding their way around the jargon!) suggested that voluntary organisations could usefully act as 'befrienders' to help parents make sense of the procedures, and that LEAs should be asked to provide funds for such a service. In fact, in December 1988, the Government gave a grant to the Voluntary Council for Handicapped Students to develop parental involvement in the assessment and education of children with special needs; and the 1989 DES Circular on special needs has called on voluntary organisations to support parents in the assessment procedure.

The conclusions reached by the House of Commons Select Committee are borne out by those of other studies. One of the most major and recent surveys, completed by a research team at London University Institute of Education, closely studied the policies and practices of five local authorities (Goacher *et al.*, 1988). On the key question of parents' rights, the team found that despite some progress most of the parents interviewed were dissatisfied and often upset about certain aspects of the way they had been treated. They felt that they had been rushed or made to accept provision they did not really want. To some extent the issues reflected the dilemmas understandably faced by local authorities in stringent financial circumstances, but parents too were experiencing impossible dilemmas. For instance, because the Government made no extra money available for special needs, parents' statutory rights were sometimes flouted by assessments being linked to existing resources rather than the children's actual educational needs. When parents insisted on a mainstream placement, LEAs would sometimes plead that they could not provide adequate resources or special provision in an ordinary school because of the extra expense: in some authorities 'parents were offered a stark choice of either a statement with resources in a special school or no statement and no resources for integration into the mainstream school' (p. 78).

Recent developments

The impact of the Education Reform Act on special needs provision has yet to be felt. Children with statements can be exempted from all or part of the National Curriculum; parents who wish to complain can use the regular curriculum complaints procedure (see p. 45) and, if still dissatisfied, complain to the Secretary of State under the 1944 Act. For children without statements, the head can exempt a child from all or part of the National Curriculum for up to six months, after which the arrangement is renewable. The child's parents, as well as the governors and the LEA, must be given full particulars and told what alternative provision is being made. When the temporary period has expired, the parent must be told either (*a*) how the child will now be involved in the National Curriculum or (*b*) that the child should be assessed for special needs. Dissatisfied parents can complain to the school governors, whose decision is binding on the head, and parents still aggrieved can complain to the LEA. It is also possible for parents to make a request for the National Curriculum to be temporarily modified for their child, and to appeal to the governors if the head does not comply.

Given the competition between schools which is likely to be generated by open enrolment, opting out, and pressure to meet the National Curriculum attainment targets, it is possible that special needs policies will suffer. Parents whose children have learning difficulties and so depress the school's average attainments may be pressurised into accepting placement in special schools or exemption from National Curriculum requirements. DES Circular 22/89 emphasises that local authorities and schools have an important role to play in ensuring that the rights of parents whose children have special educational needs are respected and developed, whether or not they have statements.

The 1988 Act does, however, give parents two new rights with respect to special needs. First, from April 1990 parents will be able to make representation to the local appeal committee if the LEA decides to *amend* a statement. Previously, under the 1981 Act, their appeal rights over statements were limited to the initial assessment stages and the annual re-assessments.

Secondly, parents should not have to campaign and appeal to the High Court, as they have done in the past, to secure support for paramedical services such as physiotherapy, hydrotherapy or speech therapy. A High Court judgement in 1986 (R. v. Oxfordshire CC, ex parte A.G.W.) ruled that speech therapy was not a 'special educational provision' and that LEAs had no power to provide the service, which was the responsibility of the health authorities. The 1988 Act, however, *empowers* LEAs to buy in such services; and a subsequent House of Lords' decision has since made clear that LEAs have a duty to provide speech therapy even though therapists are employed by the National Health Service (R. v. Lancashire CC, ex parte C.M., 1989).

In giving parents rights over their children's educational needs whilst also keeping the purse strings tight, a vast machinery of bureaucracy and appeals procedures has been erected. The problem is that this reduces, discourages and even negates the development of partnership, as envisaged in the Warnock Report. Fortunately there are some LEAs which are making strenuous efforts to involve parents more fully. A good example is the Pathfinder Project, developed by educational psychologists in Surrey for special-needs children without statements. Parents as well as teachers are encouraged to make known their concerns about any child, and teachers are asked to involve parents at a very early stage so that both parties can discuss the problem together, develop strategies for dealing with it, and define procedures for reviewing those strategies.

THE CURRICULUM AND RELIGIOUS WORSHIP

Curriculum appeals

A parent (or anyone else) can complain to the Secretary of State if it is thought that an LEA or school has acted unreasonably about any matter related to schooling or has failed to discharge its legal duties (1944 Act Sects. 68 & 99). Additionally, local appeal arrangements have been set up for school choice (see p. 58), special needs (see p. 41), and exclusions (see p. 187).

Local appeals also form part of the National Curriculum package in the 1988 Act (Sect. 23). Every LEA and grant-maintained school must have arrangements, approved by the Secretary of State, for considering and dealing with the way in which the authority or school governing bodies have discharged their functions relating to the curriculum, assessment and religious education. A parent who is dissatisfied with the decision reached by the local complaints procedure can appeal to the Secretary of State under Sections 68–69 of the 1944 Act. It is envisaged that parents will discuss their grievances informally so that the need to use the complaints machinery arises only in exceptional circumstances.

Religious education and worship

Under the 1944 Act (Sect. 25), parents can withdraw their children from religious education and collective worship in county and voluntary schools. This obviously poses problems for schools where religious education is part of an integrated curriculum, but such an arrangement does not relieve the school of its duty to comply with parental requests for withdrawal. To protect the rights of parents who want their child to receive religious education or to participate in religious worship according to a particular faith or denomination, arrangements can be made outside the school premises as long as these do not interfere with other lessons and the LEA is not expected to meet the cost. Where a child can only easily attend a church voluntary-aided school, the governors must comply with a parent's wish for non-denominational religious education to be provided according to the Agreed Syllabus.

These rights of parents are unchanged by the 1988 Education Act, but they may take on a new perspective in view of the controversial clauses formulated by the Bishop of London during the Bill's passage in the House of Lords. Although the 1944 Act had laid down that in each maintained school a daily act of collective worship must be provided for all pupils, the 1988 Act (Sect. 7) requires this to be 'wholly or mainly of a broadly Christian character' (though non-denominational except in voluntary schools). Previously, some schools had provided an assembly and religious education lessons acceptable to parents of different faiths or of no religion, more of whom may now feel compelled to exercise their statutory right of withdrawal. This could lead to feelings of divisiveness, emphasising for non-Christian children that they are 'different' and that to be properly British one must be a Christian.

However, the 1988 Act does allow a head to ask the local Standing Advisory Council on Religious Education (SACRE), set up under the Act, for permission to conduct acts of worship according to other faiths, either for the whole school or for just certain groups of pupils. This situation is likely to arise in areas where many families adhere to non-Christian religions. The school governors must be consulted first, and the DES (Circular 3/89) assumes that parents will also be consulted. The position must be reviewed at least every five years. Although this procedure should prevent large numbers of parents withdrawing pupils from religious worship, a policy which encourages separate assemblies for different faiths does not help the school to develop as a single community.

The arrangements for worship do not apply to religious education lessons, however, which, though not part of the National Curriculum, must be provided in all schools. The requirement under the 1944 Act, that these must be non-denominational in county schools and conducted in accordance with locally agreed syllabuses, remains unchanged, though new locally agreed syllabuses must reflect the fact that religious traditions in this country are in the main Christian. The Director of the Muslim Educational Trust advises Muslim parents to withdraw their children from religious education and possibly arrange for special lessons by someone competent to teach about the Islamic faith (Sarwar, 1988).

CHARGING FOR SCHOOL ACTIVITIES

The Education Act of 1944 established the principle of free school education. Nonetheless, until the 1980s the general understanding was that schools and local authorities could charge parents for 'extras'. In 1981, however, a parent won a High Court case against Hereford and Worcester LEA, who, like most authorities, had been charging for instrumental tuition. The Court favoured a wide interpretation of Section 61 of the 1944 Act, stating that instrumental tuition was part of the 'education provided' for which no fees could be charged. Similar decisions were reached by the Local Ombudsmen in cases where parents in Kent, North Yorkshire and Wiltshire had complained about charges for board and lodging on field trips.

Tightly-squeezed local authorities and schools were now presented with a dilemma: they would be risking court action if they continued to charge parents for 'extra' activities such as instrumental tuition and school visits; but if (as some decided) they discontinued the activities, parents would complain that the authorities did not value these aspects of the curriculum.

The principle of free education was also brought into public debate by the publication of reports stating that schools had become dependent on money raised by parents. According to H M Inspectorate (1985), sums collected in primary schools were in some instances well above the capitation allowances, and lessons were sometimes adversely affected by unsuitable accommodation and inadequate provision of books and equipment. As the Inspectors pointed out, 'While parental contributions benefit schools which receive them, they also tend to widen the differences in the level of resources available to individual schools, and, by their nature, cannot be relied upon when planning future developments' (para. 76). In the same year, the National Confederation of Parent–Teacher Associations published data which confirmed the HMI statements. Over 82 per cent of primary schools, for instance, were using PTA funds to provide 'essentials' such as books, computers, and redecoration of school buildings.

The 1988 Act has attempted to clarify the position about parental charges and contributions for school activities and equipment, though in doing so has created some legal anomolies. The basic principle established is that activities which are offered wholly or mainly in school time should be available regardless of parents' ability or willingness to help meet the cost, but LEAs and schools should also have the right to invite voluntary contributions and the discretion to charge for optional activities which operate wholly or partly outside school hours.

Sections 106–11 of the Act lay down detailed regulations to deal with the problem of charging. The essential points (as clarified by DES Circular 2/89) are as follows:

Activities *within* school hours:
(1) Neither pupils nor parents can be *required* to pay for, or to supply, materials, equipment or books for use during school hours. This includes ingredients for cookery and materials for CDT, though schools may make a charge if parents have indicated in advance that they wish to keep the finished product.
(2) There is nothing to prevent schools asking parents to make *voluntary* contributions provided that pupils whose parents do not contribute are not disadvantaged in any way. Thus parents may be invited to pay for a school trip, but pupils whose parents do not contribute must still be allowed to go.
(3) There are two exceptions. For instrumental tuition, charges *may* be made unless the tuition is required by the National Curriculum or an examination syllabus, but they are not mandatory. A charge can also be made for board and lodging expenses whether or not in school hours (see below).

Activities *outside* school hours, including the midday break, are deemed to be optional:
(1) Charges may be made only for activities which are arranged to meet the requirements of the National Curriculum or a public examination or the Act's provisions concerning religious education. All other activities are assumed to be 'optional extras'. For these LEAs are permitted, but not required, to make a charge (e.g. for travel, board and lodging, materials, non-teaching staff costs, entrance fees, insurance) provided the parents have agreed to their child's participation.
(2) The charge can cover the costs of teachers specifically engaged for the optional activity, but not for staff already employed by the LEA or school unless engaged on a separate contract for the activity. The charge may not include a hidden subsidy for children whose parents do not pay, though such pupils can be helped from LEA or school funds.
(3) An activity which takes place partly inside and partly outside school hours is deemed to be one or the other according to the period in which children spend most time. The timing of school trips is thus crucial: those ending on a Sunday can be charged if they begin the previous Thursday but not if the previous Wednesday!

In short, no charges are *required*, but in certain specified cases are allowed. However, charges must be remitted in the case of pupils whose parents receive Family Credit or Income Support. The policy adopted by an individual school can also be more or less generous than the LEA's policy, provided the arrangements fall within the legal constraints. Further, because the Act allows 'persons other than the governing body or local authority' to charge parents, payment for activities during school hours (e.g. a trip) can be levied directly by a third party (e.g. a travel firm). In this case, the right of the school is simply to grant leave of absence: it must not be involved in the transaction, which is between the parents and the organisation concerned, though teachers can take part. The LEA's insurance arrangements are unlikely to apply in these cases, so it is unclear just who would be involved if there was an accident and the issue may need to be resolved in the Courts.

A Labour Party survey in 1989 revealed that the charging arrangements were leading to fewer field trips and visits to museums and the theatre. Marked differences were also found in local authority practices, over half having chosen not to charge for music tuition. It is possible, therefore, that the policy may be changed. Most parents are probably happy to pay for activities traditionally considered as 'extras' provided they see them as valuable. On the other hand the fact that any charging is permitted makes it possible for the children of poor parents to feel stigmatised, while provision for those on Family Credit or Income Support makes no allowance for low-income families just above this threshold. It is also anomalous that charging is lawful for individual instrumental tuition but not, say, tuition in singing or individual sports coaching. Each is an educational experience to which all children are entitled. Further, as long as schools feel under-funded and therefore obliged to ask parents to help provide computers, science equipment and other materials, pupils in poorer areas will be disadvantaged.

ACCESS TO INFORMATION

As argued in the first section of this chapter, parents cannot easily fulfil their duty to care unless they are able to obtain information about their child's educational progress. Recent parliamentary regulations have made various provisions in this respect, details of which are given later in this book, as follows:

1 The content of the school prospectus (p. 100).
2 Access to public documents (pp. 100–1).
3 The governors' annual report and meeting (pp. 110–12).
4 Translation of documents (p. 100).
5 Results of national assessments (pp. 103–7).
6 Access to school records (pp. 108–9).

SUMMARY AND CONCLUSIONS

This chapter began by examining the moral basis for parental rights in education and suggested that these spring from the parents' duty to care for the child. These rights, however, must be commensurate with (*a*) the child's right to develop autonomy, (*b*) the general interests of the community (including the need for a common curriculum), and (*c*) teachers' professional rights. The latter, however, is in turn constrained by professional obligations to inform and consult parents about their child's progress and learning opportunities, considerations which point to the need for a model of school accountability which encourages discourse about the purposes of schools, their policies and practices.

We then reviewed a range of statutory provisions which concern parents' basic responsibilities and rights. The parent's main legal duty is to ensure that the child receives full-time education (not necessarily at school). The law in turn provides parents with a range of rights to make school attendance possible and to incorporate the parents' involvement in schooling. These include welfare provisions, decisions about special educational needs, rights of appeal over malpractice or the failure of authorities to discharge their duties, rights concerning the curriculum and religious worship, the right to secure free education, and rights of access to a range of information.

In the next chapter, we extend this discussion by considering the right of parents to send their child to a particular school and to secure a particular kind of educational provision.

Further reading

For a discussion about parental duties and rights from a philosophical perspective, see Chapter 5 in Pat White's book *Beyond Domination* (Rougledge and Kegan Paul, 1983) and Frederick Olafson's chapter in J. F. Doyle (ed.) *Educational Judgements* (Routledge and Kegan Paul, 1973).

The rights of parents in relation to the curriculum are critically analysed – though from different positions – by Mary Warnock in *A Common Policy for Education* (Oxford University Press, 1988) and by John White in his paper 'Teacher accountability and school autonomy' in A. Finch and P. Scrimshaw (eds) *Standards, Schooling and Education* (Hodder and Stoughton, 1976).

The following DES circulars spell out the implications of the legislation:

8/81: The Education Act 1981
22/89 (replaces 1/83: Assessments and Statements of Special Educational Needs
2/89: Charging for School Activities
3/89: Religious Education and Collective Worship
14/89: The Education (School Curriculum and Related Information) Regulations, 1989

For an analysis of the historical development of parents' rights, see M. E. David *The State, the Family and Education* (Rougledge and Kegan Paul, 1980). A guide to educating children at home, *Schooling is Not Compulsory*, has been compiled by Education Otherwise (address in appendix).

The provisions for special needs are explained in P. Newell *Special Education Handbook* (Advisory Centre for Education, 1988). ACE (address in appendix) also publishes summaries of each Education Act. The implications for parents' rights are included in the study by B. Goacher *et al.*, *Policy and Provision for Special Educational Needs* (Cassell, 1988).

Guidelines (with translations in Gujerati and Urdu) for parents completing profiles on their child for special needs assessment can be found in *The Parent's Contribution* by Sheila Wolfendale (NFER–Nelson, 1988). The same author provides a more detailed discussion, with examples of parents' assessments of their child's needs, in *The Parental Contribution to Assessment* (National Council for Special Education, 1988). Guidelines for LEA administrators who wish to know their statutory duties with respect to parents whose children have emotional and behaviour problems is contained in *The Role of the Administrator* by David Nicholas (NFER–Nelson, 1989).

The options on religious education and worship which are open to Muslims are discussed by G. Sarwar in a pamphlet *What Can Muslims Do?* (Muslim Educational Trust, 1988) – address in appendix.

4 | SCHOOL CHOICE

On the face of it, a policy that allows parents to choose between different kinds of school and send their child to the school of their choice seems a right one. There should always be a presumption in favour of allowing people to do what they want: the onus is therefore on those who wish to place constraints, not on those who wish to allow freedom of choice. Yet although there are arguments for giving parents a free reign when choosing their child's school, there is also a range of moral, religious, social, administrative and educational arguments for restricting parents' options.

Before some of the issues in this debate are examined, it is necessary to appreciate the main types of school that are currently available to parents of children up to the age of eleven. First of all, parents have a basic choice between *maintained* schools which are free and come under the umbrella of LEAs – the 'public sector' – and *independent* fee-paying schools, many of which are called 'preparatory' because they prepare pupils for the Public schools – the 'private sector'. Within the public sector, there are local authority *county* schools which are not affiliated to any religious group, and *voluntary* schools which are Church of England, Roman Catholic or Jewish foundations. The right of voluntary primary schools to give denominational religious instruction and conduct denominational religious worship depends upon the financial agreement made with the local authority: *aided* schools (which constitute the majority of voluntary primary schools), have the right to conduct denominational worship and give denominational instruction but have to find 15 per cent of capital expenses; *voluntary-controlled* schools have all costs met by the LEA but no denominational worship or instruction is allowed except for up to two periods a week for children whose parents expressly request it.

Under the 1988 Education Act, provision is made for a third category of maintained primary school, *grant-maintained*: both county and voluntary primary schools with over 300 pupils can apply to opt out of LEA control and instead be supported by central funds (see Chapter 5).

This chapter is concerned with three main overlapping aspects of school choice within the above framework:

1 private v. public sector schools;
2 secular v. religious schools; and
3 choice within the public sector schools.

We also consider the question of choice for parents whose children have special educational needs.

PRIVATE SCHOOLS

In the late 1980s about 5 per cent of children in Great Britain up to the age of eleven were attending independent (private) schools compared with about 4 per cent at the end of the 1970s (CSO, 1989). According to the 1989 census of the Independent Schools Information Service (ISIS), the trend towards private education is continuing, particularly for young children.

Resolution 2200 of the General Assembly of the United Nations enjoined governments to respect the liberty of parents to choose a private education for their children. The moral argument for making no restrictions on such freedom is that, because it extends the choice available to parents beyond that which can realistically be provided in the public sector, it provides more opportunity to meet children's individual needs. From her interviews with parents who had used schools in both sectors, Daphne Johnson (1987) concluded that private schools complement maintained schools, some at least offering educational provision to which parents would otherwise have no access. Independent schools were often chosen as an alternative to public sector primary schools because, for one reason or another, parents found the local authority provision wanting in some important respect. This might have been because their child had experienced an unsympathetic teacher, or that the teaching was perceived to lack sufficient rigour, or that the parent's voice was found to be unwelcome, or just that the preferred local authority school had no vacancies. Other parents particularly wanted a boarding education for their children (difficult to achieve in the public sector) or a school that catered expressly for children with artistic giftedness or which responded more effectively to problems such as emotional instability or extreme shyness.

Of course, the right of parents to have access to such choice depends upon the validity of arguments which go beyond the scope of this book, such as the place of Public schools for which many independent schools prepare their pupils, or the place of single-sex or boarding education. Yet, as the above examples illustrate, parents do not necessarily choose private education because they want more formal or exclusive schooling for their children. Park School in Totnes, Devon, for instance is a recently-established private school for juniors which parents set up because they were committed to child-centred methods and found the education in the local maintained schools sterile.

One argument against the view that parents have the right to send their children to private schools is that such a choice is not open to all parents but only those who can afford the fees (which in 1988 ranged from £1050 to £4500 a year in day independent schools for juniors). Such parental freedom creates social inequality, for the quality of education which a child receives should not depend upon parental wealth. The right policy, it could be said, is for a greater range of choice to be available within the public sector, not for the private sector to be perpetuated. As we shall see later, recent legislation has increased the opportunities for choice within the public sector but some kinds of amenity are still only available in private schools. This may be because they offer facilities beyond that which the State can reasonably afford (such as large and beautiful grounds) or is prepared to pay for (such as small classes), or because only a small number of parents want them (such as Latin lessons).

The freedom of choice which is denied to parents unable to pay fees is not just about marginal benefits or the needs of a small minority of children. Some of the educational facilities provided by many private schools are those from which almost all children would be likely to benefit. For instance, many preparatory schools have classes of about fifteen pupils, half the number found in many maintained primary schools. If children's learning is generally more effective in small classes, as was found in the London Junior School Project (Mortimore *et al.*, 1988), fee-paying schools would seem to be offering a facility which is a response to general pupil needs, not just those confined to certain individual children. Again, independent junior schools spend more than primary schools on books and materials (Travers, 1988), arguably giving the children whose parents can afford the fees a level of resources which should be available to all children. In short, it may not worry the parents of children in maintained schools that pupils in some private schools enjoy extensive grounds in the country or are able to learn classical languages; but it may appear unjust that they can receive more individual attention and have more books and materials.

Another argument against the existence of the private sector is that parents often choose fee-paying schools not so much because of their perceived educational benefits but as a way of buying special *non*-educational privileges for their children. For private schools are part of the power-structure of society: mere attendance at a preparatory and then a Public school is often enough to give pupils a head start in terms of securing the more prestigious and better-paid jobs. The privileges bestowed by private schools thus allegedly go beyond the curriculum needs of the pupils: indeed, the social and economic benefits may even be secured in those private schools where the education is inferior to that in most publicly-maintained schools.

It seems, then, that the existence of private schools institutionalises and reinforces an unacceptable form of social inequality. Yet the arguments surrounding the freedom of parents to choose a private education for their children are not easily resolved. As Pat White (1983) has recognised, parents in an imperfect democracy face a genuine moral dilemma: 'To support private schools goes against their beliefs about the place of education in a democratic society, but to let their children endure an inadequate education is likely to affect their development as morally responsible people' (p. 156). Given the powerlessness of parents in some situations to influence the kind of education available, it is not possible to say that it is 'never, or always, a parent's duty to use private schools when faced with inadequacies in the state educational system' (p. 157).

RELIGIOUS SCHOOLS

The legal basis for religious schools within the public sector was established in the 1944 Education Act:

> So far as is compatible with the provision of efficient instruction and training and the avoidance of unreasonable public expenditure, pupils are to be educated in accordance with the wishes of their parents. (Sect. 76)

The intention behind this clause was to enable parents to send their children to a Roman Catholic or Church of England school (Stillman, 1986). More specifically, the European Convention of Human Rights, which the British Government has ratified (though with the same proviso as in the 1944 Act), supports the right of parents to educate their children 'in conformity with their own religious and philosophical convictions' (Protocol No. 1, Article 2). However this does not mean that religious schools must be publicly funded.

Over the last twenty years, the proportion of pupils in church voluntary schools has remained at just less than a quarter. In 1987 there were just over one million pupils in voluntary primary schools, of whom 63 per cent were in Church of England, 38 per cent in Roman Catholic and 2 per cent in other religious schools (CSO, 1989). The latter category is made up mainly of nineteen Jewish voluntary-aided primary schools, but there are no state-funded schools (primary or secondary) for Muslims, Hindus or Sikhs.

Whatever may be the position in law, the *moral* question about the right of parents to send their children to a religious school is a particularly difficult one to resolve. Some parents choose a religious school for non-religious reasons; but we are concerned here with parents whose choice stems from their religious convictions. What is 'good' for children here must be a subject of endless disagreement since it raises fundamental questions of values and beliefs which are resolvable only by first accepting the particular ethical or religious position on which they are based.

A major problem in this debate turns on the meaning and role of autonomy in children's educational development. Is the parental duty to ensure that the child is allowed to develop the ability to form independent judgements, as enshrined in the UN Charter on Children's Rights, commensurate with the right of parents to educate their child in accordance with their own religious convictions, as enshrined in the European Conventions of Human Rights? Is a child who is educated in a school in which staff are committed to particular religious beliefs in a good position to make free choices about those beliefs in later years? Does it all smack of indoctrination?

Some critics would say 'Yes'. Callan (1985), for instance, argues that the danger is not so much that children become *incapable* of evaluating their religious beliefs but rather that they become simply *disinclined* to question them. Teachers may not set out to instil unshakable beliefs, but the ethos of the school, and the fact that certain religious doctrines may permeate the whole curriculum, could encourage pupils to accept the received knowledge uncritically. Callan concedes, however, that there are ways of reducing this risk if other religions are not taught as aberrations from the one true faith, or as sets of beliefs which only *other* people accept, but instead are studied as genuinely alternative belief systems which some children may wish to accept. The difficulty with this argument is that such an 'open' ethos would seem to remove the main characteristic that distinguishes religious from secular schools.

A contrasting view is that of McLaughlin (1984, 1985) who argues that strong religious upbringing and schooling could enhance rather than hinder the development of an ability to deliberate autonomously about religious belief. This conclusion is based on an assumption that engagement in religious experience is necessary in order to develop a proper understanding of what religion is about. However, as Gardner (1988) points out, it seems fanciful to suppose that immersion in religious practices during the formative early years will put children in a better position to make up their minds independently about matters of faith.

Many religious parents do not want their children to grow up reflecting autonomously about their own faith. Some religious groups believe that there are certain 'truths' which should not be subjected to any form of critical assessment. There are some Christians who take this view, but the problem has been highlighted in recent years over proposals to set up voluntary-aided schools for Muslim children, whose religion now attracts the third largest group of adherents in the United Kingdom after Anglicans and Roman Catholics. Although many Muslim parents currently ensure that the education which their children receive in school is supplemented through teachings at the mosque, they regard a division between religious and secular learning as unacceptable. Muslims insist that the curriculum as a whole can only be conceived in terms of Islam (which means commitment and submission to the will of God). Many, though not all, therefore support 'separate' Muslim schools, a facility which is currently limited to fourteen independent secondary schools run by the Muslim community (CSO, 1989). However, recent hard-fought attempts to set up voluntary-aided Muslim schools in Bradford, Huddersfield and the London Borough of Brent have been rejected by the local councils, as have similar attempts by Jewish independent primary schools in London. The Muslim case has been accepted, however, by both the right-wing Social Affairs Unit (Hiskett, 1989) and the Labour Party in its 1989 policy review statement, though each end of the political spectrum has groups opposed to this view.

Given the present law, the argument for allowing state-aided Muslim schools rests on grounds of equity: if taxpayers' money is used to fund voluntary schools for Christian denominations and Jews, it is unjust and hypocritical to object to similar provision for other religions. Some critics, however, fear the social consequences of any move which encourages Islamic fundamentalism and the superior role given to males. Others such as the Swann Committee (1985) believe that separate Muslim schools would be socially divisive, damaging inter-cultural understanding and tolerance.

Muslims insist, however, that the issue is essentially a religious one and not about cultural isolationism. The Director General of the Isalmic Academy believes that the Swann Committee did not grasp the essence of the position held by Muslim parents, who, he maintains:

> . . . want their children to grow up as good Muslims and they find the secularist state schools creating non-believers in spite of religious education. All subjects are taught from a secularist point of view. Children are encouraged to be critical of their own traditions and values and even of faith. Doubts are encouraged. Whereas a Muslim teaches a child to pray to God for forgiveness and to strengthen his/her faith, the rationalist teacher teaches the student to explore on his own or with reference to other faiths and ideologies. The Islamic method of removing doubts and the strengthening of faith is completely ignored. It is desirable for a Muslim child to be open-minded and be ready to admit the truth in other religions and ideologies, but it would be wrong to be critical of one's own religion without any norm to judge which is true and which is false . . . We want Muslim children to acquire that norm of judgment from Islam. (Ashraf, 1986)

The doctrinal basis for this view is found in the Qur'an:

> When God and his messenger have decreed a matter, it is not for any believer, man or woman, to have the choice in the affair (Qur'an, Sura 33, verse 36)

The liberal Western tradition, in contrast, is that:

> . . . *all* areas, beliefs, values, attitudes and so on are held by individuals according to their rational status, there being a fundamental commitment to the progressive rational development of personal beliefs and practices rather than uncritical adherence to, or determined defence of any particular set of beliefs and practices *whatever their source*. (Hirst, 1985, p. 13, emphasis added)

This latter position is inconsistent with the Muslim notion that religion should permeate the whole curriculum, respect for divine authority being the most important value in education. The Muslim concern is for the maintenance of their religious and moral values in what is perceived as an increasingly secular society.

Is there a way out of this dilemma? John Halstead (1986) thinks there is. He makes a distinction between 'strong' and 'weak' autonomy. Proponents of the former insist that each and every belief is open to challenge, religious doctrine being no exception. The latter, on the other hand, both allows for and emphasises 'reflective understanding and an informed commitment to a (perhaps pre-packaged) value system' (p. 36). Halstead concludes that this position is appropriate not only for Muslim but for *all* schools since:

> . . . it will aim at continuity between the belief system of the home and that of the school . . . [Children] will be expected to develop patterns of behaviour appropriate to the culture in which they are brought up . . . and will thus enjoy the security of belonging to a community. (p. 42)

There may be a place for schools run on the lines of 'weak autonomy': but, given that a category of belief is shielded from critical assessment of any kind and that this category permeates the whole curriculum, it seems misleading to use the term 'autonomy' in this context.

It seems, then, that the debate about separate Muslim schools is controversial largely because of incompatible views about the significance of autonomous reflection and its role in children's development. The argument is essentially between those who insist that the state should not support a form of education in which religious belief is exempt from critical scrutiny and those who insist, as Mason (1986) has argued, that:

> People with alien cultures and religion, entitled to enter this country as citizens of this state, must reasonably expect to be able to follow their own culture and faith in the same way as previous generations of English citizens were able to whilst abroad in the past. (p. 112)

PARENTAL PREFERENCES AND OPEN ENROLMENT

The problem of free parental choice

The problem of free parental choice in education has been further highlighted in recent years by moves to give parents the right in law to choose between different public-sector schools with only minimal constraints. The arguments for this policy are as follows. First, given that it is the parent who is both morally and legally responsible for the child's education, and given also that schools vary in quality and ethos, it is right that parents should be able to send their children to the school which they perceive offers the best educational opportunities and environment for learning. If parents were compelled to use the official neighbourhood school, they might effectively be forced to subject their child to an education which was known to be inferior to that in another nearby school.

A second argument relates to controversy about the educational validity of different styles of teaching and forms of internal school organisation. Education is not an exact science, and what counts as a 'good school' depends in part upon one's educational ideology. On this view, parents should be given the right to choose between different kinds of learning environments for their children, as long as alternatives are available.

Thirdly, it is argued by supporters of the free market ideology that the competition generated by encouraging choice will act as an incentive for popular schools to preserve high standards and for less popular schools to put their house in order lest they become unviable and have to close. This point was emphasised by Kenneth Baker when he introduced his Education Reform Bill to the House of Commons in November 1987:

> The Bill will introduce competition into the public provision of education. This competition will introduce a new dynamic into our schools system which will stimulate better standards all round.

Fourthly, some claim that free choice facilitates parents' involvement in their children's education, which in turn helps to improve standards. Voluntary and independent schools are often said to attract greater parental support because they have been specially chosen by parents. Lastly, catchment area boundaries create administrative anomalies, with children sometimes being required to attend a school which is further from home than another in an adjacent area.

Yet although, for these reasons, most people would support a system in which parents are given a large measure of choice, many feel that one in which the onus is on school authorities to try to meet all preferences would be counter-productive in terms of educational standards. One kind of fear is the possible adverse effects on the most popular schools. The argument is that schools which are especially sought-after could be forced to expand their intake to a point where standards are put at risk. Further, admitting children from a wide geographical area could jeopardise the development of close school–home and community relationships as well as liaison with feeder secondary schools. The London Junior School Project (Mortimore *et al.*, 1988) showed that pupils in large junior schools made poorer progress, on average, in reading, mathematics and writing, while heads of smaller schools found it easier to consult teachers and to implement whole-school policies.

A second kind of consideration concerns the less-favoured schools. The theory is that market forces will prompt these to improve. However, it could have the opposite effect, creating feelings of insecurity, reducing staff morale, taking away much-needed resources because of reduced capitation allowances, and removing support from the very parents whose involvement could help a school to improve. Further, because popularity is sometimes based on rumour rather than on objective evidence, a good school could unjustly be allowed to go under.

Thirdly, critics point to the dangers resulting from allowing parents to choose out of prejudice rather than on grounds of educational effectiveness. For instance, the Commission for Racial Equality (1987) has warned of possible damage to race relations if free choice leads to racially segregated schools.

Lastly, the unfettered operation of a free market policy in school admissions inhibits scope for educational planning. A school's reputation is not necessarily a stable phenomenon, and changes in its public standing could lead to problems in finding new staff at short notice, or redeploying teachers who become surplus to requirements. One commentator, who is sympathetic to the prospect of schools acting under the constraints of the business world, has nevertheless warned that 'the dynamic process of schools expanding and contracting will involve additional costs that do not arise in a more planned or static situation' (Chaplin, 1987).

Developments between 1944 and 1980

Although the 1944 Education Act established the principle in law that children should be educated in accordance with the wishes of their parents, LEAs were able to reject parental preferences on grounds of 'unreasonable' public expenditure, a criterion which left plenty of room for interpretation and inconsistent treatment between and even within local authorities (Stillman, 1988). During the mid-1970s, parental demand for school choice increased and the Secretary of State for Education and Science received a spate of appeals by parents dissatisfied with decisions made by their LEA. It seemed, however, that the central appeals system favoured administrative arguments rather than parental wishes since in only a handful of cases was a complaint upheld – only two out of 1124 in 1977, for example (*Where* No. 185). Yet the fall in the birth rate and consequent reductions in pupil rolls was giving greater scope for choice of school and making it necessary for administrative policies to be changed.

School choice thus became a political issue. A policy for maximising parental choice was attractive to the Conservative Party in opposition, primarily because of its general electoral appeal in shifting the balance of power away from LEAs and towards parents. Under this pressure, the Labour Government in 1978 introduced a bill which would have strengthened parental choice, but the Conservatives criticised the absence of an effective appeals system and disliked the powers which enabled LEAs to fix ceilings on school numbers.

The 1980 Act and its aftermath

In 1979 Labour lost power. The new Conservative Government quickly re-drafted the Labour bill, and the ensuing 1980 Education Act included sections on school admissions and parental preferences. The provisions undoubtedly shifted the balance towards parents. First, they were given the explicit right to express a preference for the school they wished their child to attend – even if the school was not in the authority where they lived – and to state their reasons. However, the duty of local authorities and governors to comply with the parents' choice was subject to certain exceptions. In particular it did not apply 'if compliance with the preference would prejudice the provision of efficient education or the efficient use of resources' (Sect. 6(3)).

Secondly, LEAs and governors of voluntary-aided schools were required to publish annually the rules of admission to schools. This included the number of pupils to be admitted and, most importantly, the policy for deciding which children should be given priority when a school was over-subscribed. By a subsequent regulation made under the Act schools were required to publish information about their curriculum, organisation and examination results to help parents make their choice.

Thirdly, for parents whose preference was refused, LEAs were required to set up independent appeal committees whose decision would be binding on the LEA. Governors of aided schools had to do the same, though an LEA could administer arrangements on their behalf. This meant that appeals could now be settled locally rather than by the Secretary of State. However, the appeal committees were not made strictly independent since members of the council or education committee could enjoy a majority – though only of one – over the other members who comprised teacher and parent representatives, interested lay people and those appropriate for appeals relating to voluntary schools.

These new provisions for school choice were generally very effective. In 1987 a Gallup Poll based on a sample of 1028 parents found that 93 per cent had never been refused a place at the school of their choice. Nonetheless, largely because the 1980 Act allowed local authorities to refuse a parent's choice of school on grounds of educational efficiency, room was left for official interpretation and parental aggrievement. The local appeal committees sometimes failed to satisfy parents, who complained either to the Local Ombudsman or the Secretary of State. These cases illustrate some of the school choice problems which have arisen for a minority of parents.

1 Appeals to Local Ombudsmen   Under the 1980 Act, a parent whose school preference is refused by a local appeal committee and whose complaint is based on injustice arising from *maladministration*, can take the case to the Local Ombudsman of the Commission for Local Administration. Since the Local Government Act of 1988, parents can write directly to the Ombudsman rather than going through a local councillor, as previously. However, Local Ombudsmen cannot force a local authority to act, nor can they ' idle complaints related to voluntary-aided schools. The following case (CLAE, 1988) is illustrative of complaints to Local Ombudsmen involving choice of primary school in a situation where a parent's carefully considered preference has to be balanced against the educational needs of other children and tight LEA purse strings.

Mrs X's house straddled the boundary of Manchester and Stockport. The nearest primary school for her two daughters was within fifteen minutes' walking distance in Stockport, but because rates were paid only to Manchester the parents were regarded as applying from 'outside Stockport'. In 1987 Mrs X was informed that a place was not available at the Stockport school for the younger daughter, Alice, even though the Council had earlier complied with the parents' preference by allowing the elder daughter to attend that school. Stockport Council's policy was not to give priority to children whose brother or sister attended the preferred school but to children who lived in the school's 'priority area'; Mrs X lived outside this area, even though houses on the other side of her road were in it. The Council argued that compliance with the parent's wishes would entail putting more resources into the school, which in turn would mean taking away resources from other schools: under the 1980 Act, admitting Alice would therefore 'prejudice the provision of efficient education' in the Borough.

The mother appealed to the Stockport Education Appeal Committee which agreed that Mrs X's case should be refused: there were already thirty-five children in the reception class although the admission limit was thirty, and nine Stockport children had been refused places at the school. The Local Ombudsman reviewed Mrs X's complaint, but found no grounds for maladministration on the part of the Stockport Appeal Committee. On the other hand the Ombudsman did find fault with the Committee's letter to Mrs X which had confused the mother by listing all possible reasons for refusing a school place without making clear which ones applied in her particular situation.

2 Appeals to the Secretary of State   A parent who feels that the local authority and appeal committee has acted *unreasonably* can appeal to the Education Secretary by virtue of the provision for complaints in the 1944 Act. This happened in the celebrated Dewsbury affair, which illustrates how political, racial, administrative and educational considerations can become impossibly intertwined in school choice decisions.

In September 1987 the parents of twenty-six white children refused the places offered at Headfield Junior School in Dewsbury, West Yorkshire, where 85 per cent of the children were of Asian origin. The parents claimed that they should be allowed to send their children to Overthorpe school where nine out of ten children were white. However, Kirklees Council maintained this school was full. Rather than comply with the direction of the Council, the parents had their children educated by a retired grammar school teacher in a local pub, an arrangement which continued for nine months.

The parents maintained that the basic issue for them was not race but choice. However they did claim that the presence of Asian children restricted white pupils' linguistic opportunities. They also resented the fact that, because most of the children were Muslim, Headfield School did not provide a daily act of Christian worship, even though it was a Church of England foundation.

The parents complained to the Secretary of State, Kenneth Baker, who told them that he could find no evidence to support their contention that Kirklees Council had acted unreasonably or was guilty of racial discrimination. Two of the parents then asked the High Court to conduct a judicial review. During the proceedings, fresh allegations were made that the Council had been in breach of the 1980 Act by not publishing its admission policies, as it was obliged to, and by giving the parents misleading information about the space available in the schools. Although Kirklees denied that it had not complied with its statutory duties, they evidently recognised an element of technical culpability since they reversed their decision during the High Court hearing and offered the parents their first choice of school.

Open enrolment in the 1988 Education Reform Act

The right of parents to send their child to the school of their choice has been considerably enhanced by Section 26 of the 1988 Act. The provisions in the 1980 Act for appeals and the publication of information to parents still apply. The key change is that a local authority can no longer refuse a parent's preference on the grounds that to comply would not be in the interests of educational efficiency or economy. The only grounds for rejection now are that the physical capacity of the school has been exceeded. However, the danger that voluntary schools might lose their distinctive character through having to admit large numbers of children whose parents do not share the school's religious affiliation is protected by a provision which enables the governors to come to an appropriate agreement with the LEA (Sect. 30). Typically this would state the percentage of intake which has to be of a particular denomination. Open enrolment will apply to secondary schools in the first instance, but the Government hopes that LEAs will implement the policy in primary schools before they are required to do so.

The problems which could be created by this regulation include those outlined at the beginning of this section. The terms of the Act make the overcrowding of popular schools a particular danger. This is because the physical capacity of a school is defined by its 'standard number', which means the number of pupils admitted in 1979–80 (unless the number for 1989–90 is larger or another limit is agreed by the Secretary of State). Schools which have since reduced or re-allocated their accommodation now have to find room for the extra places. Parental free choice might also encourage racial segregation, as was evident in the Dewsbury affair described above.

Because of open enrolment, competition is likely to intensify between schools, which will need to market themselves more aggressively to remain viable and retain their staff. The Government clearly foresees the possibility of under-subscribed schools having to close. The DES Circular 11/88 states:

> The number of pupils at a school may decline to a point where it becomes difficult to provide a curriculum of the desired range and diversity, and in due course meet the requirements of the National Curriculum without disproportionate resourcing. If there is no reasonable expectation that numbers will rise in the foreseeable future, the local authority should consider whether to bring forward proposals either to cease to maintain the school or to amalgamate it with another school.

The Scottish Education Act of 1981 gave similar enhanced status to parental choice as that given to parents south of the border in the 1988 Education Reform Act. Scottish parents have the right to request a school other than that to which their child has been directed by the local authority, and the request must be granted unless one of a small number of official grounds for refusal apply. Parents are also given extensive rights of appeal, not only to a local committee as in England and Wales, but subsequently to a sheriff (the Scottish equivalent of a county court judge). Moreover, whenever an appeal is upheld, whether locally or by a sheriff, the local authority must review the cases of all non-appealing parents of similar circumstances.

Two pieces of research have shown the effects of open enrolment in Scottish primary schools and point to likely tendencies in England and Wales. In a study based on three authorities, Alison Petch (1986) found that parents have taken advantage of their right to insist on a school outside the formal catchment area, particularly when to do so meant that their young child would not have to travel so far; and they have also used their right to send brothers and sisters to the same school. Petch also found that parents are much less bothered by the school's reputation in the three Rs or other matters directly related to the curriculum and teaching methods than with their young child's happiness (for example, whether friends are at the school, whether the pupils are 'rough and rowdy', or whether the school is overcrowded).

A second study (Raab and Adler, 1987) found that about a fifth of parents, many working class, have taken advantage of the new legislation. Although most parents choose schools near to home, a sizeable number avoid sending their children to the local school if it is in an area of economic and social deprivation. However there is little in the way of a two-way traffic of pupils, most schools being either gainers or losers. The result is that free choice materially affects school size. The study found that ten primary schools in Dundee and Edinburgh had effectively doubled in size through having to accept pupils outside the natural catchment area, while three schools had lost more than half their normal intake.

Taken together, these Scottish studies suggest three possible effects of open enrolment in England and Wales. One is the prospect of larger primary schools. A second is the creation of 'sink' schools in 'deprived' areas. A third is that schools which stress high attainment at the expense of the children's happiness may be the losers. At the same time, it could be, as Sallis (1988) has suggested, that parents will be more likely to settle for the nearest school if they know that their voice will be heard and that their grievances and requests will receive a sympathetic ear. In such a climate, open enrolment could become less of an issue and lose its political contentiousness.

CHOICE OF SCHOOL FOR CHILDREN WITH SPECIAL NEEDS

The statutory right of parents to express a preference for a particular school does not apply to those whose children have a statement of special educational needs (1981 Act, Schedule 3(4)). A child's statement of special needs must specify the *type* of school which the LEA considers appropriate, and it may name a particular school, which, after consulting the parent, can be in a mainstream setting (possibly the one the child is already attending); if not, the parent can ask for this to be done. A parent who does some homework and finds out which school can most suitably meet the child's needs is in a better position to make use of the right of appeal. However, unlike the committees which deal with complaints over school choice, the appeal committee for special needs cases cannot overrule the LEA decision but only ask that it be reconsidered.

The controversial nature of this debate centres around the fact that the education of statemented children can be in segregated special schools or, with suitable support, in ordinary schools. When the University of London Institute of Education carried out its survey on special needs in the mid-1980s, the majority of LEAs were placing statemented children in special schools (Goacher *et al.*, 1988); but, in the spirit of the 1981 Education Act, more local authorities are now working out phased programmes to transfer resources and staff for children with special needs to ordinary schools. Following the Fish Report (ILEA, 1985c), the Inner London Education Authority decided to adopt this policy, but some parents objected and the Campaign for Choice in Special Education was set up to ensure that parents still have the facility to choose a special school for their child.

There are two sorts of problems connected with this position. The first is ideological. Those who support a policy of integrated special education in mainstream settings, wherever this is practical, do so because they believe that segregated special schools are discriminatory and reinforce the separateness of handicapped sections of the community. Special education which is organised as an integrated part of mainstream provision is said to be more equitable, since it recognises that statemented children are entitled to the same curriculum and social opportunities as other children. On this argument, a case could be made for saying that parents should not have the right to 'choose' whether their child is denied these facilities, since they are the child's entitlement.

The second problem is a practical one. There is no doubt that many parents are concerned about special educational provision in ordinary schools. The research findings suggest that this is mainly because they are concerned about the adequacy of the resources, class size and appropriate training for teachers (e.g. ILEA, 1985c; Dawson and Kierney, 1988). It is therefore very important for LEAs to address these issues by putting properly resourced special needs facilities into ordinary schools. Given that they have only limited funds and cannot double up on all its special needs resources, the very existence of special schools severely reduces the choice available to the growing number of parents who want supported mainstream provision (Vaughan, 1989). As long as resources are locked away in special schools, integrationist policies are likely to be ineffective.

SUMMARY AND CONCLUSIONS

This chapter began by noting the range of educational provision available to children of primary school age. It then examined the moral and legal position of parents who wish to send their child to the school of their choice.

Various moral issues were identified with respect to private schooling. In particular it was suggested that parents could be faced with a moral dilemma: on the one hand it is inequitable that the more favourable staffing and material resources which are enjoyed by most independent schools are effectively unavailable to parents who cannot afford the fees; on the other hand, it would be unjust if, in the absence of private schools, parents were unable to provide the kind of education which they consider right in the light of their child's needs. The possibility that the maintained sector could satisfy the educational needs of all children in every eventuality was seen as a pipe dream – though certainly more could be achieved in this direction.

The debate about religious schools was also seen to raise many problems. One centres around controversies concerning the respective roles of parents and schools in encouraging children to develop the capacity in later years to reflect autonomously about their religious beliefs. Another is that, given public investment in schools for Christians and Jews, it seems inequitable for the same facility to be denied to those of other faiths such as Muslims.

The arguments in favour of unfettered parental choice within the public sector were seen to be associated with giving children access to school with the best educational standards, as perceived by their parents, in situations where schools may vary in quality or offer different but equally valid kinds of learning environment; with providing incentives through competition for less-favoured schools to improve; with encouraging parental involvement in education by the fact that their child attends a school which has been chosen; and with preventing restrictions through administrative anomalies. Against these arguments have to be considered various possible adverse effects on both popular and unpopular schools and the constraints on scope for local educational planning. Appeals cases and research evidence were cited to illustrate some of the problems associated with provision for greater parental choice under recent Education Acts. In the case of choice in special educational provision, the question of parental choice between special schools and supported placements in ordinary schools was seen to be bound up with ideological issues about equal educational opportunities and practical problems of resourcing.

It is clear that this chapter has raised more questions than it has answered, but this was not easy to avoid. For although we have more evidence today about the factors which make a school effective, our knowledge about this and the possible effects of parental choice leave plenty of room for controversy. Whatever the facts of the situation, disputes and dilemmas are bound to remain since they are embedded in conflicting moral, religious, educational and political ideologies.

Further reading

On parental choice and private schools
For a sympathetic exploration of the rationale for independent schools and dilemmas faced by parents, see Johnson, D. *Private Schools and State Schools – Two Systems or One?* (Open University Press, 1987). For a more philosophical treatment which centres on the question of parental rights, see the following series in *Journal of Philosophy of Education*: Cohen (**12**, 1978), Royce (**16**(1), 1982), Shaw (**17**(1), 1983), Colbeck (**18**(1), 1984), Stafford (**19**(1), 1985).

On parental choice and religious schools
For a discussion on the rights of parents in relation to religious upbringing and schools, see the following series in *Journal of Philosophy of Education*: McLaughlin (**18**(1), 1984), Callan (**19**(1), 1985), McLaughlin's rejoinder in the same issue, and Gardner (**22**(1), 1988). Arguments concerning voluntary schools for Muslim and other non-Christian children are discussed in the Swann Report *Education for All*, Chapter 8 Sect. II (HMSO, 1985). The conclusions are challenged by J. Halstead in *The Case for Muslim Voluntary-Aided Schools* (Islamic Academy, Cambridge, 1986). See also R. Jeffcoate *Ethnic Minorities and Education* (Paul Chapman Publishing, 1984).

On parental preferences and open enrolment
The background and consequences of the 1980 measures are examined in five research papers edited by Andy Stillman *The Balancing Act of 1980: Parents Politics and Education* (NFER, 1986). The arrangements for open enrolment under the 1988 Act are explained in DES Circular 11/88, whilst procedures for parents' complaints are explained in *School Choice Appeals*, a handbook published by the Advisory Centre for Education. Martin Leonard gives practical advice on how heads might manage open enrolment in *The 1988 Education Act: A Tactical Guide for Schools* (Blackwell, 1988).

5 | PARENT POWER

In the 1944 Education Act, the rights of parents were limited to matters which related directly to their own children. Parents were not given collective rights to influence the curriculum or the way schools were governed or organised. The law remained unchanged in these respects until the 1980s. As a result of the Education Acts of 1980 and 1986, parents now have the right to participate in the government of their children's school through their own elected representatives; their powers in this respect were further enhanced by the 1988 Act, which also (and more controversially) gave parents a key position in determining whether a school maintained by a local authority should apply for grant-maintained status and so secure a large measure of independence.

PARENT GOVERNORS

Developments up to 1980

The idea that schools for young children should have bodies of lay outsiders to look after their interests goes back to the 1830s when the early church elementary schools were first established. In order to receive a government grant these voluntary schools had not only to be open to inspection but also to be conducted in accordance with an approved scheme of management. Following the Education Act of 1870, managing bodies were also set up by many of the area school boards whose function was to supplement the Church's provision of elementary education. The practice of having managing bodies continued after the 1902 Act when LEAs took over the former board schools and were also made responsible for maintaining the voluntary schools.

Under the Education Act of 1944, LEAs were required to ensure that all primary schools had a body of at least six 'managers'. (Secondary schools were to have 'governors'.) The theory was that this would not only protect the public interest but help to preserve a school's individuality; but the reality was that local authorities dominated proceedings. They were able to do this because membership was left 'as the local authority may determine' (Sect.18) except in church schools which were assured a proportion of managers appointed by the foundation. Furthermore, the *powers* of managing bodies were also left undefined and in the hands of local authorities. The Act also allowed LEAs to group schools under a single set of managers, a practice which was frequently followed. Since groups often contained large numbers of schools, it was difficult for a managing body to identify with any one individual institution.

During the parliamentary debate on the 1944 Act, some MPs had urged that parents should be given the statutory right to participate in school management, an idea which had been raised by the Cross Commission as far back as 1888 but not adopted at the time because of fears of parental interference. Although the 1944 Act said nothing which ruled out parent representatives, the local authorities were loath to take up the challenge. For one thing, given that schools were their responsibility, they did not wish to lose their position of control; for another, they were under pressure from heads who saw parent managers as a threat to their professional autonomy.

During the 1960s, the cause was taken up by the Plowden Committee (CACE, 1967), by parent organisations and by the National Association of Governors and Managers. In 1969 some headway was made when Sheffield Labour Party, suffering from its defeat in the municipal elections the previous year, was anxious to promote a policy which would help it regain control of the City Council. In its manifesto the party promised 'to promote the widest participation in the running of schools by parents, teachers, trade unionists, people from all walks of life' (quoted in Bacon, 1978, p.51). In 1970, following Labour's victory in the Council elections, the new system of school management was established in Sheffield, each school having its own board which included elected representatives of parents, teachers and non-teaching staff. The example was followed by some other local authorities, and by 1975 about 85 per cent of those replying to a national survey had made some provision for parents to be school managers or governors, while 75 per cent had also involved teachers (NAGM, 1975).

However, the fact that parents had seats on some managing bodies did not mean that they were collectively represented: in many cases, they were co-opted or were simply chosen by the head, the authority or the PTA committee (DES, 1977). Where polls were organised, the turnout was generally very low. Bacon's (1978) study in Sheffield revealed that most parents there were ignorant about the school boards and that the special meetings to elect parents were for the most part badly attended. In short, the position during the 1970s was generally one in which there was little more than the illusion of parental participation in school government.

In 1974, during a Labour Party administration, a Conservative MP, William Shelton, presented a Parents' Charter Bill which included a proposal for at least three parents on the managing or governing body of every school. The parents' function, however, was to be primarily consultative and the curriculum was explicitly excluded from their preview. The bill failed to become an Act, but the Labour Government, 'prompted by a desire to steal some of the Conservatives' clothes' (Beattie, 1985), set up a committee of enquiry into school government. This was chaired by Tom Taylor, the leader of Blackburn Council and now a Labour peer, and included three parent representatives among the twenty-four members.

The Taylor Committee's deliberations were brought into sharp focus by two events in 1976. One was the affair at William Tyndale Junior School in London, where some parents protested at the 'permissive' teaching arrangements and neglect of the 3Rs but no one seemed to know where the ultimate power and final responsibility lay. The other event was a speech by the Labour Prime Minister, James Callaghan, who challenged schools to be more responsive to the needs of an industrial society. It was therefore clear to the Taylor Committee that a means had to be found to make schools more accountable to the public in general and to parents in particular.

In its report (DES, 1977), the Committee recommended that each school should be legally required to have its own *individual* governing body (primary and secondary schools alike to have 'governors') which was *representative of all relevant interests* – i.e. the LEA, parents of children at the school, teachers and the local community – in *equal* proportions. This would end the practice whereby schools were grouped and local politicians played the dominant role. Further, the Committee recommended that the *purposes* of governing bodies should be laid down, and that these should include powers over the curriculum. The latter suggestion was contentious, challenging the teaching profession's autonomy, but was grounded in the belief that the principle of partnership necessitated it. Governors were therefore to be given responsibility for setting the aims of the school, considering how they might be realised, and evaluating progress towards them. In an interview published in *The Times* (24.9.77), Taylor argued that these recommendations between them would prevent the type of situation which had arisen at William Tyndale School, since an unconventional head would have to convince the governors that he was right.

The Taylor Report, whilst suggesting an increase in parental influence, was no brief for parent power. Even so it was unfavourably received by parts of the teaching profession and by local authorities. Fred Jarvis, General Secretary of the National Union of Teachers, dismissed it as a 'busybodies' charter'. The National Union of Head Teachers was more guarded, but totally rejected the suggestion that parent organisations or governors should debate the curriculum: 'Few Governing Bodies will have the competence to set aims and objectives in a field where even the professionals find such exercises complex and can fail to reach common agreement' (NAHT, 1978, para 37). Seventeen head teachers also wrote to *The Times* (7.11.77) questioning the willingness of parents to participate, fearing 'the serious dangers of pressure groups wielding unwarranted influence'.

The 1980 Act and its aftermath

The electoral defeat of Labour in 1979 meant that parliamentary debate on the Taylor Report was continued into the Conservative administration. Unlike his successors, the new Education Minister, Mark Carlisle, bowed to the local authority argument that the composition of school governing bodies, like the local authorities themselves, should reflect the elective will of the people.

Accordingly the 1980 Education Act failed to implement the Taylor proposals for equal representation of interests and provided for only two parent governors (elected by secret ballot) in each school; teachers were allowed at least one member (two in schools with more than 300 pupils), but representation from the 'wider community' was left to LEA discretion.

The 1980 Act did not therefore substantially change the distribution of power in governing bodies. The local authority representatives, and therefore the local political party currently in power, could – and usually did – remain dominant. Nor did the Act define governors' powers, as the Taylor Committee had recommended. As before, this matter was left for the LEA to determine, and governors' meetings often continued to 'rubber stamp' decisions made by the authority or the head. The Taylor Report had also proposed that parents be given the legal right to form their own associations in each school, but this too went unheeded, as it has since.

Nonetheless, some headway had been made. For the first time, the right of parents and teachers to participate in school government had been recognised in law. Under a Statutory Instrument in 1981, parents were also given the right to see the agenda and minutes of governors' meetings, and any three governors could request a meeting. Further, to encourage schools to develop their own distinctive characters, the general practice of sharing governors was to end: as Taylor had recommended, the Act required that each school would have its own individual governing body unless the Secretary of State approved otherwise.

The gains, however, made little impact at grassroots levels. Surveys on parent governor elections conducted after the implementation of the 1980 Act revealed widespread ignorance, confusion and apathy. Investigation by *The Times Educational Supplement* (5.10.84), the Welsh Consumer Council (Woods, 1984) and the Advisory Centre for Education (*ACE Bulletin 7*, 1985) showed that the root of the trouble lay in the absence of central guidelines for the conduct of parent governor elections and the low profile which authorities gave these events. While there were certainly instances of good practice in some places, there was widespread variation in procedures: elections were sometimes by postal ballot, sometimes at a meeting; in some areas there was one vote per parent, in others one per household. Moeover it emerged that many parents had never heard of governors; and those that had did not always know whether their child's school had a governing body or what it was for. Many LEAs compounded this ignorance by preventing candidates issuing statements about their qualifications or publicising their views on issues of concern. Not surprisingly, response to governing body elections was frequently poor. Moreover interviews with elected parents indicated that some felt inhibited by the manner of the chairperson or head, and judged their presence on governing bodies to be resented.

These kinds of concern formed the background to further legislation in 1986. Meanwhile, and before the governing body sections of the 1980 Act had been implemented, the Government had issued a discussion ('Green') paper *Parental Influence at School* (DES, 1984). This dealt with two related concerns. The first was that insufficient attention had been given to the principle embodied in the

1944 Act that children should be educated in accordance with the wishes of their parents. The second was that because the powers of governors were not laid down by Act of Parliament, power was still effectively in the hands of the local authorities. The Government therefore proposed a set of measures, the most contentious of which was that the *majority* of governors should be parents of children at the school, except in the case of voluntary-aided schools where the majority would comprise the parent and foundation governors together. It was also proposed that the functions of governors should be defined to include curricular aims, discipline policy, staff appointments and dismissals, admissions, the school's spending and the use of the school's premises. Since parents were to form the majority of members, these definitions clearly added to their power. Lastly, it was proposed that the governors of each school should be made more accountable to the whole parent body by being required to distribute an annual report to every parent and to call a meeting of all parents once a year to discuss the report and pass resolutions which the governors or LEA would be required to consider.

The ensuing debate was dominated by the proposal that parents should be in the majority. This received general condemnation from the local authorities and teaching unions. Both the Conservative-controlled Association of County Councils and the Labour-controlled Association of Metropolitan Authorities embraced the principle that there should be an equal balance of interests. For the teachers, the General Secretary of the National Association of Head Teachers probably reflected the profession's general view when he criticised the Government's assumption that parents have a monopoly of wisdom in school government (letter to The *Guardian*, 25.5.84).

The parents' groups, however, were divided. In a letter to Sir Keith Joseph (28.9.84) the Campaign for the Advancement of State Education emphasised that 'education is a partnership'; whilst urging greater representation for parents, it preferred the Taylor formula, fearing that a parental majority would be provocative. Also critical was the National Confederation of Parent Teacher Associations, which wondered where all the parents would come from (*The Teacher*, 1.6.84). However, the other main parent body, the Advisory Centre for Education, welcomed the proposal that parents form a majority on governing bodies, arguing that the criticisms were misplaced when 'it is widely acknowledged that increased parental involvement in a child's schooling will be beneficial' (*Where* **200**, p.5).

In an article in *The Times Educational Supplement* (8.6.84), Maurice Kogan probably echoed the majority view: 'The Government has gone over the top and for reasons which it barely admits to itself. It does not like local authorities.'

The 1986 and 1988 Acts

In its subsequent policy paper *Better Schools* (DES, 1985a), the Government responded to the barrage of criticism by climbing down on the membership issue, but it left intact the more generally accepted suggestions for defining more closely the respective responsibilities of governors, head and LEA. The substance of the proposals were then incorporated into the Education (No. 2) Act 1986, though with some additions added by Parliament; and the 1988 Act made some further changes.

Table 5.1 Composition of school governing bodies under the 1986 Education (No. 2) Act

	Elected[a] parents	LEA appointees	Head[b]	Elected[c] teachers	Co-opted[d]	Foundation[e]	TOTAL
County and maintained special schools							
<100 pupils	2	2	1	1	3	–	9
100–299 pupils	3	3	1	1	4	–	12
300–599 pupils	4	4	1	2	5	–	16
600+ pupils	5	5	1	2	6	–	19
Voluntary-controlled schools							
<100 pupils	2	2	1	1	1	2	9
100–299 pupils	3	3	1	1	1	3	12
300–599 pupils	4	4	1	2	1	4	16
600+ pupils	5	5	1	2	2	4	19
Voluntary-aided schools							
<300 pupils	1+	1	1	1+	– (f)		
300+ pupils	1+	1	1	2+	–		

Notes

(a) Parents must be those of registered pupils at the time of the election, elected by fellow parents by secret ballot.

(b) A head may choose not to be a governor.

(c) Teachers are memberrs of the teaching staff at the school elected by fellow teachers by secret ballot.

(d) Governors are free to decide whom to co-opt, but have a duty to ensure that the local business community is represented among its members.

(e) Foundation governors are those appointed by the voluntary body to preserve and develop the character of the school.

(f) The number of Foundation governors is unspecified in the Act, but they must be in the majority by two (or three if total size exceeds eighteen) and one must be a parent.

The 1986 Act reshaped governing bodies. The position now (see Table 5.1) is that in county and voluntary-controlled schools overall control of governing bodies has been taken away from local politicians, who have to share power with parents, teachers and community representatives. Parents and the local authority are now *equally* represented and no one interest predominates. A parent, though not a teacher representative, can also be chairperson; indeed in most LEAs parents in some schools have been elected to that position (Jowett and Baginsky, 1988). By contrast, 'parent power' is a less potent factor in voluntary-aided (church) schools, where foundation governors still occupy a majority; however, in addition to at least one elected parent, at least one foundation member must be a parent. As regards the conduct of parent governor elections, there are now DES guidelines (Circular 7/87, Annex 9), though these allow a measure of choice between acceptable procedures.

The position for elected teachers remains as in the 1980 Act. In all types of school they are in the minority with only one or two elected members apart from the head; but the requirement for governors in county and voluntary-controlled schools to co-opt a given number of further members means that the representation of business and community interests is no longer left to chance. Teachers may be parent governors in the child's school or any other, and both parents and teachers can be co-opted, a controversial state of affairs since this increases their effective representation.

The combination of increased numbers of elected parent governors in all but the smallest primary schools, the elimination of local authority dominance, and the range of responsibilities assigned to governors means that parents have now more opportunity than ever to influence school decision-making. While it is the head's responsibility to manage the school's affairs, governors have the legal authority to establish certain general principles and to demand information and explanation. Governors participate in appointing the head and teachers, and under the 1988 Act, they may have considerably extended managerial responsibilities. In cases of primary schools with 200 or more pupils (and in smaller schools if the LEA, after consulting with the governors, so decides), the major budgetary powers, decisions about staff numbers and the appointment and dismissal of the head and teachers will be given to governors from 1993. The 1988 Act also makes it a duty of governors as well as the head to ensure that the National Curriculum and the law relating to religious education is observed in the school; this leaves governors with a particular responsibility under the 1986 Act to consider remaining teaching areas and to ensure that the school's curriculum reflects the interests of the local community. It is entirely in the hands of governors whether sex education is included in the curriculum and, if so, what its content and organisation should be; and with the head teacher and local authority they must ensure that whenever teachers raise political issues, there is 'a balanced presentation of opposing views' and no 'pursuit of partisan political activities'. Governors also have the important responsibility to prepare an annual report for parents, with whom they must hold an annual meeting (see pp. 110–13).

Parental power?

On the surface, at least, it would seem that, through the school's governing body, parents now have the facility to bring a new and distinctive dimension to school decision-making. Not only are they now assured of representation, but with teachers can outvote the local politicians, and they are numerically strong enough to make their influence felt in important policy matters.

How far the changed balance of representation has given parents genuine power is a matter open to dispute. Whitehead and Aggleton (1986) suggest that Conservative politicians have wanted increased parental participation less because they see intrinsic merit in enhancing parents' political rights and more because they assume that parent governors will tend to support centralist policies to raise levels of managerial efficiency and teacher accountability. At the same time, the teachers' unions are torn between an ideological commitment to more openness and a concern to protect their professional autonomy. There is also the danger that governing bodies, though ostensibly possessing greater autonomy, will become even more dependent on the school's and other managerial expertise because of the increasing complexity and amount of business which they are now required to transact. One recent report has suggested that parent governors tend to come from the limited few who already take an active part in school affairs, and that for the great mass of parents the elections hold no interest (Browning, 1989).

Certainly much remains to be done if parental participation in school government is to work effectively. First, there remains the difficulty of eliciting parent participation. The DES has spent £110 000 on advertising through newspapers and leaflets, and its guidelines require LEAs to ensure that pre-election publicity is designed to maximise participation. Some education authorities have responded positively by such means as newspaper advertising, posters, radio phone-ins and the distribution of promotion literature in various languages. Yet the response from parents, though high overall, has been patchy. In a survey commissioned by the DES (Jeffries and Streatfield, 1989), more than a quarter of rural primary schools had found it difficult to recruit enough parent governors. In contrast, only one in fourteen primary schools in metropolitan areas had experienced this difficulty, but few parent governors came from underprivileged backgrounds or from black or Asian communities. A survey among Exeter primary schools, where parental participation was high, also showed that the majority of parent representatives occupied professional or managerial positions (Golby and Lane, 1988). It would appear, therefore, that 'parent power' is more a phenomenon of the white urban middle-classes.

Secondly, although the majority of schools give parent governors full support, letters in the agony columns of the educational press suggest that there is resistance in some quarters. For instance, chairpersons sometimes appear to discourage their parent members participating fully in appointment interviews or nominating co-opted members; heads are sometimes unwilling to discuss matters openly and may resist negotiating an agreed means whereby parent governors can elicit parental views.

A third problem is knowing who parent governors represent. Research carried out by Brunel University before the 1986 Act (Kogan *et al.*, 1984) revealed that parent governors generally felt they were untypical of parents in general – not least because they had put themselves forward for election – and they had difficulties in canvassing the views of their electors. The link between teacher governors and their constituency was understandably less tenuous. A more recent survey has revealed that large numbers of parent representatives are teachers from other schools, blurring the parent and teacher constituencies (*The Times Educational Supplement*, 21.10.88). Yet parents may well wish to elect one of their number who is also a teacher because they value being represented by someone who is well informed about schools. While it would therefore be a mistake to debar such candidates, it is important for ordinary parents to know that their voice is being heard on governing bodies.

Lastly, the new responsibilities of governors are such that many parents may feel unable to give the time which is needed, especially if this means a period off work and loss of earnings. Apart from meetings and other governors' business, time is needed for training which is essential if governors are to feel confident about making a contribution. Governors who are 'ordinary' parents are especially affected here since they are least likely to be accustomed to committee work and undertaking public responsibilities. It is LEAs who (under the 1986 Act) have the responsibility to ensure that every governor is offered the training they need and free of charge; but although most authorities have made a start, recent surveys show that much remains to be done (Roberts *et al.*, 1988; Pryke, 1989).

The better training courses are run on workshop lines and are based on individual schools or a small group. Besides covering information on the law of education, curriculum issues, special needs and community links, they deal with the skills of selecting staff, monitoring the curriculum, chairing meetings and financial management. To encourage good practice by spreading the lessons of local initiatives, a coordinated national agency called Action for Governors' Information and Training (AGIT) has been set up (without Government funding) at the Community Education Development Centre in Coventry. This consortium, for which the Open University has produced materials, includes the National Consumer Council, CASE, the NAGM and local authority associations.

The role of the school in helping parent governors

However helpful the LEA and a training programme may be, the head and staff also have an important role to play in making it possible for parent governors (and other members of the governing body) to fulfil their responsibilities. Parent governors are more likely to want to participate, and to do so constructively, if they find the job at once manageable and challenging. School staff play a vital role here by encouraging openness and dialogue and demonstrating that the parents' view is important. This section therefore concludes with a list of ways in which schools can do this:

– By helping to locate relevant resources, for example DES leaflets and guidelines, and by identifying members of staff who can explain and advise on particular matters.
– By inviting governors into the school. This needs to be more than a general 'You're welcome to come along any time' kind of statement, for many governors feel diffident about just dropping in. Invitations should be to those events which are likely to give governors insight into the workings of the school: perhaps a project which some pupils are conducting, a staff meeting about a curriculum issue, a group planning an event, or an in-service day.
– By establishing agreed procedures whereby, without incurring ill-feeling, governors can learn the concerns of parents and teachers, consult with them about issues and report back. Schools should not resist setting up PTAs since these give parent governors a structure in which to discuss the views of parents and teachers.
– By arranging with the chairperson for teachers (and not only the elected members) to

attend governors' meetings from time to time to explain some aspect of their work.
- By ensuring that minutes (including unconfirmed minutes) and agendas of governors' meetings are easily available and that parent governors have facilities to put up notices and meet parents.
- By keeping parent governors in the picture about possible developments, particularly those which may be controversial among parents (e.g. changes to the way children are grouped, a new approach to the teaching of reading, fresh strategies to deal with behaviour problems).
- By ensuring that the school has a general policy of parental participation so that parent governors' elections and activities are not isolated incidents of involvement.

SCOTTISH SCHOOL BOARDS

Scotland has its own education system and its schools have not had governing bodies. At the end of the 1970s, school councils were set up, but these were advisory bodies only and did not relate to any one school but, at best, a secondary school and its feeder primaries. Further, although the councils included parent and teacher representatives from each school, their members were in a minority.

The local authorities, mostly Labour, thus remained in a controlling position. In 1987, however, the Conservative Government announced its intention to give parents the opportunity to become more closely involved in the running of schools. The school councils would be replaced by school boards, one for each school and with parents having majority membership, with powers to take a central role in school management (SED, 1987). The plan was to give the boards 'floor' functions to include the right to be consulted over the curriculum, to control capitation allowances, and to veto the head's appointment. There was then the possibility of graduating to 'ceiling' functions, whereby the boards would assume greater financial control and have the right to 'hire and fire' the head and staff. By holding the majority vote, this would have given parents considerable power.

Following a period of extensive consultation, the Scottish Education Minister, Michael Forsyth, responded to the main criticisms by parent and teacher organisations by backing away from the proposals concerning curriculum powers and staff appointments. The Schools Boards (Scotland) Act of 1988 provides for individual school boards with elected parents in the majority, elected teachers and co-opted community representatives making up the remaining members: in schools of up to 500 pupils the numbers are, respectively, four, one, and two. Their 'floor' functions include only *helping* to appoint staff (others being to encourage links with parents and respond to their views, to receive reports from the head and education authority and to make representations to them, and to approve plans for buying books and materials); and although more functions can be taken on, these specifically exclude powers to 'hire and fire' and to decide what is taught or how children are assessed.

OPTING OUT

The most controversial provision in the Education Reform Act 1988 allows for schools in England and Wales to break away from local authority control and instead become 'grant-maintained', receiving finance from central funds and run by governors as a private company. In February 1989 the Government published the Self-Governing Schools (Scotland) Bill to introduce a comparable scheme north of the border.

The Government went ahead with its proposals in spite of overwhelming opposition from education officers, teachers, local government, the Church and the major parent organisations. These groups saw grant-maintained schools as part of a 'privatisation' plan to reduce the power of local authorities, and suspected that 'opted out' schools would attract special social status. In an open letter to the Education Secretary in October 1987, the Bishop of London, Dr Graham Leonard, argued that no democratic government should forget the need to ensure a balance between the powers of central and local government. Only certain right-wing organisations (principally the Hillgate Group and the Centre for Policy Studies) plus six Conservative local authorities came out positively in favour of opting out (Haviland, 1988), a view which was taken by merely 18 per cent of 1479 people interviewed in a Marplan poll (*Guardian*, 9.2.88).

Eligibility and responsibilities

Apart from all secondary schools, primary schools with more than 300 pupils may apply to the Education Secretary for grant-maintained status. Eligibility among primary schools is thereby restricted to about 14 per cent of county schools, 4.5 per cent of Church of England schools, and 7.4 per cent of Roman Catholic schools (Gay, 1988). At a later date, smaller schools might be able to opt out too, but nursery and special schools are not eligible.

If the application is successful, the local authority loses control of the school. The property of former county schools is transferred to the governors, the assets of former voluntary schools remaining with the trust. The governors of a grant-maintained school manage all the school's affairs, including its budget, staff employment, admissions and special needs; they also take over from the LEA the duty to provide the major support services for the school (e.g. advisers and in-service training) though the LEA remains responsible for providing additional support for children with statements of special need, for welfare, educational psychology and careers services, and for free transport and clothing allowances.

In the case of a former county school, the governing body includes a new category of member called 'first' governors, appointed by the other governors and including at least two parents of pupils at the school. A former voluntary school continues to have foundation governors appointed by the providing body. First and foundation governors together are sufficient to outnumber all others.

The minority membership comprises five elected parents, at least one but not more than two elected teachers, and the head.

There are important respects in which a grant-maintained school is not independent. In particular it must follow the National Curriculum and national testing arrangements, it cannot charge fees, it cannot change its general size or character from that of the original school (e.g. become selective, change the age-range or adopt a new religious basis) without the Secretary of State's permission, and it must pay teachers on the same basis as in LEA schools.

The procedure for opting out

A request to seek grant-maintained status can be initiated either by the parents themselves (the number being equal to at least one-fifth of the school roll) or by the governing body. There is an important set of conditions which must be observed (1988 Act, Sect.60–3), but these do not include consulting the head or staff of the school. The governors must then organise a secret ballot to secure the agreement of a simple majority of the parents. In July 1988, the House of Commons overturned a House of Lords amendment which would have made grant-maintained status conditional upon a favourable majority of *all* parents, and not just those who actually vote. Instead the Government instituted a new hurdle: if less than half the parents vote, a second ballot must be held within fourteen days, the decision to 'opt out' then resting on a simple majority irrespective of the turnout. This extra provision reduces the risk of a small group of parent activists holding the reins, but the future of the school could still be determined by a minority of the parents (though the Secretary of State has stated that he takes account of the level of parental support in deciding whether to approve applications (Hansard, 26.2.89)). By June 1989, sixty-two ballots had been held (all secondary except for one nine-to-thirteen middle school), with forty-seven in favour.

A school wishing to surrender its grant-maintained status will not be allowed to 'opt in' to LEA control, but may apply to be closed. In a case of mismanagement the Secretary of State can intervene by appointing two extra governors to help put things right; he can withdraw the grant if this is ineffective or if the school fails to recruit enough pupils to remain viable.

An independent Grant-Maintained Schools Trust, financed by individuals and companies, was set up in 1988 to advise parents, governors and heads. At the same time the Advisory Centre for Education launched its own Advice Unit to help parents assess the benefits of grant-maintained status from a wide perspective, including effects on surrounding schools and the prospects for children with special needs.

Arguments for and against opting out

In defending the idea of grant-maintained schools, the Government rested its case on two factors – maximising parental choice and stimulating higher standards through the generation of competition between LEA and opted-out schools. These perceived benefits are also emphasised in literature put out by the radical Centre of Policy Studies (Lawlor, 1988) and the Institute of Economic Affairs Education Unit (1989). The Education Secretary Kenneth Baker clearly saw grant-maintained schools as a weapon in cases where parental rights and standards were said to be placed in jeopardy by left-wing councillors, particularly in deprived inner-city authorities such as Haringey and Brent. At the North of England Education Conference in January 1988 he said:

> Grant-maintained schools will be a threat to the complacent and to the second best . . . I would expect local authorities to respond to the creation of grant-maintained schools by making greater efforts to satisfy the needs and wishes of their customers.

In the event, however, the first batch of schools to apply for grant-maintained status were not those in extreme left-wing areas. Typically they were institutions defending their grammar school status or facing prospects of amalgamation or closure under reorganisation plans by local authorities, the majority of which were Conservative-controlled.

The power of parents in the opting-out procedure has attracted much criticism. There is an important sense in which, because a publicly-funded school is an asset of the whole local community, its future should not be bound by just one part of that community. It is true that the 1988 Act gives electors in general the opportunity to make objections within two months on the publication of a proposal; but the decision to make an application in the first place is very much in the hands of those parents whose children are currently at the school. Their main interest is likely to be their own children rather than the just allocation of resources to meet the needs of all pupils in the area.

Another problem is that opting-out reduces scope for LEAs responding to reduce costs by reorganising or closing schools in response to demographic changes. In October 1988, the Education Secretary announced in Parliament that there were in England approximately 620 000 surplus primary and 800 000 surplus secondary places which, if removed, would save £240 million a year (Hansard 138 (201), col. 999). For instance, the decision to allow Castle Hill Middle School in West Yorkshire to opt out botched the plans of Kirklees LEA to switch from nine-to-thirteen middle schools to junior and eleven-to-sixteen comprehensives. Further, a school opting-out increases the cost of services in the LEA by diminishing its resources. The government grant payable to the authority is reduced to recover the cost of the maintenance grant now paid from central funds to the grant-maintained school; but the LEA cannot in turn reduce pro rata overheads on resource centres, advisers and other services.

The Roman Catholic Church and Church of England roundly condemned the opting out provision from the start, fearing the destruction of the historic partnership between Church and State. The Act makes little concession to the Church: although trustees must be informed of any proposed ballot of parents and have the right to object if any application for grant-maintained status is made, a voluntary-aided church school can opt out without the consent of the trustees.

Nonetheless, for voluntary-aided church schools there is the obvious attraction that, without losing any powers, the governors will no longer have to fund 15 per cent of money for maintenance and repairs. The Church of England Board of Education, however, warn that in the longer term dependence on central funding could work to the disadvantage of church schools:

> Apart from the question of whether it is right or not for the Church to have certain privileges for its schools without bearing significant costs . . . the absence of any continuing financial input from the Church could strengthen the arm of any future government wishing to abolish church schools. (National Society, 1988)

Other religions might also stand to benefit from opting-out. At a press conference in May 1987, the Education Secretary recognised that the possibility of achieving grant-maintained status could lead to the first state-funded schools for Muslims and Hindus. This could be attractive to those primary schools in which the vast majority of pupils are of Asian background, as in some areas of Newham, Brent, Birmingham and Bradford. A similar opportunity might be available for Orthodox Jews. However, although in these circumstances the ethos of a grant-maintained school could be unmistakably Muslim or Hindu or Jewish, a school cannot immediately change its official religious status upon opting out: a separate application would have to be made, and the Secretary of State has said that he would not normally approve proposals for a change in a school's character within five years of its acquiring grant-maintained status.

A county primary school might see advantages in opting out in order to have greater freedom in its spending powers and staffing. However under the 1988 Education Act, governing bodies of LEA-maintained primary schools of over 200 pupils are in any case given considerable financial and managerial autonomy, including the power to determine their own staffing complements and appoint teachers. A school might feel that opting out could result in having more spending money: however, the Secretary of State has insisted that 'the aim will be to treat grant-maintained schools no more and no less favourably than LEA-maintained schools' (DES News 348/88): grants for capital spending will be treated on a case-by-case basis, and maintenance grants will be equivalent to what the LEA would otherwise be spending on the school. There might conceivably be extra money through the special purpose grants, but these would normally be provided to parallel special support and training grants to LEAs and to cover expenses which would not have arisen had the school not changed its status (DES Circular 10/88). Grant-maintained status might also appeal to parents and governors who do not like the LEA's political intervention in the curriculum – but here again governors under the 1986 Act now have power to modify the local authority curriculum statement.

For most primary heads, therefore, the price to pay for the small amount of extra independence gained is too high in view of the new responsibilities which they would have to take on once links with the LEA were severed. Not surprisingly, evidence to date suggests that the primary sector is not much interested in opting out. By the end of June 1989 only one school with primary-aged children, Castle Hill Middle School in Mirfield, West Yorkshire, had applied (successfully) for grant-maintained status.

SUMMARY AND CONCLUSIONS

This chapter first sketched the developments in which parents, by the Education Act of 1980, eventually won the statutory right to influence decision-making in schools by having their own elected representatives on governing bodies. Yet it was not until the 1986 Education Act that the numbers of parent governors balanced the representation from the LEA, from which a position of dominance was thereby arrested. The same Act defined the purposes of governors (since extended by the 1988 Act) and required governors to distribute an annual report and hold a meeting at which parents could demand consideration of specific issues.

Problems still remain, however, not least those of eliciting parental participation from all sections of the community, of ensuring that parent governors receive support from the head and fellow governors, and of providing training in the skills needed for assuming the increased managerial responsibilities which governing bodies have been given. The school has an important part to play in helping parent governors to realise their rights, and various suggestions were outlined.

Discussion then moved to the rights of parents to secure a measure of independence for a school by removing it from LEA control and securing grant-maintained status. Only a small proportion of primary schools are currently eligible and few seem interested. Only time will tell whether the vociferous objections which have been made to the opting-out clauses in the 1988 Act have foundation, though the controversy over the right of one section of the community to determine whether a school is no longer subject to the control of that community raises issues of general principle.

Whether the plethora of legislation of the 1980s represents a genuine shift of political power in favour of parents is a matter of dispute. Certainly there has been plenty of Government rhetoric to suggest that parents now have a real chance to influence educational decision-making. Soon after the passing of his Education Reform Act, the Education Secretary Kenneth Baker told a conference of parents, 'I have given you more power than you have ever had, or ever dreamed of'. (*The Times Educational Supplement*, 25.11.88).

Yet parents have not had it all their own way. There are some areas in which they have failed to achieve the statutory rights they have been seeking: they have no right to be represented on official national decision-making bodies as is the case in some other parts of Europe; they have no right to establish a parent-teacher association if the head objects; they have no right to be consulted when their child's behaviour is causing concern; and they have no right of access to the class teacher even by appointment. Nor has the reality of the right to participate in school government always matched the statutory provision. These matters are among the issues which have been responsible for the growth of parent organisations, a topic to which we now turn.

Further reading

For discussion about parent governors, see Joan Sallis *Schools, Parents and Governors: A New Approach to Accountability* (Routledge, 1988).

Although based on research carried out before the 1986 Act, *School Governing Bodies* by Maurice Kogan *et al.* (Heinemann, 1988) is a fascinating study of authority and power relationships, and its revelations about the diverse roles which governing bodies play is still of relevance.

A training pack for school governors is obtainable from the Learning Materials Office, The Open University, PO Box 188, Milton Keynes, MK7 6DH. It consists of a guide for group use, a set of ten workbooks and a video. The BBC also produces an information pack. The first module is called *Getting Started* and consists of an audio cassette, providing first-hand accounts of governors' experiences, plus a book giving advice on duties and responsibilities.

DES Circulars 8/86 and 7/87 plus Annexes spell out guidelines for the conduct of parent governor elections and provide model articles and instruments of government. The DES (1988) has also published a free brochure *School Governors: A Guide to the Law*. See also C. Lowe *The School Governors' Legal Guide* (from Croner Publications, 173 Kingston Road, New Malden, Surrey).

The case for opting out is spelt out by Sheila Lawlor in *Opting Out: A Guide to Why and How* (Centre for Policy Studies, 1988) and by the Institute of Economic Affairs Education Unit in *Opting to Grant-Maintained Schools* (1989). Extracts from representations to the Secretary of State concerning the original opting-out proposal are printed in Chapter 4 of J. Haviland *Take Care, Mr Baker!* (Fourth Estate, 1988). Issues that parents and governors must consider in opting-out decisions are suggested in *Considering the Options* by Rick Rogers (ACE, 1989).

The provisions for opting out in the 1988 Act are explained and discussed in Chapter 4 of Stuart Maclure's *Education Re-formed* (Hodder and Stoughton, 1988), while official guidance is given in DES Circulars 10/88 and 21/89. The Government's plans for opting out in Scotland are critically analysed in *Self-Governing Schools: Extending Choice for Parents* (Scottish Consumer Council, 314 St Vincent St., Glasgow G3 8XW, 1989).

6 | PARENT INTEREST GROUPS

THE PURSUIT OF INFLUENCE – NOT POWER

Within schools, parents are generally interested in working *with* teachers: they want to achieve better home–school relationships but not to dictate school policy. This is also the position of the main parent organisations. A promotion leaflet on home–school associations put out by the National Confederation of Parent–Teacher Associations (NCPTA) states:

> HSAs do not encourage parents to interfere in the methods of teaching or the internal management of the school. It is essential that parents respect the professionalism of the head and staff.

The Scottish Parent Teacher Council similarly works for partnership rather than parent power. According to its recruitment leaflet, the qualifying criterion for membership is 'the desire to promote parent–teacher cooperation for the benefit of children'.

Thus, although the term 'parent power' has become part of the media vocabulary in recent years, the majority of parent organisations do not see their activities in that light. As we saw in the last chapter, the belief that parents have more to gain from cooperating with teachers than in occupying a position of dominance led most parent groups in England and Wales to oppose Government plans in 1984 to give parents a majority vote on school governing bodies. We also saw how the Scottish Parent Teacher Council, while supporting parental majorities on the new school boards set up in 1989, successfully cooperated with teachers in getting the Government to back down from its original proposals by which parents, by their built-in majority, would have made decisions on the curriculum and have the right to hire and fire.

The belief that teachers and parents must work together was tested almost to breaking point in 1987 when strikes forced many schools to close for periods during term-time. Whilst condemning the teachers' militant strategies, James Hammond of the NCPTA argued on BBC television that the responsibility for teacher unrest lay with the Education Secretary since it was he who had provoked the teacher unions into action by depriving them of negotiating rights. Further, in a twenty-seven point letter to the Prime Minister, the NCPTA asked for an inquiry into teachers' pay and status.

Yet if the parent organisations renounce the idea of parent power, most are politically involved, acting as watchdogs and making their influence felt in Government circles. None of the parent bodies is aligned to a particular political party, though some have attracted the support of individual MPs on one side of the House or the other. Nonetheless, through articles, speeches and evidence presented to ministers, opposition has been voiced over levels of Government spending, and representations were made about some proposals in the Education Reform Bill (especially testing and opting out) not least because of fears that they could encourage confrontation between parents and schools.

The perception of a need for greater political involvement has presented the parent organisations with a dilemma about their membership. On the one hand, they recognise that improvement in the quality of their children's education is dependent upon parents and teachers working in partnership: on the other hand, there is concern that the Government is inclined to brush aside their opinion on the grounds that it is influenced by the self-interested views of an articulate minority of teacher members. Although in 1987 the NCPTA changed its constitution to give parents a two-thirds majority on the executive committee, all the organisations welcome professionals within their ranks and have resisted attempts to make their names suggest otherwise. At the annual general meeting of the Campaign for the Advancement of State Education in 1985, Joan Sallis moved from the chair that the word 'Parents' ' should be inserted before 'CASE'. Her argument was that politicians might listen more to demands which came from a body whose name reflected the fact that most members were parents; but the motion was defeated, the feeling being that the organisations should be seen as a forum for everyone who cares about the state of education. Again, during industrial unrest in the mid-1980s, the NCPTA was under pressure from some of its parent members to drop the 'T'; but those efforts never succeeded, largely because most parents believed that the pupils' interests were better served by teachers and parents working together.

The teacher unions have reciprocated by adopting a distinctly pro-parent view in many of their more recent publications. In contrast to its opposition to parent governors recommended by the Taylor Committee in 1977, the National Union of Teachers ten years later urged its members to build on their relationships with parents and so make more constructive a policy which in the past had 'remained well-intentioned but distant' (NUT, 1987). Similarly, the National Association of Head Teachers (1988) has argued for a 'contract of partnership' in which schools and parents would commit themselves to an agreed set of obligations and responsibilities, the development of parent–teacher relationships being 'too vital to leave to chance or spasmodic effort'.

GROWTH OF PARENT INFLUENCE SINCE 1960

Although the millions of parents in this country form a potentially formidable pressure group, it is only since the 1960s that parents have become a serious political force. Until then the parent movement was concerned above all with informing and educating parents about what was good for their children. The only major organisation was the influential Parents' National Educational Union (PNEU), founded by Charlotte Mason in 1887 to spread the 'principles of physiological-psychology', to help less capable parents become involved in their children's education (Beattie, 1985, p.168). (The PNEU is now an international service, largely involved in supporting familes who are educating their children at home.) In the inter-war period parent–teacher associations were formed in a small minority of schools; but these saw their function as limited to cooperating with teachers, not as a pressure group for lobbying MPs or in otherwise seeking political influence. In 1930 the Home and School Council was founded to coordinate the activities of parent–teacher associations; but many of these never joined, being more interested in supporting individual schools than in developing centralised policies. The HSC finally folded up in 1951 and has no connection with the present-day organisation of that name.

The changing stance of parent organisations during the 1960s has been attributed by Beattie (1985) to two main factors. The first was the consumerist movement: 'As with restaurants or vacuum-cleaners, informed choice was expected in the long term to improve the quality of the product' (Beattie, 1985, p.173). The second factor was the growth of comprehensive schools: not only were parents now invited to choose between selective and non-selective schools, but, faced with the prospect of radical changes in the secondary system, they felt that they had the right to be heard. Moreover, their opinion became important in winning local and national elections. This in turn led to the need for political parties to find policies which would win them parental support, as happened in Sheffield in the late 1960s (see p.66).

During the 1980s, parent organisations became increasingly outspoken in their attacks on Government policy. Paradoxically, attempts by Conservative governments to stimulate an interest in 'parent power' sometimes only served to fuel discontent because the rhetoric of parent participation often failed to match the reality of the situation. This happened when local authorities failed to make adequate arrangements for electing parent governors following the implementation of the 1980 Act (see p.68) and when parents found that they were not being involved in decisions affecting special educational needs in the manner promised by the 1981 Act (see pp.42–3). The need was thus seen to mobilise group opinion and to use the resources of parent groups to publicise the view that rights in law must be rights in practice.

During the mid-1980s, the Government's desire to reduce state expenditure as a response to the country's economic problems led to widespread complaints by parents and teachers about inadequate resources. Frustration reached its peak over salary restrictions and the eventual suspension of pay negotiations in 1987. Although the ensuing disruption in schools infuriated many parents, it also acted as a catalyst for others who saw that they had as much to gain as the teachers by pressing for better government funding of the education service. As the leader of one parent group put it, the failure of teachers to enlist the support of parents means that 'we would all go down together' (Allen, 1986, p.8). In March 1987 the main parents' organisations lobbied MPs and jointly mobilised a rally at Central Hall, Westminister in an effort to enlist support for more books, smaller classes, the improved maintenance of school buildings, and the rights of teachers to be represented in salary negotiations.

Matters became further embittered in the debate surrounding the Education Reform Bill in 1987. Government claims concerning the importance of the parent's voice were greeted with cynicism by many parent groups when their critical views on national testing and the abolition of the Inner London Education Authority were declared 'unrepresentative' by the Education Secretary. Joan Sallis of the Campaign for the Advancement of State Education took up the challenge: 'Real parents have no status, and the moment they have any real proposals to make they become subjected to abuse and slander' (*The Times Educational Supplement*, 18.9.87).

Following the Government's proposal to abolish the ILEA, representatives from various London parent groups combined in the spring of 1988 to campaign for a ballot to test parental opinion. This was resisted by the Education Secretary, in spite of his espousal of parental rights, on the grounds that the break-up of the ILEA was a constitutional matter for Parliament to decide and that a popular poll could become the object of a propaganda offensive in which the genuine wishes of parents might be ignored. The parent groups therefore organised their own ballot, supervised by the Electoral Reform Society. Funds were raised in schools and by a gala performance by West End stars. In spite of a nineteen-to-one result against abolition (based on one vote for each child at school) and a 56 per cent turnout, the Government went ahead with its abolition clauses in the 1988 Act. The majority view among parents was of little consequence when the ruling party enjoyed a majority of over 100 in the Commons.

THE THREE MAIN INTEREST GROUPS

The three main parent organisations in England and Wales are the National Confederation of Parent Teacher Associations (NCPTA), the Campaign for the Advancement of State Education (CASE) and the Advisory Council for Education (ACE). Together in 1967 they set up the Home and School Council to publish a range of booklets on home–school relations, and the National Association for Primary Education (NAPE) has since added its support.

NCPTA

Founded in 1956, the NCPTA is the largest parent body in England and Wales, its membership having increased from a little over 1000 affiliated home–school associations in the mid-1970s to well over 6000 in 1985. Its journal *Home and School*, issued three times a year, contains articles, written mainly by professionals, to explain educational issues for parents (e.g. the use of computers in schools) or to put forward a point of view (e.g. on national testing, school uniform, competitive sport). The General Secretary, James Hammond, is also President of the affiliated Parent–Teacher Association of Wales which he helped to found.

The confederation eschews the notion of parent power and is emphatic about the importance of schools and parents working together. Its principal objective, according to the official explanatory leaflet, is 'the promotion of essential partnership between home and school; child, parent and teacher; parents, local education authorities and other interested bodies'. These objectives are pursued not only through home–school associations but through area federations whose representatives liaise with officers of the LEA and involve themselves in policy discussion. At the same time the Confederation emphasises the responsibility of parents to support their children and each other. Hence, according to its Public Relations Officer, home–school associations should recognise that they can help the shy parent to gain confidence and the 'switched off' disillusioned parent to take an interest (Naybour, 1985).

If pressure is mild with respect to school staff, it is tough with respect to Government policy and national provision. No longer content to encourage parents to raise funds and organise social events, the NCPTA now urges its affiliated home–school associations to engage parents in debate about educational developments and to monitor the effects of Government policy on schools. The Confederation discusses education policy with Government officials, the teacher unions, the TUC and other national organisations. In the mid-1980s, the NCPTA was particularly active over the level of state funding for education, revealing that parents were supporting the state system to the extent of 30 per cent of capitation in primary schools and 9 per cent in secondary schools, with over 80 per cent of schools using funds from parents to provide essentials such as books, computers and school furniture (NCPTA, 1985).

The NCPTA believes that the Government needs to put more effort into encouraging genuine parent–teacher partnership rather than parent power. In its blueprint for the development of parental involvement in education, *Parents – Partners in a Shared Task of Education* (NCPTA, 1986), the Confederation called for a national structure of grant-aided parents' organisations supported by Government grant. Besides stimulating parental interest in school and reinforcing the importance of learning in the home, these bodies would offer Government ministers a parental view of educational issues. Further, it was argued that parents should be represented on all local authority education committees and sub-committees – though without a vote – and that each LEA should appoint an officer expressly for developing home–school links. Heads and teachers, it was insisted, should not only be obliged to form home–school associations but be given time by the local authority to initiate home–school activities. At the same time home–school liaison should become a standard topic for all school staff appointments, and staff contracts should contain clauses to make staff accountable to the governors for activities designed to involve parents. Area federations, each with a full-time development officer, should also be set up in each LEA to disseminate material and run meetings, conferences and workshops for parents.

Like the other main parent groups, the NCPTA opposed many of the proposals in the Education Reform Bill. Although it welcomed financial delegation as a means of giving schools more autonomy, it stipulated in its submission a list of safeguards to prevent the extra responsibilities becoming unacceptably onerous. It was not convinced that the best way to improve standards was through the kind of National Curriculum proposed and through national testing. It was even more critical about proposals to allow schools to opt out of LEA control, and soon after the Act was passed the Confederation's General Secretary urged LEAs to 'launch an aggressive marketing offensive which explodes some of the myths surrounding opting out' (Hammond, 1989). In November 1988, James Hammond told a conference that the Education Secretary, Kenneth Baker (who was present as a guest speaker) was being unfair to members in claiming that the Education Reform Act had given parents unprecedented power when they were still denied the right to set up their own forum in every school.

In 1988, the Confederation appointed Philip Woods, a sociologist from the Welsh Consumer Council, to a new post of General Manager. Woods (1988) sees parents as 'consumer-citizens' who need special support to develop the capacity to engage in effective participation. It is, he says, in the interests of the teacher unions and professional organisations to fund 'a strong and informed parent movement which places a high value on education'; and the Government should help to fund a national representative association which, akin to the National Union of Students, would include *every* parent who was a member of a school association.

In short, the NCPTA has changed from a body of affiliated PTAs whose main purposes were fund-raising and social activities to a more centralised and politically active institution. Whilst sticking to its policy of working jointly with teachers and resisting pressure to become an exclusively parent organisation, it also demands the attention of ministers by claiming to represent the interests of parents as a national watchdog of the education system and as a group which has the right to be consulted about developments in national education policy.

The equivalent to the NCPTA in Scotland is the Scottish Parent Teachers' Council. The SPTC strongly supported the Government's proposal for giving parents majority representation on the individual school boards, in contrast to the NCPTA's attitude to the equivalent proposal in 1984 for governing bodies of English and Welsh schools. However, wanting parent influence in education rather than control, it was against the proposal which would have allowed the boards to petition the Minister for greater powers over finance and staffing. The modified proposals which in fact emerged suggested that the Government had listened to the SPTC's concerns (see p.74).

CASE

The Campaign for the Advancement of State Education (CASE) was established in 1962, building upon a local group of parents in Cambridge set up two years earlier.

Like the NCPTA, it is not a unitary organisation but a federation, though not school-based. Although there are some national members and affiliated colleges and institutes of education, most members come from the fifty or so area groups which work within a broad policy framework. Reports of local initiatives and activities are reported in *Parents and Schools*, issued termly. CASE acknowledges that it is dominated by middle-class parents and would like to be more representative of parents in general. It wants partnership with teachers, who are included in its membership, along with local councillors and others interested in education; but in doing so it emphasises the importance of each partner pulling its weight. In 1987, when she was its President, Joan Sallis chided heads for not doing more to make a success of the annual parents' meeting established under the 1986 Act, and she criticised the teacher unions for wanting their members to boycott the meeting (*The Times Educational Supplement*, 23.10.87).

In the 1960s CASE was mainly concerned in campaigning for comprehensive education and parent governors. When the Labour Party in 1965 asked all local authorities to declare their plans for comprehensivisation, CASE was instrumental in ensuring that parents were required to be consulted. Today the Association presses for general improvements in state schools and the right of parents in general to be involved in educational decision-making at local authority and government levels as well as in schools. To these ends it passes resolutions for government action and meets politicians. For instance it met DES officials for two-and-a-half hours in 1984 to discuss the Government's proposals about the reform of school governing bodies. It also urges parents to attend all school meetings, to arrange meetings themselves, and to write letters to the Prime Minister, MPs, local councillors, the chairperson of the local education committee, and local newspapers.

The activities of the Sutton group in Surrey can serve as illustrative of local CASE endeavours. In recent years, surveys have been conducted and discussion documents produced on local provision for the under-fives, on information contained in local primary school brochures (see p.101), on secondary school examination results, and the working of the 11+. When Sutton Council drew up various options for the reorganisation of secondary education, the CASE group set up special advice clinics to help parents complete the Council questionnaire, and it prepared a detailed submission supporting proposals for a fully comprehensive system. Not surprisingly, it opposed Wilson Grammar School's application to opt out of local authority control in 1989. Sutton CASE is typical in enlisting the cooperation of local branches of the teacher unions to exert pressure on the local authority to provide, for example, more resources in primary schools. The group also encourages parents to stand as school governors, for whom courses are run, and gives help with school choice appeals.

Although CASE is not formally associated with any political party, support among MPs tends to come from Labour and the Democrats. In 1986 the Confederation organised a massive distribution of a leaflet highlighting cuts in government spending on education and the deficiencies in resources for schools, as reported by HMI and the NCPTA. In the same year the Confederation supported the recommendations of the all-party House of Commons Select Committee report on primary education which had recommended increased provision for under-fives, a national policy for four-year-olds, better staffing, resources and buildings, a curriculum which positively recognised cultural diversity, and a cautionary approach to national testing.

During the run-up to the 1987 General Election, CASE presented a 'Parents' Manifesto' for members to draw on at election meetings and to present to their MPs. The education spokesperson of each political party was presented with a copy in a scroll, tied with a purple ribbon! The manifesto included demands for better books and equipment for schools, more support staff and improved teacher–pupil ratios, better communication from schools to parents (including parental involvement with their children's learning), measures to improve teacher quality and to improve school buildings, and pre-school provision for all children.

CASE was highly critical of the short time offered by the Education Secretary for consultation on the Education Reform Bill and opposed many of the proposals. Although supporting the idea of a common core curriculum, it maintained that the National Curriculum as proposed was too prescriptive and subject-centred. It opposed national testing, and some parents at the annual conference in 1987 even threatened civil disobedience by promising to withdraw their children from the tests. In its submission concerning opting out, CASE was no less forthright, insisting that it was morally wrong for the community control of a school to be ended by one generation of parents and governors.

Recent motions affecting primary education passed unanimously at annual general meetings have included: the need for teachers to have better salaries; the provision of nursery education for all three-year-olds; the rectification of resources revealed by HMI to be inadequate; opposition to vouchers or any attempt to privatise education; demands for better state funding of schools, ending the need for parents to 'subsidise' the provision of educational materials and facilities; and assurances from the DES that teacher-training and in-service courses include working with parents.

In trying to make its voice felt in government circles, CASE has great difficulty in being recognised as a body which genuinely represents the interests of parents at large. When in 1988 the Democrat leader, Paddy Ashdown, enlisted the support of the Confederation in tabling a motion asking MPs to listen to parents in their constituencies, forty-two Conservative members signed an amendment objecting to 'the attempts by CASE to promote its ideological and left-wing opposition to this Government by seeking to speak on behalf of parents'. As we shall see later, other groups have been set up in response to pressure from parents on the Right; but the NCPTA and CASE remain the largest and most active parent organisations.

ACE

The Advisory Centre for Education was founded in 1960 by the sociologist Michael (now Lord) Young. In contrast to the NCPTA and CASE, ACE is a single organisation with no federal structure. Its principal aim has always been to disseminate information so that parents can discuss educational issues and make choices from a basis of knowledge. This is achieved through its bi-monthly magazine *ACE Bulletin*, formerly called *Where*, which had a circulation of 3500 in 1988. A survey in 1987 showed that the majority of readers were involved in educational management and school government, few being parents only. Hence ACE is not an organisation *of* parents but one which works *for* parents.

Michael Young had also founded the Consumers' Association and *Which?*, and much material in the early issues of *Where* was about school choice with about 14 per cent of its space devoted to independent schools (Sellick, 1985). ACE even published a *Good Schools Guide* in 1967. The philosophy today is quite different, focusing on the rights of all parents and also school students. Unlike CASE's *Parents and Schools, ACE Bulletin* is not a grass-roots publication but a platform for experienced professionals to represent the rights of parents. Apart from feature articles, there are sections on government and local authority initiatives and a detailed digest giving particulars of the contents of relevant journals and recently published reports and books; Joan Sallis also has a regular column for parent governors. Additionally ACE publishes handbooks and information sheets to help readers get to grips with such matters as special needs, school choice, how to face prospective school closures, how to be an effective governor, and the contents of recent Education Acts. ACE also makes its views known in a more popular format through radio and TV programmes and women's magazines, and it has a regular column in *Special Children*, a magazine which focuses on special educational needs.

An important part of ACE's work is giving free advice to individual parents. Up to half the calls in one week concern special education, the next largest category being appeals over school choice and exclusion, with an increasing number of requests concerning confusions arising from the Education Reform Act (*ACE Bulletin* 29, 1989). A special advice service for special education was set up in 1985 to provide support for Bangladeshi parents living in Tower Hamlets and experiencing problems because of their home language and racial abuse; and a national conference on the special educational needs of Asian children was organised in 1988. Another special advice service was set up in 1988 to give guidance on opting out.

Besides providing information and advice, ACE monitors local and national developments, exposing malpractice and deficiencies in the law, and urging the Government and local education authorities to provide an education system which is fairer and more responsive to the needs of parents. Since the 1981 Act, the Centre has been unrelenting in fighting for the rights of parents whose children have special educational needs, pressing local authorities to produce properly planned and adequately resourced schemes for the integration of these children into mainstream schools. Exasperated at the behaviour of Hertfordshire LEA which had ignored eight years of campaigning to provide speech therapy for deaf children at local secondary schools, ACE proclaimed in a headline on the front page of its *Bulletin* in September 1986, 'Pressure not partnership the key to meeting special needs'.

Like the NCPTA and CASE, ACE has exposed inconsistencies and inadequacies in arrangements for the election of parents on governing bodies, but was alone among the main parent groups in welcoming the Government's 1984 proposal (later scrapped) for parents to be in the majority on governing bodies (see p.69) – though its present staff would prefer a balanced representation. Campaigns have also been fought for fairer procedures in cases of suspension from school (including the right of appeal), the right of parents to have access to their child's school records, and the abolition of corporal punishment. Like the other two main organisations, ACE was highly critical of some of the proposals contained in the Education Reform Bill. In briefings for the House of Lords, it argued that market forces should not be allowed to shape the future of education. In particular, it was concerned that the Bill seemed to ignore many problems related to children with special educational needs, such as safeguards for their provision in schools which opted out of local authority control.

ACE is less sensitive than the other two main organisations in criticising the policies of schools, though it does not normally name its targets. Although the early editions of *Where* advised parents to steer clear of anything that smacked of interference in the way a school was run, *ACE Bulletin* has taken schools to task over the handling of suspension cases, corporal punishment, the extent to which parents are welcome in school, and school uniform regulations.

RECENT INTEREST GROUPS

The late 1980s saw the growth of more parent organisations. In Scotland, Education Alert (EA) was launched in March 1987 in Aberdeen, with help from the business community. Its founder, Diana Daly, was struck by the higher morale among teachers which she had experienced in Western Australia, and believed there was a need to provide a public forum which would work for the revival of teacher morale, improvements in state education and consensus on educational developments. EA does not see itself as a pressure group: 'building bridges' and 'plugging the information gap' are the declared approaches.

Unlike its counterparts south of the border, EA has pulled back from campaigning against the Government policies, partly because it saw no chance of the Government deferring its legislation in 1987/88 and partly because the Scottish proposals were at first not so contentious as in England and Wales (though the Government has since controversially introduced plans for Scottish schools to opt out of local authority control). Furthermore, a summary of the proposals was distributed in condensed form to every teacher and parent by the Scottish Education Minister, Michael Forsyth, who allowed a much longer period for consultation than ministers provided for the more radical proposals in English and Welsh schools. On the other hand, EA is by no means politically inactive. For instance, with the Lothian Parents Action Group it has asked for a detailed review of Scottish education and the setting up of a Scottish Select Committee on education in the House of Commons. The idea is to provide a coherent framework for educational developments in contrast to the piecemeal approach which successive governments have adopted in recent years.

New parent groups in England and Wales can be divided into three broad categories:

1 those which have been set up in response to problems emerging in the wake of the 1981 Act and its provisions for 'integration' in special education;
2 radical-Right organisations working towards the realisation of unfettered parental choice in education; and
3 groups taking action against the perceived inadequacies of Government provision.

An example of a group in the first category is 81 Action, set up in 1986 as the result of the initiative of Elizabeth Wallis, Information Officer for CASE, who recognised the need for a national forum to support parents of children with special needs. The group offers information and legal advice, links up local support groups, encourages parents to use their statutory rights to influence decisions affecting their children's educational opportunities, and urges the authorities to fulfil their statutory obligations to promote partnership between professionals and parents. The group's president is the Labour MP David Blunkett, whose message at the first annual conference in October 1987 expressed concern about opportunities for children with special needs in relation to the National Curriculum, opting out, and financial delegation to schools.

The London-based Parents Campaign for Integrated Education is another example of a group of parents concerned about special needs provision. As its name suggests, it was formed to press for greater commitment to implementing the integrationist policies of the 1981 Act. Working with teachers, these objectives were effectively achieved in the ILEA. Out of this organisation has grown Parents in Partnership (PIP) which campaigns nationwide for other authorities to follow the ILEA's example. PIP helps parents of children with special needs to get in touch with each other, to choose a suitable school and to liaise with teachers; it also offers assistance with assessment and statement processes under the 1981 Act. Above all it works for partnership with professionals and organises conferences to this end.

In contrast to PIP's integrationist policies, the Campaign for Choice in Special Education seeks to preserve the existence of special schools to complement the option of supported mainstream education. This group reflects the fears of some parents about placing children with special needs in ordinary schools, but has been described by Vaughan (1989) as 'a campaign to preserve segregation, not to promote choice'. The problems raised by this position were discussed briefly in Chapter 4.

The second category of new parent groups attracts supporters from the radical Right, who want unfettered parental choice in education. The Campaign for Choice in Special Education is also within this category, but the Parental Alliance for Choice in Education (PACE) is the most important example. Founded in 1985 by Fred Naylor 'to provide a rallying force for all fighting to defend parental rights in education', it has the support of Baroness Cox, a prominent Conservative spokesperson on education in the House of Lords. The group argue that the right of parents to educate children as they choose, as enshrined in the 1944 Act, had been undermined since the mid-1960s. To quote one of the group's council members:

> As choice and types of variety of schools diminished . . . all the characteristics of the monopolist emerged in triumphant local authorities . . . The system was as responsive as the GUM store in Moscow and was equally firmly supplier and not consumer-led. (Peach, 1987)

PACE is a registered company limited to fifty members, but has branch groups of 'supporters'. It advised the parents involved in the Dewsbury case (see p.60), threatening to take the Government to the European Court of Human Rights, and it supports the cause of Muslims to run their own state-aided voluntary schools.

The Campaign for Real Education, formed in 1987, is another group which, though not aligned to any political party, is orientated towards policies of the radical Right. Its members, who are not limited to parents, challenge 'the gradual erosion of the traditional curriculum which emphasised literacy, numeracy, respect for and appreciation of our history and culture and which encouraged a healthy competition amongst pupils'. It argues that higher standards are impeded when schools 'neglect the "basics" for the sake of political ideology', as manifest in activities such as peace studies.

Also included in this category are ad hoc groups which have emerged in protest against an unacceptable local authority policy. The Harringey Parents Association, for instance, was set up in June 1987 when the authority put up posters advertising a 'Lesbian Strength and Gay Pride Week' as part of its 'positive images' campaign for homosexuals. Its members threatened to press for primary schools to opt out of LEA control if the 'positive images' policy continued. The Harringey association is a rare example of a parent pressure group proper, using the threat of sanctions in pursuit of its aims; most parent organisations are 'interest groups', content to use publicity and persuasion rather than to employ sanctions (Macbeth, 1984).

The third category of new parent groups are those which have emerged in response to the perceived inadequacies of national educational provision. The main example is ALPAG, the All London Parent Action Group, formed in 1986 to coordinate the actions of individual parent groups concerned about levels of investment in schools. Liz Allen, the organisation's main inspiration and then Publicity Officer for CASE, explained the aims of the campaign as 'a simple, no-nonsense ticket in support of state education, proper pay for teachers and massive new investment in education' (Allen, 1986). Under the banner 'Crisis in Education', the group has campaigned and lobbied MPs for higher teachers' salaries and more resources for schools. Although it has worked in association with CASE, ALPAG's strategies are more populist and militant: 'ALPAG . . .

was founded upon parental frustration and anger; we have no evidence that this Government is prepared to listen to argued reason, but it might just be swayed by a popular movement of "ordinary" parents' (Collier and Henry, 1986). In spite of their anti-Conservative stance, ALPAG is avowedly non-political, maintaining that it would be equally concerned if similar difficulties arose under a different government. The Action Group produces a newsheet *Schoolwatch* to keep parents informed on the current educational scene, to suggest where members can get help and advice and, most of all, to give parents the means of sharing their experiences and views.

Another group in this category is Parents' Initiative, a forum created in 1986 to promote a better-resourced and more accountable education system. Supported by a range of parent and teacher organisations as well as the National Association of Governors and Managers, it is currently concerned with implications of the changes brought about by the Education Reform Act, sending out information leaflets on issues such as Local Management of Schools and the National Curriculum.

THE EUROPEAN PARENTS' ASSOCIATION

The European Parents' Association (EPA) is a consortium of national parent organisations. Set up in 1983 as the result of an idea of Dr Alistair Macbeth of the University of Glasgow, its aims are to represent parents' associations to international authorities, especially the European Commission, the Council of Ministers and the European Parliament; to collect and disseminate information and stimulate relevant research; to elaborate education policies; and to promote parents' and teachers' training for a more constructive dialogue between home and school.

Full membership of the EPA is open to parents' organisations which are concerned with the education of children at school and whose objectives are in accord with those of the EPA. Individuals and other organisations whose aims do not run counter to the EPA's can also join as associate members. A secretariat has been established in Brussels, and an Administrative Council consists of two members from the five largest countries (France, Germany, Italy, Spain and the UK) and one from the others. The UK is represented by the NCPTA and the Scottish Parent Teacher Council.

The problem here is that EPA membership is for parents only, teachers being excluded. This issue, it will be recalled, presents a major dilemma for British organisations. The NCPTA wants the Europeans to recognise the value of teachers and parents working together as political partners; but against this is the view that governments may be more likely to listen to the organisation if it knows that its policies represent the distinctive view of parents.

EPA resolutions have called for measures to bring coordination between health services, school and family; for the parental participation in curriculum development; for collaboration between teachers and parents in the battle against

AIDS; and for greater action in relation to educational disadvantage, particularly as it affects girls, physically and mentally handicapped children, the children of migrant workers and the socially under-privileged.

SUMMARY AND CONCLUSIONS

In this chapter we have seen how parent groups no longer see their purposes simply in terms of supporting individual schools but in terms of articulating the concerns of parents to those in authority and in demanding the right to be heard. This does not mean that they speak with one voice, as the divergent aims of the more recently-formed parent groups demonstrate; but parent organisations have become more centralised and politicised, monitoring developments in education at national and local levels, disseminating information and pressing for changes in the law and in local authority practices. It is difficult to gauge just what the groups have achieved. Over the Education Reform Bill the voice of the main groups was not only ignored by the Government but denigrated; on the other hand some aspects of recent legislation – for example access to information, more parent–governors, better facilities for appeals – certainly reflect the group's objectives. Much of this, of course, is the outcome of efforts by the political parties to win votes, but the content of electorally appealing strategies has no doubt been informed by the policies of parent organisations.

It is likely that the voice of the parent will become increasingly important with the opportunities created under the 1986 and 1988 Education Acts. It is true that the main parent bodies are not interested in parent power as such; but given the greater facilities for making an impact on educational policies, over time parents are likely to respond rather than remain passive. The emergence of parents as a sizeable force in governing bodies, the increased scope for school choice, and the provision for initiating moves for a school to opt out of local authority control are all likely to lead to greater parent action against unpopular local authority policies. Yet parents have still been given no means of exerting comparable pressures on central government. This contrasts with Germany where the Government requires parents to participate in its educational decision-making, and where government-financed *statutory* parent organisations have been set up for this purpose.

The likely effect of the new measures on individual schools is more problematic. The fact that parental participation in school government is now numerically substantial and legally guaranteed could serve to make parents more militant, particularly if a school's future is threatened by parents using their newly-won rights to send their children to another school. Alternatively, parent governors could use their presence to engender a spirit of partnership with the school staff, enlisting more general support from parents in general. This is certainly the direction favoured by the main parent groups. Much, however, depends on how relationships with parents are handled and whether their questions and complaints are seen as coming from 'problem parents' or 'parents with problems'.

Fortunately there is still every sign that parents in general are interested in partnership but not in taking over, and may even feel threatened at such a prospect because they lack the time and necessary expertise. Yet most want to participate in school life to the extent that they are listened to and receive a positive response to their legitimate grievances. They also desire to be more informed about the curriculum and the best ways of helping their children. When parents have the organisational structures to make an impact on school policy, there is always the danger that they will become defensive if they feel that their legitimate interests are being ignored. For political as well as educational reasons, 'working with parents' is vital.

Further reading

Two books compare the activities of parent organisations in different European countries. Nicholas Beattie's *Professional Parents* (Falmer Press, 1985) compares the development of parent groups in France, Italy, West Germany and England and Wales. Alastair Macbeth's *The Child Between* (Office for Official Publications of the European Communities, Brussels, 1984) considers home–school relations in nine members states of the European community.

The main sources for recent and current developments are *ACE Bulletin* and *Parents and Schools*. These are published respectively by the Advisory Centre for Education and CASE (see p.189 for addresses), but also include the activities of other parent groups from time to time. Each is also a very useful source of information on educational developments in general.

PART III

COMMUNICATION
AND DIALOGUE

7 | COMMUNICATING INFORMATION

As earlier chapters have shown, parental rights have been considerably enhanced in recent legislation. Although some of the developments have been criticised for being more politically than educationally motivated, there is today a more general recognition of the moral right of parents to be involved in decision-making about their own children's educational opportunities and in the development of school policy.

Yet rights are sterile unless the right-holders have the requisite knowledge, skills and motivation to take advantage of their rights. To some extent central directives can be a stimulus in these respects. For instance (as we shall see in this chapter) LEAs and schools are now obliged to provide certain sorts of information to facilitate parental choice and teacher accountability; and (as we saw earlier) each LEA now has a duty to ensure that governors (including parent–governors) are given opportunity for free training, an enterprise which in turn is supported by government grant. Yet partnership between home and school is not guaranteed as a result of Acts of Parliament and statutory orders, which in any case are focused more on making schools accountable than on providing the facilities for teachers and parents to work in closer collaboration. In the last analysis, the realisation of parental rights depends upon the willingness, enterprise and initiative of the professionals and local administrators to make partnership work. Without this, laws and pronouncements about parental rights and school accountability are invitations for confrontation and frustration.

In this chapter we concentrate on some of the issues involved in providing information for parents of current and prospective pupils, looking not only at what is required in law but also at what is necessary as part of sound professional practice. In subsequent chapters we look at initiatives which go a step further by developing teacher–parent collaboration and parental involvement in children's learning. It is recognised, however, that this division of material into that which is about 'informing' and that which is about 'discussing' and 'doing' is somewhat arbitrary since the two go hand in hand when the emphasis is placed upon the importance of professionals and parents *sharing* their knowledge and expertise.

SCHOOL PROSPECTUSES AND NEWSLETTERS

School prospectuses

The publication of a school prospectus (or brochure) has traditionally been accepted practice in private education; but, as a consequence of recent legislation to reinforce parental choice and school accountability, the prospectus is now also a feature of schools in the maintained sector. Under a regulation issued under the Education Act 1980 schools were required to publish information for parents. Further regulations under the Education Reform Act 1988 have amended and extended this requirement, and the position now is that primary schools, in an annual prospectus, must give parents the following information:

1 *General information about the school:*
   – the school's name, address and telephone number;
   – names of head teacher and chairman of governors;
   – classification of school (e.g. a county primary, a voluntary-aided primary);
   – arrangements for parents of prospective pupils to visit the school (if any); and
   – religious affiliations (if any).

2 *Information about the curriculum:*
   – a summary of the governing body's statement of curricular aims;
   – the arrangements for sex education (and how to see the full policy statement on this);
   – a summary for each year group giving the content and organisation of the National Curriculum, religious education and other subjects;
   – procedures for complaints about the delivery of the curriculum; and
   – for schools in Wales, arrangements for the teaching of Welsh and use of the Welsh language.

3 *Information about teaching arrangements:*
   – particulars relating to pupils with special educational needs;
   – the way children are grouped;
   – homework requirements;
   – the hours spent on teaching each week;
   – dates of school terms and half-terms for the next school year;
   – the school's policy on charging for school activities; and
   – the length of school sessions (which is linked to the charging system – see p. 47).

4 *Information about social matters:*
   – arrangements for pastoral care;
   – arrangements for discipline and school rules;
   – extra-curricular activities; and
   – the policy regarding school uniform.

The information must be published free of charge and made available to parents on request and for reference by any person. It must give the date at which the information was correct with a warning that there may be changes. LEAs and governing bodies must decide whether there is a need to provide information in languages other than English and issue translations if necessary. The prospectus must also state how parents and others can have access to key educational documents, copies of which schools are now obliged to hold. These documents include circulars issued by the DES and LEA, HMI reports on the school, and the schools schemes of work and syllabuses.

Of course, schools are free to provide further information over and above the statutory requirements. Possibilities include the following:

- health and welfare (including free meals and transport);
- school resources (e.g. the buildings, facilities such as a swimming pool, computers, laboratories);
- arrangements for starting school and transition to secondary school;
- ways in which parents can be involved in the life of the school;
- arrangements for multicultural education and whether there are bilingual teachers on the staff;
- arrangements for gifted children and those with special needs;
- assessment and reports to parents; and
- medical matters including procedures followed when a child is ill.

School prospectuses differ greatly in style and presentation, some consisting of just a few typed sheets while others are glossy picture-packed brochures. They also vary in their coverage of information: many omit to mention important aspects of the school's life and work, even leaving out items which are legally required. In a recent local survey, the Sutton Campaign for the Advancement of State Education (1989) found that primary schools frequently undervalued what they had to offer: few supplied information about their art and craft work, and there was very little reference to multicultural education, equal opportunities for boys and girls or special educational needs. Although most prospectuses indicated that children may be withdrawn from religious education and worship, not one said anything about alternative provision for children of non-Christian religions. On the other hand, many schools referred to corporal punishment, even though this sanction is now illegal! In an earlier but more extensive survey of 560 primary school brochures from all over England (Weeks, 1987), a large number failed to mention anything at all about the curriculum!

Undoubtedly the way a prospectus is presented affects the reader's initial attitudes towards the school. Do the photographs, drawings and cover convey the impression of an interesting school? Does it have a nice 'feel' about it in terms of size of paper, legibility, typeface and layout? Is the language welcoming and unpatronising? Is there an opening letter from the head which conveys the school's respect for pupils and their parents? Do statements about the school convey a sense of achievement without sounding complacent? Does the choice of words and illustrations have racist or sexist overtones? Is the prospectus clear, readable, free from grammatical errors and spelling mistakes? Is it informative without being overwhelming or jargon-ridden? If minority parents live in the area, is it available in suitable translations? It is also important to consider the distribution of the prospectus. Is it available in the local library, citizen's advice bureau, where pre-school groups meet?

Given that the main readers are to be parents, the prospectus must above all reflect their concerns and needs. The question which should constantly be at the front of the minds of those revising a school prospectus is therefore this: If I were a parent about to decide where my child should be educated, what impressions of the school would I pick up from this prospectus and does it tell me the kinds of things I want to know? Indeed it is a good idea to involve current parents in the preparation of the prospectus because they can raise issues and suggest ideas that reflect their perspective and which might otherwise be overlooked. It is also wise to employ a consumer test by asking parents (including some who do not know the school) to give their honest opinion on the draft.

Newsletters

Many primary schools send home a regular newsletter. This keeps parents informed about matters like term dates, parents' evenings, special events, new developments in the school, and staff changes. The head can also use newsletters to appeal to parents about particular issues, invite their views, and encourage their involvement in school affairs.

Many of the points already made about the content and presentation of prospectuses apply also to newsletters, which will convey *a* school image even if it is not the intended one. If the emphasis is on chiding parents for their children's disruptive behaviour and breaches of uniform regulations, or bemoaning the levels of contributions to the school fund and attendance at parents' evenings, the implicit message is that parents are problems; if the newsletter is compiled by the head only and written in an official style, the image conveyed may be that of an authoritarian institution. Apart from its content, a newsletter's presentation can help to project a positive school image. There are now computer software packages available which enable newsletters to be produced with a range of various type-faces and even in newspaper format. Sources are given at the end of this chapter.

There are, of course, occasions when a head needs to write a straight letter to parents. Newsletters, however, should fulfil a wider purpose by inviting contributions from all those who participate in the life of the school – parents, governors, teaching and non-teaching staff, pupils, outsiders closely associated with the school – thus helping to promote the idea of the school as a community. Items concerning pupil activities such as drama, music and sports events could well be written by the pupils themselves, whilst those concerning parents could be written by parent representatives. A column devoted to parents' and pupils' *views* about a matter would not only generate interest but help to convey the message that the opinions of everyone matter and are being actively sought. It is obviously important here to ensure that pupils and parents from all kinds of backgrounds are involved; if the writers are confined to those with the most obvious gift for language, the result may be divisive by creating an elite band of contributors, and so defeat the purpose. Indeed, both in what is said and who writes it, newsletters can help to reinforce the school's equal opportunities policies with respect to race, class, gender and special educational needs.

Performance Indicators and National Assessments

Central to the programme of education reform set out in the 1988 Education Act are the related aims of encouraging parental choice and raising educational standards. For these to be realised, the Government argues that it is necessary for schools to provide two sets of information:

1 information on school effectiveness according to agreed 'performance indicators' by which the school is made accountable to parents and the general public. Such information is also required to facilitate school choice; and
2 information on the achievements of individual pupils by which their parents and teachers can monitor progress and plan a suitable programme of work.

Apart from the requirement in the 1980 Act that secondary schools publish their examination results, performance indicators relating to the social aspects of both primary and secondary schools have been suggested (Coopers and Lybrand, 1987; CIPFA, 1988). These would involve publishing school ratings for matters such as pupils' behaviour, rates of suspension, vandalism, indictable offences; absenteeism, lateness and truancy; participation in school and outside activities, including sport; and the pupils' and parents' opinion of the school. It is not easy, however, to arrive at suitable criteria for quantifying the respects in which a school should be judged successful or unsuccessful. Moreover, achievements in some aspects of a school's endeavours which matter a great deal to parents and pupils – such as whether the children are happy and feel valued and secure, whether visitors feel welcome, relations with parents and the community – are virtually impossible to reduce to ratings without losing the essence of the qualities being evaluated. During the course of pilot work conducted in the late 1980s, the DES concluded that the quality of life in schools was too complicated to be expressed in a series of ratings. Instead, it has decided to issue a simple checklist to help schools review their performance each year (*The Times Educational Supplement*, 14.7.89).

The Education Reform Act generated a special performance indicator, both for individual pupils and for schools, in the shape of National Assessments. In June 1988, the Government announced to Parliament that parents will be told, as of right, the results of their child's assessments at the end of four 'key stages' covering the period of compulsory schooling, that is 5–7, 7–11, 11–14 and 14–16 years. This information is to be used in two ways: *summatively* to convey to parents and teachers what a child knows, understands and can do in relation to the National Curriculum attainment targets; and *formatively* so that parents and teachers can identify the children's strengths and weaknesses and plan the next steps for their education. The Government also announced that aggregated test results for each school must be published about pupils of eleven years of age and over so that parents and the wider public can make judgements about attainment in a school or LEA; publication of the results for seven-year-olds is not required but is strongly recommended by the Government. The separate arrangements which have been made for Scotland are less comprehensive, with testing confined to English and mathematics and only at ages eight and twelve, the point of transfer to secondary education.

Much controversy surrounds the appropriateness of quantified, published performance measures for general use. Supporters see them as an incentive to improving standards, ensuring that the public get value for money and generating information by which schools and LEAs can develop strengths and attend to weaknesses. Critics, however, regard them as intrusive monitoring by criteria which, while giving the appearance of objectivity, are easily open to misinterpretation, discouraging pupils who do not perform well and generating league tables which encourage unfair comparisons between schools with different qualities of pupil intake. The Government therefore set up a Task Group on Assessment and Testing (TGAT) headed by Professor Paul Black of King's College, London and including the former Chief Inspector for Primary Education, Norman Thomas. In its reports (DES, 1988a and b), TGAT argued that, in the interests of both justice and effectiveness, the nature of the assessments and the manner of their reporting must command the *confidence* of the teaching profession, parents and the general public alike. Its recommendations were broadly accepted by the Government and, though not received without criticism, allayed the worst fears about the narrowing effects which externally-imposed paper-and-pencil tests could have on the primary school curriculum. In Scotland, primary testing in English and mathematics will also be conducted on the TGAT principles.

There are a number of factors which could affect the faith which parents, teachers and others place on the National Assessments:

1 Validity An assessment is valid if it really represents what it says. A reading assessment based only on word recognition would be an obvious example of an invalid indicator of general literacy. The National Assessments can be said to be valid in two main respects. First, they are to be based on *both* externally-devised 'standard assessment tasks' (SATs) *and* assessments by the children's teachers. The reported results will be the outcome of moderation exercises where teachers from groups of schools resolve discrepancies between the internal and external assessments. Parents and the general public would lack confidence in a system based on teachers' judgements alone, while reliance on external tests carried out over a limited period of time might not do justice to the child's everyday progress. Secondly, the National Assessments are valid in so far as external assessments, as well as the teachers', are planned to reflect the actual curriculum which the children follow. By selecting from a bank of items, teachers will be able to choose SATs which best match the work which the pupils have been covering and which test practical, investigative and oral skills as well as knowledge revealed in paper-and-pencil tasks.

2 Reliability An assessment is reliable if consistent results would be obtained on repeated occasions. TGAT therefore decided that the SATs should be carefully piloted in trials and regularly re-appraised in the light of the moderation exercises. The risk that the tasks would be unreliable by children not doing justice to themselves would be minimised by devising them to look like interesting and typical classroom work. As the Task Group recognised, the reliability of assessments is particularly a problem with the seven-year-olds because their varied pre-school learning experiences and limited amount of formal schooling could unduly affect the results, making comparisons between schools erroneous. For this reason, it is regrettable that the Government has recommended the publication of school assessments at this age.

3 Usefulness For the assessments to command the confidence of parents, teachers and the public, they must be useful in judging a school's effectiveness and for providing formative, diagnostic information on individual children to guide the next step. To this end, the Government has accepted the Task Group's recommendation that the SATs should be *criterion-referenced*, reporting how far the children have reached specified assessment targets, like an Associated Board music exam or a driving test. The alternative would have been to make the tests norm-referenced, like the 11 + and the standardised tests traditionally used in primary schools; but these are less useful for parents and teachers since their purpose is to compare children with each other rather than to reveal how much they know and can do. On the other hand, although the assessments are not designed to meet norm-referenced criteria, the publication of aggregated results is bound to encourage parents to compare their own child's achievements with those of others.

All the same, the usefulness of the results is restricted in two respects. The first concerns the *range of type of achievements* which are covered by them. Because of the problem of finding methods of assessment which do justice to the nature of some subjects and avoid distorting curriculum opportunities through the backwash effects of testing, the assessments do not cover all the foundation subjects of the National Curriculum. However, in order to reduce the risk of parents and teachers focusing their attention unduly on achievement in those areas which are formally assessed, TGAT made two recommendations. One was that assessments for individual children should be reported to parents in the context of a description of the child's achievements across the whole curriculum. The other was that the aggregated school results, which are to be made public, should be published 'only as part of a broader report by that school of its work as a whole' (DES, 1988a, para. 132).

The other matter which restricts the usefulness of the assessments is that the *range of levels of achievement* among pupils is not reflected in a school's aggregated assessments. This is because results for each school are to be published as simple averages of the pupils' results. Two schools, however, could produce the same average result, but in one case it might reflect a normal distribution of results and in the other a skewed distribution which came about by the specially good or weak achievements of some pupils.

4 Interpretation There are two aspects to this problem. The first concerns the large number of scores which will be yielded during the course of assessing achievement towards the large number of attainment targets. On the one hand, it is important that parents are not presented with so much information that they are overwhelmed, misinterpreting it or not grasping its significance; on the other hand, it is important that parents are not given such a small amount of information that variations in a child's performance are masked. To try to get over this difficulty, reported results for each subject will refer to clusters of related attainment targets called 'profile components'. For instance, there are three profile components for English – speaking and listening, reading and writing. This information should give parents enough knowledge about the breadth of their child's attainments without blinding them with statistics. The results are to be reported on a scale of levels of achievement, numbered 1 to 10, which cover the full range of possible progress between the ages of five and sixteen. Children of seven years would normally be expected to achieve a Level of 1, 2 or 3, with 1 suggesting that additional help is needed to overcome weaknesses and 3 suggesting that help is needed to develop strengths. Children at eleven years would typically be at Levels 3, 4 or 5, but some may be at 2 or 6. Parents will also be told the proportions of children in the same age group who reached each Level, both at the school and nationally.

The second main issue which concerns the interpretation of National Assessments is the extent to which parents and the public can make fair judgements about a school's teaching effectiveness. The problem here is that pupils' attainments are influenced not only by the quality of a school's teaching but by a complex range of background factors. Unless these are taken into account, the National Assessments could mislead parents into making erroneous comparisons between standards of teaching in different schools. In studies such as the Junior School Project (Mortimore *et al.*, 1988), a number of background factors have been found to be particularly important in making fair comparisons between teaching effectiveness in different schools. These include variations in levels of attainment and behaviour at entry to school, whether parents are in manual or non-manual occupations, the pupils' pre-school experience and length of time which they have spent in the infant school, whether English is a second language, position in the family and family size, and poverty.

The Task Group therefore recognised that parents and the general public would need help in comparing the results of schools which have differing social, economic and cultural backgrounds or initial levels of attainment. It was therefore suggested that the LEA prepares a statement about each school, drawing attention to background factors which could affect the pupils' performance. The difficulty here is that it is the ratings themselves which are likely to dominate public perceptions of school effectiveness: a school with a large proportion of socially-disadvantaged pupils could therefore be unfairly victimised if results are presented without adjustment for background factors. A recent study has illustrated this problem. Using the data from twenty-one secondary schools in one LEA, Goldstein and Cuttance (1988) have shown how adjusting raw scores to take account of social advantage and disadvantage not only reduces apparent variations in effectiveness of one school compared with another but reveals that some schools with 'advantaged' intakes are underperforming.

The furore which can be created by publishing primary school assessments without adjustment was illustrated in December 1987 when, as part of a series on the academic achievements of local schools, the *Croydon Advertiser* published league tables based on the borough's junior school test results. Not surprisingly, letters from head teachers and the Director of Education complained of the sensational way in which the information was presented, the inaccuracy and incompleteness of some statements and the dangers of over-simplifying complicated issues.

Much care will therefore be needed to prevent misinterpretation of the National Assessments both with respect to individual children and comparisons between schools. Teachers therefore have the important responsibility first to understand the meaning of the assessments themselves and then to explain this to parents. It will clearly not be enough to rely on written communication: meetings will be essential to explain terms like 'Standard Assessment Task', 'Profile Component' and 'Level', and to help parents make fair comparisons between classes in the same school and with other schools. It would probably be more meaningful for schools to point to progress in relation to their own past performance than to compare themselves with other schools in the area.

ACCESS TO RECORDS

Primary school teachers keep records about each pupil. These may contain not only particulars about educational attainment and behaviour but also notes concerning medical problems and the pupil's temperament, character, personality, and family background. The purpose of these records should be 'to record progress, diagnose need and define provision' (ACE, 1988). Traditionally, although records have been open to welfare officers, social workers, educational psychologists and even the police, they have been kept secret from parents. However this is now changing.

Why have parents previously been denied access to records about their own child? One argument frequently heard is that if teachers, social workers, doctors and other professionals know that parents may see what they write, they could feel inhibited about recording sensitive but potentially useful information. They may resort instead to general and less informative statements, and keep a separate set of confidential records for their own use.

Constructive teacher–parent relations, however, depend upon mutual trust, a notion which is incompatible with an insistence that pupils' files must remain confidential to the professionals. Further, secrecy allows no check against the possibility that recorded information about the child or the home may be false, out of date, or based on a misunderstanding. It also enables heads, teachers and other professionals to write biased comment or make unfounded allegations which the parent cannot challenge. Evidence collected over the years by the Advisory Centre for Education has revealed cases of inaccurate and unfair statements on pupils' record cards. Such 'information' on primary school records could be damaging to the child's future education and career since the content is usually passed on to secondary schools.

The general principle behind the move towards open files is that parents have a moral and legal right to information about their own children if they are to fulfil their responsibilities of care. It is also important that teachers feel accountable for what is placed on records, and that parents are given the chance to point out any inaccuracies or misleading statements.

During the 1980s, some LEAs decided to give parents right of access to their child's records. The Tomlinson Report (1987) to the ILEA recommended that records should also be open to the pupils, regardless of age, since 'teachers find that involving children in recording their progress and the thinking, talking and writing this requires is a valuable part of the educational process' (p. 71).

In spite of local initiatives, however, it was not until the end of the decade that schools were statutorily obliged to give parents access to their child's school record. The Data Protection Act of 1984 gave everyone the right to inspect and obtain a copy of any computer records which hold information on them, but this did not affect most school records which are kept on paper. Section 27 of the 1980 Education Act enabled the Secretary of State to issue regulations concerning the keeping and disclosure of pupil records, but a consultative document was not issued until 1987, the regulations themselves not appearing until two years later. Comparable provision is planned for Scottish schools (SED, 1989).

The Education (School Records) Regulations 1989 cover pupil records in all maintained schools and non-maintained special schools, except data held on computers. They place the responsibility for maintaining and disclosing records with school governors. However, day-to-day responsibility can be delegated to the head and teaching staff provided arrangements are issued in a statement (with translations if necessary) and made available for inspection.

First of all, schools are obliged to keep records for each pupil and to ensure that the information is updated at least once a year and transferred (on request) to the pupil's next school. The contents, although not prescribed in detail, must meet two distinct but related purposes: one is to enable parents and other teachers to have information which shows how the pupil is progressing in relation to each National Curriculum attainment target; the other is to enable teachers to present evidence to support their assessment of the pupil's level of attainment for the key stage assessments. In addition to meeting these curricular requirements, schools may, if they wish, include other information which they find helpful in giving a full picture of the child, such as attendance data and material on behaviour, emotional development and home background. However, a teacher's subjective comment 'should be sufficiently well-founded to bear scrutiny by the parent' (DES Circular 17/89, para. 18).

Secondly, the Regulations require schools to ensure that, with certain exceptions, parents have access to any material in their child's record which comes from a teacher, educational welfare officer (EWO), or local authority employee. ('Parent' includes separated and foster parents, divorced parents with joint legal custody, and other adults who act in the parental role, governors having the responsibility to sort out any disputes over right of access.) A teacher may, however, keep private personal notes on a pupil provided that these are not shared with others. The main exceptions to parental access which apply to primary schools are reports from social services departments (except from an EWO), medical reports, information relating to child abuse (whether actual, alleged or suspected), reports to juvenile courts, and material concerning other pupils (e.g. those involved in an incident). Schools will not be required to give parents access to records made before September 1989, though they may do so if they wish.

Parents wishing to see their child's records must make their request in writing, when they can also ask for a copy (for which governors may charge to cover the cost). The school must respond within fifteen days (except during school holidays). A parent can ask for an entry on their child's record to be corrected or deleted if it is felt that the information is factually inaccurate or misleading. The school must comply if it agrees with the parent's verdict; otherwise it must allow the parent to add his or her own comment to the entry. Parents can appeal to the governors if they are not satisfied.

These provisions should go some way in preventing pupils becoming the victims of prejudiced judgements when transferring to secondary schools. However, certain problems remain. One concerns the information provided by professionals outside the school (e.g. social workers, psychologists or doctors) which the school need not disclose to parents. This provision was made to cover delicate situations such as suspicions about child abuse. However, even if one grants a need to protect some information, that is no grounds for keeping secret all records of outside bodies. It is likely to cause anxiety to those parents who have reason to believe that there is such a record. In any case it is inconsistent with the provision in the 1981 Education Act which gives parents of 'statemented' children rights of access to all professional records.

Of course, there is little point in giving parents access to records if these do not have a carefully considered purpose and contain information which is clear, comprehensive, accurate, helpful and up to date. This implies that LEAs and schools need to be clear about the aims of record-keeping and ensure that the design of record forms helps these aims to be realised. For instance, it is important for records to distinguish fact from opinion and to show whether opinion is more than simply one teacher's view. Moreover, to prevent parents misinterpreting an entry, it is important to ensure that a teacher explains the record to them and discusses it.

There is a further point too. If parents are to be involved in their children's learning, then records ought also to hold information to which the parents themselves have contributed. This idea has recently been taken up by Manchester City Council (1988), which has decided to introduce profiling for all its primary school pupils. This new form of comprehensive record-keeping also includes samples of children's work. The intention is to get teachers and parents working together to identify and develop each child's strengths and areas for improvement.

SCHOOL REPORTS

Now that parents are given access to their child's school records and profiles it could be asked whether there remains a special function for issuing the traditional school report once or twice a year, a practice which many primary schools have abandoned. The only large-scale study of reports which has so far been undertaken has focused on secondary schools (Goacher and Reid, 1983); but some of the issues raised in this survey have relevance for the primary schools wanting to review their reporting policy. Perhaps the most important finding was that, while parents in general valued reports, used them to monitor progress, and discussed them with their children, many said that the content could be more useful. In particular they wanted more detailed information on what their child had been doing and specific advice on how to help their child improve.

These requests suggest that, if reports are to continue, it is important that they should *involve* parents as much as *inform* them. Parents should be able to express a view on what the teachers have written, how their child feels about the report, and how the school could provide further information and guidance. Some schools therefore invite parents to contribute to the report, but it is important that this practice is not just a formality. If partnership between home and school is to be a reality, what parents say in response to school reports must be followed up.

Apart from these considerations, it is obviously important in any school review that attention is given to the language of reports. Are they free from jargon which parents may not understand? Is the meaning of grades and relative terms like 'average' clear to parents (and to teachers!). Are words and phrases consistent with anti-racist and anti-sexist policies? Are reports made intelligible for parents who do not read English or who have difficulty in doing so? If parents' are invited to record their comments, is it clear that they can do so in any language?

Given that it is for parents that reports are primarily written, their value, function, range of content, frequency and format should constitute part of the discussion which takes place during parent meetings.

THE ANNUAL REPORT AND PARENTS' MEETING

Under the 1986 Education Act, school governors must each year send a written report of their activities to parents of pupils at the school (using 'pupil post' if they want to). The report should be available in other languages if required. In practice, reports are as often drafted by head as by the governors, though frequently by both.

The annual report is intended to be a brief, straightforward, and factual document. Section 30 of the 1986 Act lays down certain items which must be included, and those which affect primary schools are as follows:

– particulars about each governor, e.g. name, an address for contact, type of governor (e.g. elected parent) and term of office;

−name of the chairperson and the clerk;

−notification of the annual meeting and its agenda;

−what the governors have done to carry out their responsibilities during the year;

−how the school has spent its money;

−how the school has strengthened its links with the community and local police; and

−arrangements for the next election of parent governors.

Following the 1988 Act, the report will also have to include the aggregated results for National Assessments at eleven years. Under a regulation issued under this Act, changes to information presented in the school prospectus must also be given, particularly term and half-term dates.

There is, of course, nothing to prevent other information about the school being included in the annual report to give a more complete account to parents and to engage their interest. The Advisory Centre for Education (1987a) suggest that additional items might include:

−the school's particular strengths;

−areas of weakness and how these are being tackled;

−policies on sex education, special needs and equal opportunities;

−educational visits;

−record-keeping policies;

−courses which teachers have attended to improve their professional competence.

Governors are also obliged to invite the parents to a meeting, to be held within a fortnight of issuing their annual report. The purpose of the meeting is both to discuss the report and the way the LEA and head teacher have discharged their functions. The intention is to make the governors, local authority and school more accountable to the parent body.

Governors can invite anyone to the meeting who is likely to be useful, including teachers and non-teaching staff and a representative of the LEA−but the DES suggests that it would generally be undesirable to invite the press or the general public (Circular 8/86). Parents can raise any matter which has a bearing on the life of the school and, provided the number attending is at least 20 per cent of the school roll, they can pass formal resolutions which the governors and LEA are required to consider. ACE (1987a) suggest that the invitation to the meeting includes a tear-off slip for parents to suggest matters which they want raised. This would give the governors a chance to inform themselves on the issues, though it is important that this practice does not prevent parents raising matters at the meeting without prior notice.

As the DES has noted, skilful chairing would be called for if criticisms were to be made of individual teachers:

> Particular care will be needed in the handling of anything which involves criticism of a named individual, such as a member of staff. The Chairman should try to ensure that any such discussion is kept calm, positive and reasonably brief. Taking early delivery of the point for further consideration by the governing body or LEA might be the

most appropriate solution. The person criticised should be offered the right to reply, either at once if he is present or subsequently to the governing body, the head teacher or the LEA, as appropriate. (DES Circular 8/86, para. 13(c))

In the event 'teacher bashing' has not been prevalent, criticisms in the first round being directed more at the LEA and Government. However, attendance has generally been very poor and usually insufficient for resolutions to be passed. Nonetheless, it is clear that many meetings have generated useful discussion (Earley, 1988; Fletcher, 1989). Topics raised have included discipline, sex education, special needs, the needs of brighter children, policy on race and gender, homework, school uniform, school meals, charging for activities, parking arrangements for collecting children, safety in the playground, prospects of testing at seven and eleven, the admission of rising-fives, mixed year-groups, access to test results, the importance of spelling and grammar, and the right of parents to withdraw their children from sex education.

At the best of times, parents will feel that attending the annual meeting is not worth the effort if they do not see it being of direct benefit to them – particularly if they have to arrange a baby-sitter or miss their favourite TV programme! They will also effectively be encouraged to stay away if they have been sent a dull, closely-typed report announcing a meeting which has a formal-looking agenda. Conversely, they are more likely to attend – and to make positive comments when they do – if their normal perception of home–school relationships is favourable. The annual meeting should be just one of many ways in which teachers and parents get together.

Although parents are now represented on governing bodies, the annual meeting is probably the only occasion when the general body of parents can meet the governors (and, by invitation, staff and LEA officials) to exchange ideas and influence decision-making about school arrangements. But it is the school which needs to take the initiative in engaging parents' interest, which undoubtedly is influenced by the degree to which parents believe that the governors really want to know their views. What, for instance, were parents to make of the following statement in the annual report of a primary school covered in a survey by Mahoney? (1988, p. 8): 'The teachers labour in vain, their commitment and dedication go for nothing, when opposed by the indifference and carelessness of parents . . . There have been no grave epidemics'.

From the proceedings at a conference on the first round of annual reports and meetings (Earley, 1988), it would seem that parents might express greater interest in the annual meeting if:

– the annual report is attractively set out (perhaps in question and answer form), interesting (not just lists and budgetary tables), and sent with a covering letter which uses welcoming, personal phrases such as 'We invite you . . .' and 'We look forward to meeting you . . .';
– meetings begin with refreshments and informal chat between parents, governors and teachers to break barriers;
– it is known that the evening will include such events as an exhibition of children's

work, demonstrations by pupils, a film about the school trip, a proposed video for sex education or solvent abuse;

- the parents' questions are received positively and not taken as implying personal criticism or greeted by a defensive wall;
- governors refrain from simply presenting information and responding to questions but also raise issues for discussion (e.g. 'We would like your views on . . .'); and
- a crèche and child-minding facilities are available.

PROMOTING A POSITIVE SCHOOL IMAGE

Forbat (1988) distinguishes between a school's *image* and its *reputation*: both are views held by outsiders, but whereas reputations emerge over time, images are deliberately created and positively promoted. A school which suffers from a bad reputation may do so unfairly or for good reason, but if it wishes to attract pupils it will need to change that reputation. Its success in doing so will depend, of course, on the extent to which changed practices (and possibly personnel) allow it to be deservedly held in higher regard, but the process will be assisted by the cultivation of a positive image.

The need for schools to think in terms of advertising their strengths and special features has been emphasised by provision in recent legislation. The advent of open enrolment, whereby parents are encouraged to choose between schools (see p. 61), means that no staff can afford to ignore their school's reputation. When the policy is one in which education is market-led, one school's popularity could mean another's closure as they compete for customers. Adverse criticisms made by HM Inspectors, whose reports on individual schools have been published since 1983 and are frequently summarised in the Press, place school practices on a public pedestal, while the publication of National Assessments will make each school continuously vulnerable to public opinion. Additionally, primary schools face mounting competition from independent schools whose numbers have increased over the last decade.

Many teachers find the whole idea of image-building distasteful. Apart from the fact that it may use up energy which might otherwise be spent on educating the children, they wonder about its morality, particularly if facts about the school are selectively and aggressively presented, exaggerated or even invented. But the process does not necessarily involve 'being economical with the truth' or 'massaging the statistics': an alternative way of looking at the problem is to regard it as an incentive to put right the factors which seem responsible for any shortcomings in the school's reputation and to develop constructive relations with the community in general and prospective parents in particular. At its worst, image-building is an exercise in covering-up and public deception: at its best it is an exercise in self-improvement and public education. As Usher (1985) has pointed out, 'private' schools, which keep themselves to themselves, engender myths; whereas 'public' schools, which are open and share their successes and failure, engender support and understanding (not least when things go wrong!).

How might a primary school go about developing a positive public image? For a start, it is important for the governors and head teacher to ensure that one member of staff (who need not necessarily be the head) has particular responsibility for the development of communication with parents, prospective parents and the public at large. This officer then needs a group to collect, discuss and generate ideas and to undertake specific tasks. Apart from the public relations officer, such a group might comprise the head/deputy/another teacher, a parent governor and another governor, and a non-teaching member of staff such as the school caretaker. Consideration should also be given to the involvement of, say, two pupils from the top year: after all, nothing affects a school's reputation so easily as the pupils' feelings about their school. Satisfied (and well-behaved) pupils are the school's best advertisement.

The first task of the group is to find out, as objectively as possible, just what kind of image the school currently enjoys. Of course, the staff and governors will have a rough idea about this, but their perceptions are understandably coloured by their involvement in the school. So the group needs to conduct an investigation to answer questions such as the following:

1 What is it that makes parents choose or reject the school?
2 What is it that the pupils and teachers themselves admire and dislike?
3 What makes some parents choose alternative schools (including private schools)?

The collection and analysis of such data (in which the pupils can play a major part) constitutes the basis for developing a more positive school image – strengthening the good qualities, eliminating the bad, and bringing to the public's attention those positive features of the school which they may not know about. It is also important not to regard such an investigation as a one-off affair: the school needs to monitor its public image.

Brunt (1987) has emphasised the importance of finding out the extent to which a school lives up to the expectations of different sections of the community. What are the perceptions of parents from different ethnic groups and of working-class and middle-class parents? This does not mean that the school should pander to parents' tastes, regardless of what they are: some parents may be avoiding the school because of its multicultural programme or because it emphasises 'real books' rather than reading schemes, but the expression of such views does not itself constitute a reason for changing the school's considered policy. It might, however, suggest that the rationale for the policies needs to be communicated more effectively. The school has to make a judgement as to what changes it should make which are consistent with its educational principles. However, no school should be so complacent that it neglects to review its aims and objectives. Indeed in some cases poor enrolment may reflect the public's perception that the school lacks commitment to a clear set of educational principles.

A second task for the group is to review the arrangements for the school's public events – sports' afternoons, drama and music events, the annual parents' meeting, summer fêtes and Christmas bazaars, charity-raising efforts – to ensure that on these occasions the best possible image is put forward. Is the advertising wide enough? Do the posters and invitations present the school in a good light? Are visitors made welcome when they arrive? Do the pupils themselves play a major part in receiving guests and looking after them? Should the local press or local radio be informed or invited? It is certainly worthwhile cultivating a good working relationship with the local media, getting to know individual reporters and maintaining regular contact. Such a relationship could pay dividends by lessening the impact of bad publicity which any school can encounter from time to time.

Part of the school's public image is portrayed in the face presented to visitors. A third task for the 'image group' members is therefore to walk around the school imagining themselves in the position of a prospective parent. What impression is conveyed by the entrance area (and can it be easily found)? What will a visitor make of the notices about enquiries, of the display areas, of the library and other resource areas, of the playground, of the corridors, or of the state of the furniture? Where bilingual visitors can be expected, are there signs of welcome and direction in relevant languages? Is there an inviting place for visitors to wait, or do they have to stand in the corridor beside the pupil on report for bad behaviour? Above all, what impressions do the children create, and what hidden messages does this convey for teachers to ponder over? Those entering the building for the first time will be quick to perceive whether the school is welcoming and purposeful, and whether the children are happy and mindful of visitors' needs.

Fourthly, the group might examine the extent to which the school is involved in the general life of the community. Are community representatives invited to talk to the children and are the children, in turn, involved in community life? Apart from its intrinsic, educational value (see pp. 134–5), the extension of the school into the community and the community into the school can help to develop constructive public relations. Some primary schools mount special exhibitions of children's work in the local library and other centres such as churches, mosques and temples.

Fifthly, the presentation and content of the school's regular information bulletins need to be reviewed – not only the prospectus but also newsletters and other forms of internal communication which current parents may show to parents of prospective pupils. These materials carry important messages about a school – what it values, what it ignores, how much it cares about its relationships with parents, pupils and the community.

Lastly, a film or video of the school in action can help to project the desired image (as well as providing a valuable educational experience for the children who help to make it). The content might usefully include interviews with current parents who know the questions that need answering. The film or video could be shown at meetings for parents of prospective pupils and copies made available for loan.

SUMMARY AND CONCLUSIONS

This chapter has addressed a range of issues concerning the primary school's responsibility to provide information for parents. *Morally*, the school has an obligation to provide information which will facilitate their accountability to parents, and an obligation to keep parents informed of matters which enable them to care properly for their children. *Professionally*, teachers should give parents information which engages their interest and involvement, so maximising the effectiveness of their teaching. *Legally*, each school has a duty to:

1 produce a prospectus, the contents of which must meet certain minimum requirements and be revised annually;
2 hold and make available to parents key national and local educational documents as well as the school's syllabuses;
3 report to parents their child's National Assessments at seven and eleven years and to publish its aggregated results (compulsory at eleven and strongly recommended at seven years);
4 give parents free access to their child's records;
5 issue an annual report from the governors who are required to invite parents to an annual meeting which, if quorate, can pass resolutions which the authorities must consider.

Politically, given policies of open enrolment and the growth of the independent sector, schools need to keep the public aware of their ethos and achievements in order to improve their image and so attract custom.

In the course of discussing each topic it has become clear that the school cannot fulfil its communication responsibilities to parents just by providing information: there must also be discussion with parents and a respect for their point of view. The next chapter, therefore, considers the development of dialogue between home and school.

Further reading

Schools revising the information they provide for the parents of prospective pupils would do well to consult *Planning Your School Prospectus* by Felicity Taylor (Advisory Centre for Education, 1987) and/or *Your School Brochure* by Alan Weeks (New Education Press, 1987). The relevant DES Circular is 14/89.

The production of school newsletters can be given a more professional look by means of computer packages which allow printing in a range of typefaces and in columns. A simple one to use is *Front Page Extra*, suitable for the BBC, RML 480Z and Nimbus computers (Newman College Computer Centre, Bartley Green, Birmingham B32 3NT). More sophisticated is *Newspaper*, suitable for the RML 480Z and Nimbus computers (Software Production Associates, PO Box 59, Leamington Spa CV31 3QA), though it is not easy for young children to use. Two multilingual word-processing packages are 'Allwrite' for the RM Nimbus (Inner London Educational Computing Centre, John Ruskin St, London SE5 0PQ) and 'Modern Language Folio' for the BBC micro (THATT Services, Whitechapel Technology Centre, 75 Whitechapel Rd, London E1).

The problems of reporting National Assessments to parents are explored in the Report of the Task Group on Assessment and Testing (DES, 1988).

A full discussion on the issue of opening records to parents can be found in the Tomlinson Report, *Informing Education* (ILEA, 1987) (obtainable from the Advisory Centre for Education). The relevant DES Circular is 17/89.

Governors' Reports and Annual Parents' Meetings edited by Peter Earley (National Foundation for Educational Research, 1988) is a very useful collection of papers for schools wanting to attract parental interest.

Schools looking for ways in which to project a positive image might wish to consider making a film or video for parents of prospective pupils. A discussion of some of the issues involved can be found in Barbara Tizard *et al. Involving Parents in Nursery and Infant Schools* (Grant McIntyre, 1981).

8 | DEVELOPING DIALOGUE

Home – school relations are not just about keeping parents well informed, though this in itself is of first importance: they are also about working *with* parents. This means sharing ideas, skills and knowledge, openly discussing issues, and exploring ways in which parents can be more effective in facilitating their children's educational development.

Janet Atkin and her colleagues (1988) distinguish between a philosophy of home – school relations which is based on effective ways of 'handling' parents and an alternative, more constructive, philosophy which is 'parent-centred'. The latter involves:

1 understanding the needs of parents as *they* perceive them, and finding out how they assess the quality of current home – school relations;
2 acknowledging that parents have the right to be consulted about, and involved with, their children's educational development;
3 developing an active partnership in which teachers and parents share the same goals and work together;
4 using parents as a resource to complement the knowledge and experience of teachers and other professionals; and
5 believing that parents, as persons, deserve the respect of professionals.

The remaining chapters of this book look at ways in which communication between schools and parents is an *interactive* process. It is not a matter of schools *surrendering* to parental pressures: such a policy would involve devaluing teachers' professional skills and insights. Nor is it a matter of teachers *telling* parents how they can best support their children's education: such a policy would ignore the parents' skills and insights. Rather it is a matter of *each partner valuing the skills and insights of the other* in a process of working together within a framework of mutual understanding. Thus, teachers need not only to inform parents of the school's goals and practices but be prepared to change and modify these as a result of their involvement with parents. Conversely, parents need to respect the knowledge and experience of teachers and be prepared to change and modify their perspective on educational goals and practices.

None of this supposes that parents and teachers are homogeneous groups with distinctive perspectives which need to be 'brought together' in some kind of compromise package deal. Parents as a group do not think alike any more than teachers do. Nonetheless, an effective home–school relations policy should not only encourage parents to think more constructively about their role in schooling but also prompt teachers to think more clearly about their own educational beliefs and strategies and the justification for them.

ADJUSTING TO SCHOOL AND TRANSITION TO SECONDARY SCHOOL

Adjusting to school

Some adults can still recall the period when they started school. Some of these memories bring back feelings of anxiety and helplessness about an unfamiliar and bewildering situation; being separated from parents who were often not allowed in the building, and in spite of it all being made to feel guilty for failure to put on a brave face. In an article published in 1966, Moore reported that eight out of every ten children at that time found difficulty in adjusting to infant school.

The extent to which starting school poses a threat to children's feelings of security and self-worth is affected by the quality of early contacts between home and school. Tizard *et al.* (1981, p.128) see these as having four main aims:

– to make the child's transition to school as easy and pleasant as possible;
– to show parents that they are welcome, and can feel comfortable there;
– to explain the school's aims and methods to the parents; and
– to provide staff with opportunities to learn from parents about their child.

Many infant school teachers visit the parents of new children in their homes during the term prior to entry (see section on Home Visiting below). In at least one authority, the parents of children already in the school help in this activity (Jowett and Baginsky, 1988). Apart from giving the child the opportunity to meet the head or class teacher on home ground, a visit from the school provides an informal setting for the parents to discuss school matters and for the teacher to learn about the child's life in the home setting. Blatchford *et al.* (1982) found that teachers who visited the homes of children about to start school were welcomed by parents almost without exception. Whether or not a home visit is arranged, it is now generally regarded as good practice for children to visit the school before they officially start and for their parents to stay with them as long as necessary at the beginning of the first term. Some children do not need a parent to stay long on the first day, or even at all, but others find the process of adjustment easier if they do. It helps, too, if the first few days are staggered so that children and their parents can be given more personal attention.

Many parents still feel that, even if they are allowed to stay in the classroom when their child begins infant school, the delay in parting would only make it harder for the child. Yet, as the Thomas Report put it recently, while there are sensitive judgements to be made it is wiser to err on the side of over-sensitivity rather than the opposite (ILEA, 1985a). It is not just that the parent's presence is important for the sake of the child's feelings of security, but also that the parent is given the means to become familiar with the work and life of the school. Incidents can be discussed with the child from an informed perspective. Equally, it is important for the child to see his mother or father being part of the school and being welcomed by the head and teacher. In infant classes where the territory between the professionals and the parents is broken down by involving parents in the class on a regular basis, the presence of parents of reception children is simply part of the fabric.

The child's feelings of security are helped enormously through the preliminary visits with a parent, particularly if these can introduce the child to various aspects of the school situation. More than one visit helps children (and the parents!) to adjust gradually and get to know the head and reception class teacher. Joining a family assembly, which in many schools is a regular occasion anyway, helps the child to become familiar with being in a hall with a large number of people.

Tizard *et al.* (1981) recommend a 'pre-school club' for prospective entrants. This is not an alternative to a regular pre-school group the child may already be attending; rather it is a special facility by which children and their parents, once or twice a week, can familiarise themselves with the school environment and the staff and meet other parents and children. Indeed, parents could help to staff the club, which could be advertised in local clinics, launderettes, libraries, and other places which parents are likely to visit. Clearly there will need to be play materials for younger siblings. The club can be used to disseminate information on social services, courses in early child development, and ideas for pre-reading and pre-writing activities. Most importantly, it is a means by which dialogue among parents and teachers can begin. Full-time working mothers may find it difficult to attend, but those working part-time will be able to do so if the timing of the club meetings are varied.

Endeavours to help new children and their parents recently prompted the staff of Birstall Primary School near Leicester to publish an attractive book which parents can share with their pre-school child. It was written by two of the parents, Janet and Allan Ahlberg (1988: details under Further Reading). Another way of helping to introduce both child and parent to the school is to provide a video of typical activities. This could be shown to a group of incoming children and their parents, and/or lent out for home viewing and discussion, and will be all the more useful if available with commentaries in minority languages. Some primary schools involve children in making videos anyway, so for them the task should present no special problems.

Transition to secondary school

Studies on transition from primary to secondary schools have traditionally ignored the parent's perspective. The assumption has been that improvement in this area is a matter which the teachers can settle alone. Recent investigations, however, have broken new ground by including the parent's point of view.

The London Secondary Transfer Project, involving approximately 1600 pupils, is the most extensive investigation which has yet been undertaken on improving transition from primary to secondary school, and it importantly included the views of parents (ILEA, 1985d). The project revealed that although about 85 per cent of those interviewed were generally satisfied with transfer arrangements, almost a quarter expressed particular worries. The most common concern was about bullying; others included the bad influences of other children, prospects of a longer and more arduous journey to school, teachers' expectations being too low, discipline, parent–teacher liaison, racism, the expense of school uniform, loneliness and friendship problems, and the large size of the school. In some cases the anxieties reflected difficulties which the child was already experiencing at primary school, and the fear that the secondary school would fail to respond positively or even exacerbate the problem. The seventeen project bulletins produced over 200 recommendations, most of which go beyond the immediate concerns of this book, but two issues directly affect primary schools in their relations with parents.

The first of these concerns information. Parents found the booklets issued by the secondary schools confusing, particularly in matters related to the curriculum, and tended to look to primary heads and teachers for advice. However, the primary staff did not always possess the relevant knowledge; moreover their perceptions of the secondary curriculum and teaching methods were often stereotyped and negative, and based more on supposition than direct evidence. The report therefore recommends that primary schools should find out the kinds of questions which parents ask at this stage and acquire the relevant information from the local secondary schools. Another recommendation was that as many primary teachers as possible should visit the secondary schools to which their pupils go so that they can give parents advice which is based on first-hand experience.

The second issue concerns the finding that parents often thought their children 'marked time' in the pre-transfer year. To counter this tendency, the report urges primary and secondary schools to forge curriculum links. This is not altogether easy when each secondary school has a large number of feeder schools, but the problem would be eased if primary and secondary schools exchanged curricular information, which many do not. The report also suggests that both parents and children would benefit if the pre-transition year was made more like that of secondary schools (e.g. more subject-centred), with content and teaching methods fitting in as far as possible with the local secondary school practices. Since the National Curriculum covers the whole of compulsory schooling, it should be easier in future for primary and secondary teachers to force curriculum links.

Another recent study, 'The Development of Effective Home/School Programmes' Project at Nottingham University School of Education, has been concerned with parents' perspectives about many aspects of schooling, of which transfer is one. Bastiani (1986) has reported that many of the parents interviewed, being used to the personal atmosphere of the primary school, were frustrated by their experiences of secondary schools' bureaucracy. In particular, they found that home–school relationships at transfer were dominated by impersonal written communication which emphasised the school's public image rather than the parents' and pupils' immediate concerns. The latter included an understanding of secondary school routines and classroom life and ways in which parents could be utilised and incorporated into the life of the secondary school from the start.

In their liaison with secondary schools, primary schools could be instrumental in eliciting and conveying their parents' concerns so that the secondary schools' response better matches the parents' needs. Evidence that this 'listening to parents' philosophy pays off is provided in an evaluation report of an induction programme for new pupils in a comprehensive school (Worsley, 1986). This gives a convincing account of the benefits of working in close liaison with parents at transfer, particularly through meetings with the pupils' form tutors at the end of the primary school summer term. It is especially important for primary schools to help parents who are concerned about the prospects of the secondary school coping with their child's learning, behavioural and emotional needs, or their physical and sensory disabilities, or special talents. These parents need to know what special support the secondary school will provide.

MEETING PARENTS INDIVIDUALLY

All schools have arrangements of one kind or another for discussing each child's progress with the parents. This is important from the standpoint of parent, teacher and child. *Parents* have the right to know how their children are progressing and how teachers are trying to meet any problems. They also need the opportunity to talk to teachers about their concerns. *Teachers* will be more successful when they understand what the parent feels about the child's progress and the school's approach to teaching and learning, and when there is opportunity to discuss ways in which the parent can help the child. It is only through face-to-face discussion that a teacher can really understand the parent's perspective, knowledge of which may be particularly imperfect with respect to ethnic minority parents, single parents, and those whose children have handicaps of one kind or another. *Children* need to know that their parents and teachers are sharing ideas and working in the same direction.

Nonetheless, as noted in the last chapter, recent research findings suggest that parents are frequently ill-informed about their child's progress, even in situations where they are given access to their child's records and have discussions with the teacher. In a study in Handsworth, Birmingham, some West Indian and Asian parents complained of being 'fobbed off' by the teacher's remark that 'he's doing all right' when it later emerged that the child was experiencing learning problems (Tomlinson, 1984). Again, in their interviews with London infant school parents, Tizard *et al.* (1988) found that 26 per cent of reception class children and 34 per cent of top infants were reported by their teachers as presenting behaviour problems: yet only 12 per cent of reception and 22 per cent of top-infant parents had been told about this. The London Junior School Project (Mortimore *et al.*, 1988) found considerable variations between schools in the frequencies of home–school contacts, a small minority of parents having never met the class teacher at all.

How can we explain the fact that many parents know so little about their children's progress and problems, and what approaches are likely to be fruitful? First, some parents just don't come in to school. However, this is not necessarily because they are not interested. Unpleasant memories of their own school days may lead them to assume that teachers will talk to them in the same manner as teachers spoke to them as children, being over-directive and making them feel inferior and inadequate. They may have reason to hold such beliefs if the school has directly involved them only when things have gone wrong, or has not respected their point of view, or in trying to understand their difficulties has only made them feel inadequate. Other parents may not visit because they lack confidence, have a poor command of English, or prefer to leave educational guidance to the teacher. It is also the case that work patterns and the need to arrange baby-sitters make it difficult for some parents to attend at the time the school offers. Clearly, therefore, it is important for invitations to be friendly and welcoming and issued in translation where necessary; invitations to social evenings usually elicit a better response and help teachers and parents to meet more informally. Flexibility in the scheduling of meetings is also desirable, and visiting the parent's home (discussed in a later section) is another possibility. As Rundall and Smith (1982) have argued, 'The problem is not that all these parents are unreachable, but that we have not yet been able to reach them' (p.67).

Some primary schools do not issue formal invitations to discuss the children's work because they believe that communication will be more productive if parents know that they can drop in whenever they want to see the teacher and inspect the child's work. The motive here is commendable; the problem, however, is that the parent who feels diffident about taking the initiative, or thinks that meeting the teacher is unnecessary, is going to get left out. It may therefore be a mistake to assume that the adoption of a 'drop in any time' policy obviates the need for formal invitations; both practices are important. It may help if the invitations set out the sorts of topics which the teachers would like to raise, and among these should be what the parents think about their child's progress and their feelings about the school. Parents are more likely to respond to invitations to visit the school if they know that the teacher will attend to what they are saying, show concern for and respect their feelings, and not do all the talking or be judgemental. Some in-service courses have helped teachers to develop the relevant skills here by asking pairs to role-play an interview between a parent and a teacher. Experience also shows that parents are much more likely to want to discuss issues with teachers in the context of home–school curriculum projects. As many reports have shown, virtually all parents, not least those in predominantly working-class areas, will take advantage of this kind of opportunity (see next chapter).

A second reason why parents can be ill-informed about their children's progress at school is that some teachers deliberately withhold information because they fear the parent might handle the difficulty by severely punishing the child. This is particularly likely over a child's aggressive behaviour, when the teacher knows that punishment is not the answer. Yet there seems little point in holding any discussion with the parent unless there is an honest appraisal of the child's progress and a sharing of the problems. Some teachers will also avoid talking about a child's difficulties because they feel that the parent may interpret the situation as a sign of the teacher's professional incompetence. The problem is compounded when the parent, sensing the teacher's defensiveness, feels unable to be frank and open about the child's difficulties, and may be put off coming to school at all. Parents in general do not want their children to see them as 'troublemakers'.

There are no easy answers to these problems of honest relationships, but some kinds of physical conditions make it much easier to talk to parents on a basis of equality. Sitting on opposite sides of a table in a classroom, particularly if other parents (who may appear more confident and have brighter children) are waiting in the same room, does not offer the best kind of environment for frank and open discussion; nor does it help if parents have been kept waiting in a corridor. There is, of course, much to be said for seeing parents in the classroom since they can see the environment in which their children learn and have easy access to their work; but parents' privacy needs to be safeguarded, and for daytime interviews a parents' room (which can serve also for group meetings and the dissemination of information) is an invaluable facility. It is also important to ask open-ended questions to invite the parent's opinion and to give parents time to express their concerns, which they may feel reluctant to do if they have a feeling of being hurried.

Obviously relations are more difficult to develop when parents are critical and hostile. Rundall and Smith (1982) make a number of suggestions for teachers who are placed in this position. One is to try to appraise the situation honestly and consider if the parent might have a genuine complaint, in which case it will be necessary to admit fault and deal with the matter. Another is to ask oneself whether the parent's apparent hostility arises from poor skills in assertiveness or from the difficulty in accepting that his or her child has real learning or behavioural problems: 'These parents need to be allowed the opportunity to ventilate. They need to be accepted and listened to, and told that their anger is normal' (p.80). It is also important to resist allowing the parent's hostility to arouse visible anger in you. This is not easy but can often be achieved by making yourself talk slowly and softly, letting the parent know that you recognise the feelings being expressed. Equally, do not show fear which may reinforce the parent's hostility, but try to remain calm and composed, maintaining a positive attitude.

Whatever arrangements are made for meeting parents, it is important for schools to evaluate these. Bastiani (1988) has commented that 'teacher–parent interviews . . . seem trapped in a suffocating network of unexamined assumptions and conventions, which effective evaluation would need to recognise and clarify' (p.215). Setting aside a 'Baker day' for this purpose could be productive, providing the discussion is based on some hard data. Monitoring the questions which parents commonly ask, listing their comments and discussing these with parent representatives is therefore very important. Maybe some parents would feel easier relaying suggestions to the parent governors rather than to the head or a teacher.

SHARING THE CURRICULUM

There are a number of respects in which parents are now being given greater access to the school curriculum. The National Curriculum attainment targets and programmes of study are generally available, and under the 1980 Education Act and subsequent ministerial orders, schools are required to provide parents with written information about their curriculum programmes (see p.100). At the same time, an increasing number of primary schools are taking the initiative themselves to give parents a more participatory role in the curriculum.

It is possible to distinguish between five different kinds of ways in which parents are being given greater insights into the primary curriculum and are working more collaboratively with teachers. These are:

1 explaining the curriculum and teaching approaches to parents;
2 engaging parents in workshop activities which deepen their understanding of subject-matter;
3 incorporating parents in curriculum decision-making processes;
4 inviting parents to develop their role as educators of their children; and
5 involving parents in classroom activities.

The first three of these are discussed in this section, the other two in later chapters.

Explaining the curriculum to parents

In a number of respects, the primary school curriculum has changed since parents were at school themselves. For instance, there is generally less formal instruction and instead a greater emphasis on investigative work and encouraging children to assume more responsibility for their own learning. Furthermore, new developments are taking place all the time, such as the use of computers and word-processors, greater attention to health and sex education, and the institution of new programmes of study and assessment processes under the National Curriculum. Parents have the right to understand what teachers are trying to do and what developments are being planned.

Many primary schools, therefore, hold evenings to explain new teaching methods and curriculum arrangements, and often invite a local adviser or other professional 'expert' to deliver the talk. These events are usually more successful when the speaker is well briefed about what to do, makes effective user of audio-visual aids, tries to respond to the parents' concerns and gives plenty of opportunity for discussion. Unfortunately, the parents are sometimes disappointed since what they get is a lecture ridden with unfamiliar jargon and delivered by a visiting expert who has no direct knowledge of what the class teacher is doing. Parents are also not always clear how what is said relates specifically to their own children.

For these reasons, more and more schools are organising events in which there is more interaction between one parent and another and between parents and the class teacher. Displays of resources and children's work, with flexible times for viewing, also helps to give parents more of the kind of information they are seeking and free the teacher for discussion with individuals. There can also be opportunities for parents to use equipment themselves. For instance, using computer software, particularly with the help of some pupils, helps to demonstrate its value in the classroom.

Curriculum workshops

Many primary schools run workshops for parents, often on a regular basis. They are particularly useful when the teacher arranges for the parents to engage in activities which are similar to those in which the children themselves participate, for this provides a meaningful context for discussion about curriculum philosophy and investigative teaching methods. It also contributes to parent education by developing understanding of the subject itself, as for instance in using first-hand historical material or in using mathematical apparatus. Moreover, the parents usually find it fun!

What are the principles which need to be observed for a successful curriculum workshop? First of all, such occasions need to be informal and provide plenty for the parents to do. They are therefore usually more successful when they involve a small group of parents or at least allow a larger meeting to break up into smaller units. Although inviting small numbers may mean that the evening has to be repeated, the arrangement should facilitate discussion not only with the person taking the session but also between the parents themselves. Secondly, it is probably better if the evening is run by the class teacher or another member of staff rather than, say, a local adviser. This allows the agenda to be tailor-made to fit the programme of work which the children are following and it gives parents and teachers a chance to get to know each other better.

Thirdly, workshops are more successful if they are planned to help parents acquire understanding such that they are better able to help their children and talk intelligently to them about curriculum activities (a matter which is developed in the next two chapters). The parents should go away feeling that they have not just been informed about new concepts and teaching approaches but have engaged in discussion and practical activities which makes them more aware of their own thinking processes. Lastly, it is important to evaluate each session so that future occasions can be more responsive to parents' needs. Keeping the group small will make it easier for parents to voice their own ideas for future events; and a questionnaire is usually helpful, particularly if it includes opportunities for parents to make suggestions.

Having a say in the curriculum

The establishment of the National Curriculum and increase in the responsibilities of governors has restricted teacher autonomy in curriculum planning. The idea that parents should 'interfere' with what scope is left may seem anathema to many teachers. However, as some primary schools have found, curriculum decisions are made with greater confidence when the parents' perspectives are known and their ideas and suggestions taken into account. One junior school described by Sutcliffe (1986) includes PTA representatives in some curriculum planning meetings since, as the head put it, 'It's a renewal of credibility and trust'. He feels that mutual understanding between parents and teachers is furthered when the school incorporates parents into its decision-making processes.

Parents usually welcome involvement in planning programmes which relate to areas about which they are likely to have strong or ambivalent feelings, such as sex education and multicultural provision. Liaison between teachers and parents means that pupils are more likely to receive a consistent message at home and school. Combes and Craft (1987) have recorded a variety of ways in which primary schools elicit the parents' help on sensitive topics or those which relate immediately to the home. Examples include the following:

- inviting parents to complete a health education questionnaire, data from which is then analysed and used to revise the school's health curriculum;
- a joint venture by a group of parents and teachers to make a video about safety in the home;
- viewing written and audio-visual resources in sex education, followed by a staff-parent discussion session. The parents are able to borrow videos, are told when they will be shown in school, and are invited to discuss them with their children at home.

HOMEWORK

Opinion is divided about the value of giving homework to primary school children. (The term, of course, needs to embrace any work directed but not supervised by the teacher outside the timetabled curriculum, even if this is not done at home.) A survey by HM Inspectors which included eighty-six primary schools found practice varied a good deal even among teachers of the same school (HMI, 1987); but many parents would like it set regularly, particularly in the top junior year (Newson and Newson, 1984). It is not the purpose of this section to enter this controversy, but we should note briefly the main claims for homework. These include its potential to develop the practice of independent study and the qualities of perseverence, self-discipline and initiative; to allow practice of skills introduced in class and to enable the teacher to concentrate on activities which need his/her presence; to explore materials and resources outside the school; and to forge links with parents and other adults (DES, 1985b). For older primary pupils, it also begins to familiarise them with the demands of secondary education.

At worst, of course, homework creates *dis*harmony between parents and teachers and children. Parents complain when it is not set, or too much is given, or the work is unsuitable, or the children are not adequately prepared in class; teachers complain when parents do not cooperate in seeing that work is completed on time; and children complain that they do not understand what they have to do, that it is burdensome and takes too long, and that it causes friction at home. At the very least, therefore, the school must communicate its homework policy to parents in the school prospectus, newsletters and special leaflets. This, of course, presupposes that the staff have developed a policy in the first place, which very few have (HMI, 1987).

Better still, however, is to develop the policy *with* parents. Discussion about the purposes of homework, the kinds of activities which are suitable at different ages, the time which pupils should spend on homework, and the role which parents should play are all issues which need thrashing out. For the success of homework depends much on parents' understanding of the kind of thing expected and its purpose and teachers' understanding of problems which pupils may have in completing work at home. Governors have a legal duty here as part of their responsibilities for the curriculum, but the groundwork needs to be done by teachers in consultation with parents in class meetings, the PTA or even a consultative group. Homework policy also needs to be kept under review as teachers try out new ideas and test parents' reaction at meetings to discuss their children's progress.

Curriculum workshops, discussed in the previous section, provide opportunities for exploring the kinds of tasks which parents and their children might undertake together. The next two chapters are devoted to home–school projects in reading, writing and mathematics, but the scope for involving parental participation clearly goes beyond the basic skills, for example, visits to museums, churches, mosques and temples; making observations and collecting data for work in environmental studies; talking to parents and grandparents about family history, and their experiences as children.

HOME VISITING

Historically, home visiting by teachers has been seen as a reactive device to 'get to' parents who do not come into school on their own accord and whose children have attendance or behavioural problems. More recently, home visiting has also been used proactively as an integral part of programmes concerned with the educational development of all children and not just those with problems.

Pre-school schemes

Since the mid-nineteenth century, health visitors have given support to the parents of young children, but over the last twenty years or so teachers have been involved in schemes for visiting the homes of pre-school children, typically in areas of social hardship or in cases where the child has special educational needs. Since the first interventionist scheme was started in the West Riding of Yorkshire in 1970, a range of schemes have developed in the UK. These programmes have interest for primary school teachers because they demonstrate some of the main issues involved in home visiting.

Although each scheme has its distinctive purposes and mode of functioning, Gillian Pugh identifies four needs to which all pre-school home visiting tries to respond:

- the need to break down barriers between professionals in health, education and social services, between professionals and volunteers, and between professionals and parents – and to see the family as a whole;
- the need to shift the focus of support away from the individual child, towards the child within the family, and the relationship between parents and their children;
- the need to reach out to those who are not using the services and who are not coping well, to listen to what they are saying, and to build on their inherent strengths and abilities;
- the need to encourage growth rather than dependency, and to involve parents in planning and running their own community support networks. (Pugh, 1983, p.14)

The Portage scheme to help parents teach skills to their severely-handicapped children is one of the best known endeavours of its kind. Set up in 1969 in Portage, Wisconsin, it was imported into the UK in 1976, and there are now over 300 such services in this country. The parent and home teacher together identify specific everyday skills which the handicapped child is to acquire. The procedure is written down and modelled by the home teacher while the parent watches. Subsequently the parent keeps records of the progress made, and receives further supporting visits from the home teacher, who suggests future targets when this is thought appropriate. In a survey of the South Glamorgan Portage scheme (Land, 1985), all parents viewed the service positively, particularly when the child was seen to acquire new skills. They also valued the psychological support which the scheme provided and the recognition that they were not the only family experiencing difficulties.

The Portage project is based on behavioural psychology, providing practical direction in a highly structured way with clearly defined objectives and much use of checklists and record cards. An example of less directive but nonetheless planned work with pre-school parents is the Lothian Educational Home Visiting Project (McCail, 1981). The aims of this pioneering venture were partly to improve the cognitive development and language in two- to three-year-old children who lived in 'disadvantaged' areas and partly to encourage the mothers to appreciate the significance of their educational role by helping them to become more involved in their children's learning.

The home teachers were all experienced infant or nursery teachers based in local schools. For about an hour a week, over nine months or so, they each visited between ten and twelve families, at first talking to the mother and reading stories and playing games with the children, then gradually encouraging the mother to participate. The mothers were also encouraged to visit the home visitor's school, partly to participate in the children's activities there and partly to take part in informal further education studies such as hostess catering, family swimming and child development. The idea was thus two-fold: to 'close the gap' between home and school; and to help the mother develop interests outside the home and so become more personally fulfilled and therefore a more effective mother.

An independent evaluation (Raven, 1980) showed that, compared with other mothers in the area, those who had taken part in the project changed their attitudes more markedly towards their children and schooling. They enjoyed closer relationships with their children, becoming more aware of their needs, realising how much enjoyment there was to be had when parent and child play together or share books, and learning that they could influence the kind of person their child was to become. Through getting to know a teacher personally, they came to value schooling more and to understand the importance of their own role in their children's education. As a result, the children were better prepared for school. Another finding was that the home visitors themselves felt changed persons: not only did they increase their understanding of the problems of low-income and often poorly-housed families, they also altered their views of working-class parents, seeing them no longer as antipathetic to schooling but potentially resourceful and able to work cooperatively with schools in the education of their children.

Many pre-school home visiting schemes can now be found in various parts of the country. Reports (see, for example, Aplin and Pugh, 1983) show that home visitors will be maximally effective if they regard their role not as one which involves working directly with the child but of providing a supporting, caring relationship with the family, who in turn are better able to provide a supportive home environment for the child's development. Since many of the mothers may at first be unresponsive and have difficulty in relating to their children and to other adults, home visitors will be accepted and in a position to provide help only by first demonstrating that they have come to listen and share the mother's feelings.

Primary school schemes

From the perspective of parents whose children are at primary school, a teacher's visit is often important for social and psychological reasons: it helps to lessen parents' worries, to reassure, and to deal with misunderstandings and problems about school. From the teacher's perspective, home visiting can often help to provide insight into a child's learning and behavioural difficulties and can give an opportunity to meet more members of the family.

Teachers sometimes fear that they will be unwanted in their pupils' homes. They think that parents and children may be embarrassed by the teachers' presence, or even resentful that their privacy has been invaded. Reassuringly, the evidence suggests that while this is often so when children are in trouble with the school, almost all parents welcome visits which have a positive purpose and are not recriminatory (Hannon and Jackson, 1987b). Home visiting helps to meet the needs of those parents who are anxious about visiting school. They are usually more relaxed and confident in their own setting and therefore feel more able to raise matters which they might keep quiet about in school with other parents and children around. These matters might relate to aspects of the curriculum which the child finds difficult or boring, to behaviour problems or to family difficulties. All the same, it is important that home visits are offered to parents and not imposed, and that the family has a say in what kind of information (if any) about the visit is recorded.

Even if home visiting is seen as desirable, many schools will say that their teachers have no time to do it. Undoubtedly special arrangements need to be made, but if the activity is seen as a priority it is worth trying to see if the timetable can be adapted and the staff redeployed in order to release teachers to visit homes.

Home visiting is also one of a range of strategies which are sometimes used in home–school reading projects (see next chapter). It is also used in programmes to increase understanding with minority parents, an issue to which we now turn.

THE NEEDS OF BLACK AND ETHNIC MINORITY PARENTS

Underlying principles

In Chapter 2, attention was drawn to evidence suggesting that some teachers hold stereotypic views of black and minority families whom they see as 'disadvantaged' and disinterested in their children's schooling. The effect of such attitudes is low levels of expection and consequent under-achievement, particularly among black pupils.

Yet, as many studies have shown, minority parents generally have both high and realistic educational aspirations for their children (e.g. Rex and Tomlinson, 1979; Tizard *et al.*, 1988). Further, any lack of involvement in school affairs is not necessarily a sign of disinterest in education. Among some Asians and Chinese, for instance, respect for teachers' opinions and guidance, the shyness of mothers and long hours of work, explain why visits to school are few and far between in some cases. At the same time, as Tomlinson (1984) shows, minority parents want to define their own problems and take their own initiatives. Because of their different cultural backgrounds, many hold distinctive expectations about schooling and are critical of mainstream provision in this country. For this reason, some groups have set up supplementary schools, and Muslims have campaigned for their own voluntary-aided schools to ensure that their children are exposed to a curriculum and ethos which is consistent with their cultural values and religious beliefs.

In a series of books reviewing research into the education of minority children, Monica Taylor has shown that although minority parents express a range of beliefs about schooling, many have strong feelings that some schools could respond more sympathetically to their concerns about teaching arrangements and the purposes of education. For instance, many Afro-Caribbean parents see British schooling as too liberal and lacking in discipline (Taylor, 1981). Some Asian parents 'view the school as a potent agency in the erosion of their values', while orthodox Muslims 'feel schools are threatening the maintenance of their religious beliefs and cultural practices' (Taylor and Hegarty, 1985, p.400). There is also mystification and misunderstanding about teaching styles and the value which primary schools attach to play and the 'integrated day', as evidenced in reviews of perceptions held by Chinese parents (Taylor, 1986) and Cypriots (Taylor, 1988). In a study of a group of Punjabi Sikhs, Bhachu (1985) explains how the competitive nature of Punjabi culture gives special emphasis to the instrumental role of education in securing upward social mobility, achieving social status and getting a job.

Some minority needs are difficult to meet because they are based on fundamental beliefs which are difficult to reconcile with traditional assumptions held in the West (see pp.54–6). However, a major source of tension and misunderstanding appears to be lack of information. As Tomlinson (1984) points out, because British educational values are different from those in many other parts of the world, minority parents are especially dependent upon the school explaining its processes. On top of social and economic pressures which many have to endure, they are vulnerable to misunderstandings and inappropriate decisions regarding their children's special educational needs, which often arise from language problems and cultural differences. Chaudbury (1986) has described how Bangladeshi parents, for instance, do not understand the concept of 'special educational provision' and 'assessment for special needs'.

Fortunately, the quality of relationships between primary schools and minority groups, although still imperfect, is generally improving through a variety of approaches, examples of which we will now discuss.

Approaches

Multicultural policies

First of all, it is important that the parents have confidence in the school's policies to combat racism and to promote inter-ethnic understanding through the curriculum. The school brochure and other forms of written communication should make this clear. Although, as has been noted, there may be conflicts of interests, the school's practices are more likely to appear credible when minority parents know that representatives from local community groups have been involved in the formulation of policies, are regularly invited into the school to talk to teachers and pupils, and are members of the governing body. Community groups might also be asked to suggest how parents and their children could be best helped during the period of starting school.

Informal meetings

A dialogue with minority groups might be set up by inviting representatives to talk to the staff about their perceptions and expectations of schools. Howard and

Hollingsworth (1985) have described the range of strategies which the staff of one infant school developed to involve minority parents, for example, coffee mornings, classroom visits, pre-school playgroup, after-school story sessions in different mother tongues, and community weeks. Many difficulties were encountered, such as misreading community needs, language barriers, pressure on teachers' time, openly expressed antagonism from some white parents, unexpected pressures to help out with family problems, poor attendance at some sessions, and the realisation that every year the task begins anew. In spite of all this, the writers conclude that the staff's efforts were worthwhile since they had 'eliminated the inhibiting fear that made parents hesitant to visit the school'.

Translation services

All local authorities with bilingual populations should employ services for the translation of written communication into Chinese, Urdu, Bengali, Gujerati, Hindi, Punjabi and other relevant languages and for an interpreter to be present at interviews. This is especially important when children are being assessed for special needs. Where official translators or trained interpreters are unavailable, the services of members of the community, other parents or older children can sometimes be enlisted; but, if the volunteers have little understanding of educational terminology and the education system, they are unable to help parents *understand* the communication (Rehal, 1989). Volunteers are therefore no substitute for translators who are familiar with educational issues.

Pre-school centres

Some authorities have developed multi-lingual pre-school centres where parents can meet each other, community workers and representatives from local schools. Taylor (1988) refers to a report by Hunter-Grundin describing the well-patronised pre-school centre in Haringey, which was set up to facilitate discussion among parents, disseminate information and advice, and foster understanding between different cultural backgrounds.

Home–school curriculum projects

These provide an informal but structured forum in which the parents are valued as a resource in their children's education. These schemes, examples of which are described in the next two chapters, generally have a high take-up rate among minority parents.

Parental involvement in the classroom

Minority parents constitute an important resource for teachers. In their account of parental involvement at an infant school in Tower Hamlets, Clover and Gilbert (1981) described how the parents came into the school to tell stories about events in their home countries, their festivals, food and childhood memories. These stories were translated into English, illustrated and photocopied for borrowing. Such activities generate a good deal of discussion among parents, children and teachers. They increase understanding of and respect for different cultures, helping minority children to feel proud of their heritage, and generally to improve the quality of home–school links.

Home–school liaison workers

Some local authorities have created special posts for home–school liaison work to increase the social understanding of teachers and minority families. An important example of such work is the 'Parents in Partnership' project set up in Lancashire, Kirklees and Bradford by the Community Education Development Centre in Coventry. The early developments have been described by McLeod (1985). Specially appointed home–school liaison teachers (HSLTs) liaised between predominantly Muslim families and twenty-four primary schools and language centres, teaching the pupils part-time and building relationships with the teachers. With the involvement of representatives from the Muslim community, they helped to develop curriculum policies in areas such as language, religious education, and art. Another aspect involved visits to homes, both before and after school entry, to explain school policies, practices and routines, to encourage adult/parent education, to discuss religious and cultural issues, and to help parents gain information and advice about special educational needs. The parents were also involved in the schools, introducing their pre-school children to routines, attending adult education classes and helping in the classroom.

Many parents and teachers received valuable help through these activities, though, as can be imagined, many problems were encountered and the role of in-service training proved vital. Some HSLTs were not easily accepted in schools, and some of the LEAs' expectations of them were unrealistic. Perhaps the most important outcome of the project was that it enabled the HSLTs to gain a greater understanding of the issues, and as a result they found it necessary to re-appraise their role. Because they often worked among families who were undergoing considerable stress, the more successful realised that welfare and educational roles could not realistically be separated, since the parent's social concerns needed to be addressed as much as the child's educational development.

COMMUNITY SCHOOLS AND CENTRES

Since the early 1980s, designated community primary schools and centres have developed in some local authorities such as Liverpool, Rochdale, Leicestershire, Coventry and, more recently, Devon. In addition, other non-designated primary schools have cultivated an explicit community orientation.

Community schools represent the belief that education is something in which the whole community should be involved. Midwinter (1984, p.25) has explained the underlying principles thus:

> At its full tide, community education is the reverse of the conventional. It calls upon the school to cease to be a cloistered and inward-looking institution and to become the bustling headquarters for often widespread outreach activity. It calls upon the teacher to act, not as the minder/mentor of children, but as steward of the 'educative community'.

Two head teachers of primary community schools (Bird and Croson, 1988, p.176) have put it this way:

> Community education . . . involves the sharing of power, . . . professional expertise being used to free people in their minds and actions rather than entrap them in institutionalism.

There is no one formula which characterises the work of community primary schools. Indeed, as one of the main progenitors says, because of differing local policies, community needs, and resources, 'such an idea is inimical to the whole concept of community education' (Rennie, 1985, p.15). Accounts of individual schools (see under 'Further Reading'), however, show that at least some of the following features are likely to be found:

- an open atmosphere in which parents and others are always welcome and someone is available to see them;
- regular meetings for parents and other members of the community;
- the involvement of parents as a matter of course in decision-making processes and school activities;
- a family room with supporting crèche facilities for meeting parents and holding informal group meetings;
- facilities for refreshments and disseminating information and advice;
- a playgroup or other pre-school facility on the same site to enlist parental involvement as soon as possible and ease the process of transition to school itself;
- visitors to classrooms and voluntary helpers, e.g. representatives of ethnic minority groups, local business and commerce;
- home–school curriculum projects of the kind described in the next two chapters;
- home visiting by teachers and/or community workers linked to the school;
- holiday play schemes and other events;
- clubs for senior citizens and the unemployed;
- the incorporation of provision to respond to local community needs, e.g. parent and adult education and clubs for senior citizens, community groups, the local branch library or swimming pool; and
- participation in local radio.

Besides community schools, family and community centres have been established in some cities. The flagship in this enterprise is the Coventry Education Development Centre, an independent charity established in 1980 under the directorship of John Rennie. This has a national network of training programmes in community–school management, home–school relations, work with under-fives workers, and other aspects of community education and care. Its Family Education Unit has sponsored projects in various parts of the country to explore ways of developing home–school relationships. The main examples are 'Parents in Partnership' described in the previous section, the 'Home-Based Early Learning Project' in Coventry and Hounslow, and the 'Family Education Project' in Salford and Leicester. The FEU produces videos and a comprehensive range of publications such as practical guidelines, resource packs, evaluation reports, a newspaper *Network* and the *Journal of Community Education*.

At Priesthill in south-west Glasgow, the 'Partnership in Education' project was set up in 1983. A group of tutors under the Project Coordinator, Sister Doreen Grant, engage local teachers and other professionals, parents and children in a range of activities, such as curriculum workshops and the involvement of parents in classrooms. These are based around principles which include the raising of awareness, the sharing of skills and knowledge, supporting learning opportunities in the home and cross-professional links.

The Liverpool 'Parent Support Programme' was set up in 1979 as a local authority initiative. Parent centres, each with a part-time teacher and an outreach worker, have been established in over thirty primary schools in the area. The project has no central director since the work of each centre is the responsibility of the head teacher, but John Davis of the Department of Education, Liverpool University, has been appointed as an evaluator. Each centre is equipped for parents and pre-school children and makes resources available to parents 'to support and reinforce their responsibility as partners in the education of their children' (Davis, 1988).

The Newham Parents' Centre, established in 1975 in the East End of London, has a support network to give advice on parents' legal rights and their children's special needs; it also helps parents to recognise and practice their own special knowledge and skills and to support each other in a crisis. It runs an education shop, selling books and play materials, distributes a termly newletter on local educational initiatives, and publishes a user-friendly guide on educational law. A range of projects has been developed to promote training, access to further and higher education, community care, adult literacy/numeracy, and parent-child reading workshops. These ventures are especially important in a borough which is the second most deprived in England and Wales and where only one per cent of the population has professional status.

SUMMARY AND CONCLUSIONS

This chapter has described various ways in which dialogue between parents and teachers is being facilitated in many local authorities and primary schools. Through arrangements for starting school and moving on to secondary school, for meeting parents individually, visiting them in their homes and running curriculum workshops, and for engaging the support of black and ethnic minority groups and utilising the skills and resources of the local community in general, the concept of partnership is being gradually realised.

Dialogue and partnership is not about parent power but parent *empowerment*, enabling parents to work with teachers and so play a fuller part in the educational development of their children and in the life of the school generally than would otherwise be possible. In the next two chapters this theme of parent empowerment is taken further by considering ways in which many primary schools are helping parents to develop roles as educators of their own children with respect to reading, writing and mathematics.

Further reading

A book with many practical suggestions in this area is *Listening to Parents* by Janet Atkin, John Bastiani and Jackie Goode (Croom Helm, 1988). This could be supported by the series of readings in J. Bastiani's *Parents and Teachers Vol. 2: From Policy to Practice* (NFER–Windsor, 1988).

On the early years of schooling, see *Involving Parents in Nursery and Infant Schools* by Barbara Tizard *et al.*, (Grant McIntyre, 1981). A charming book which schools could recommend parents to share with their child who is about to start school is Janet and Allan Ahlberg's *Starting School* (Viking Kestrel, 1988). The text and 163 illustrations deal with various concerns such as the playground, dinner time, toilets, and where to hang your coat, while the children portrayed appear authentic by not being invariably happy and cooperative.

For advice on talking to parents individually and in groups, see *Working with Parents* by Roy McConkey (Croom Hill, 1985). Rundall and Smith have written a useful chapter on working with difficult parents in *How To Involve Parents as Educators in Early Childhood Education* (edited and published by Brigham Young University Press, 1982).

Practical suggestions for organising workshops and other curriculum events for parents can be found in Roy Long *Developing Parental Involvement in the Primary School* (Macmillan, 1986) and in *Sharing Mathematics with Parents*, published by the Mathematical Association and Stanley Thornes.

Examples of 'tried and tested' schemes for conducting workshops and establishing community links in health education have been compiled by Gill Combes and Ann Craft in *Parents, Schools and Community* (Health Education Council, 1987), distributed by the Community Education Development Centre, Coventry).

For a critical assessment of the Portage scheme, see P. Sturmey and A.G. Crisp, 'Portage guide to early education: a review of research', *Educational Psychology*, 6, 139–57. An account of the Lothian Home Visiting scheme is contained in *Mother Start* by Gail McCail (Scottish Council for Research in Education, 1981); see also *Perspectives on Pre-School Home Visiting* edited by Geoff Aplin and Gillian Pugh (National Children's Bureau, 1983) and the series of Partnership Papers published by the National Children's Bureau.

Relations with ethnic minority parents are discussed by Sally Tomlinson in *Home and School in Multicultural Britain* (Batsford, 1984). Readers wishing to know more about recent research should consult the series of reviews by Monica Taylor and Seamus Heggarty (particulars in References). The problems faced by minority parents in assessment for special needs are discussed by A. Rehal in the journal *Educational Psychology in Practice*, January 1989.

The work of individual community schools is described by John Rennie in *British Community Primary Schools* (Falmer Press, 1985) and by Paul Widlake *Reducing Educational Disadvantage* (Open University Press, 1986). For a series of papers giving a critical framework in which to evaluate developments in community education, see G. Allen *et al. Community Education: An Agenda for Reform* (Open University Press, 1987). See also articles in the *Journal of Community Education*.

The NCPTA has recently produced a video *Parents Partners in a Shared Task: Welcoming Parents into School*, which can be hired or bought. This illustrates ways in which staff can make their school more welcoming and develop home–school links.

9 PARTNERSHIP PROJECTS IN CHILDREN'S READING

The idea that parents can help children learn to read is nothing new. Indeed, contrary to what teachers sometimes suppose, several studies have shown that the great majority of working-class as well as middle-class parents help children with their reading (Newson and Newson, 1977; Hewison and Tizard, 1980; Tizard *et al.*, 1981). Until fairly recently, however, most schools have been content to encourage mothers and fathers to read and tell stories to children and have refrained from involving them in the teaching of reading as such.

The Bullock Committee on the teaching of English (DES, 1975) devoted a large part of its report to the teaching of reading. Yet, whilst the Committee was in 'no doubt whatever of the value of parents' involvement in the early stages of reading' (para. 7.1), this acknowledgment is made mainly in the context of parents talking and reading to their children. The only explicit remark about parents hearing children read is a warning that they should not use published reading schemes, no doubt because this might cause confusion if a scheme was different from the school's. The neglect of parental involvement in home-based curriculum activities in the 1960s and 1970s was also apparent in a standard text on home–school links, *Linking Home and School*. Even the third edition (Craft *et al.*, 1980), described by the publishers as 'a uniquely comprehensive and updated review' of recent developments, failed during the course of twenty-five articles to address the role of primary schools in enlisting parents' cooperation in children's reading.

The 1980s, however, has seen a growing recognition of the value of home–school reading programmes. The recent NFER national survey on parental involvement in education found that a substantial number of schools in over half the LEAs in England and Wales were organising such work, usually in primary but sometimes too in secondary schools (Jowett and Baginsky, 1988). In one London borough, over half the primary schools were operating structured home-based reading programmes in 1986 (Hancock, 1987).

The first part of this chapter will examine some of the early research and later developments. It will only be possible to review a few of the many projects which have been mounted in various parts of the country, but the accounts should provide a flavour of schools' experiences in running home–school reading programmes as well as evidence about their success. In the second part of the chapter we shall consider a range of problems and issues which affect teachers who are thinking about introducing such a scheme.

PIONEERING WORK AND PROJECTS

The Dagenham and Haringey Studies

The fact that working-class parents frequently hear their children read without any prompting from the school is now more generally appreciated as the result of three studies carried out in the mid-1970s by Jenny Hewison and Jack Tizard (1980). It was found that in about half the homes of 267 seven- to eight-year-olds in Dagenham, the mother, without any intervention or encouragement from the school, was regularly hearing her child read. Moreover, a comparison of test results in reading comprehension showed that the children who were receiving such help at home were generally making better progress in reading than their classmates, and their superior level of performance could not be explained in terms of higher intelligence.

These findings were impressive, not least because they challenged the view that working-class families are often uninterested in their children's educational progress. However, in the absence of a controlled experiment the results could not be accepted as conclusive evidence to support a theory that parental help with reading makes a unique contribution to children's reading development. Such a study was carried out in the late 1970s by Jack Tizard, Bill Schofield and Jenny Hewison (1982) under the auspices of the Thomas Coram Research Unit in the University of London. The project, which lasted two years, involved 248 six- to eight-year-olds in six multiracial infant and junior schools in an economically disadvantaged area of the London Borough of Haringey. To establish baseline data, all children were given standardised word recognition and reading comprehension tests before the project began, and to monitor progress, tests were again given at the end of each year of the project. Finally, to assess whether progress had been maintained, tests were also given one year after the project had ended, and a follow-up study was conducted two years after that.

The schools were randomly assigned to three groups – two schools in which parents were involved, two schools in which the pupils were given help by an extra teacher, and two schools in which no special help was provided and which acted as a control. In each of the first two groups, the children in one class of top infants were involved in the experiment, the other classes acting as within-school controls.

The project worked like this. The class teachers sent home books between two and four nights each week. They indicated on a card the amount of reading to be covered, and the parents recorded on the same card what had been accomplished. The books were those which the child was currently reading at school, but sometimes these were supplemented by other material and even written work. At first the teachers checked progress by hearing the child re-read this material in class. This practice was soon abandoned, however, because the children were reading so much more than anticipated. During home visits, the researcher observed while the children read to their parents; in one school the parents also sometimes observed while their children read to the researcher. No general meetings between researchers, teachers and parents were called and no special training was given to the parents, but specific advice was given by the researcher or class teacher as needed. Virtually all parents – some of whom did not read English and a few of whom did not read at all – continued to cooperate throughout the two years of the project.

Analysis of the test scores at the end of the two-year project clearly showed that those children who had read regularly to their parents made significantly greater improvement than the controls, and that this difference was maintained one year after the project had ended. Improvement was also noticeable amongst children who had been failing to read when the project began. It was also found that the reading levels of more than half the children in the experimental groups were above the national average. By contrast, in keeping with the usual standards achieved in the area, only one-third of the controls had reached this level of achievement. The results for children who had received extra teacher help were mixed, but in general were not much better than those of the controls, who had received no extra help. Moreover, in a follow-up investigation just before the children transferred to secondary school, it was found that nearly two-thirds of the home collaboration group were reading at or above the national level, whilst the proportion among controls had altered very little (Hewison, 1988).

In short, the Haringey project clearly demonstrated that a partnership between parents and teachers in the teaching of reading can be remarkably fruitful. Even parents who did not read English or even read at all could help by being good listeners and providing encouragement. The project had also shown that improved results could be obtained without involving parents in a programme of special training, apart from advice and (for some parents) demonstrations. At the same time the evidence suggested that providing extra help in school is not likely to improve children's reading attainment, suggesting that it was the involvement of parents that was crucial. The project was also significant in two ways which went beyond the findings from test results. First, it had shown that parents in multiracial inner-city schools will respond positively to initiatives which involve them in the education of their children when they are given support and a structure in which to work. Secondly, reports from teachers suggested that home collaboration has a general positive effect on children's motivation to learn and on their classroom behaviour.

The Belfield Project

Shortly after the start of the Haringey Project, another home collaboration scheme was set up at Belfield Community School in Rochdale, Yorkshire. The catchment area of this school was predominantly working class, with levels of unemployment and overcrowding three times the national average. One of the teachers, Angela

Jackson, acted as the project coordinator. A researcher from Sheffield University, Peter Hannon, monitored and evaluated the project which operated for five years from 1978 to 1983 and involved over 100 children and their families.

The programme, described by Hannon and Jackson (1987a), was launched by the head teacher who called a general meeting of parents. Those who did not come were visited in their homes. Pupils from five to eight years of age took home reading books which they read to their parents for a few minutes on five nights each week during term time. The teachers wrote down on cards what the parents should do; the parents in turn ticked a box if the work had been completed, and added any comments which they wished to communicate to the teacher. The parents' comments might include difficulties experienced by the child or parent, or suggestions for the teacher. Support was provided throughout by various means − visits to the children's homes, occasional meetings, informal contacts, letters from the school, and a leaflet listing suggested 'Dos and Don'ts'.

As in the Haringey project, it was found that working-class parents would readily cooperate in a scheme to help their children in reading and would maintain their involvement over several years. From his interviews with a sample of the parents and all the eight class teachers who had participated in the scheme, Hannon (1986) concluded that the vast majority of children had read almost daily to a parent or other adult in the house. This was typically the mother, but often the father and sometimes a grandparent, brother or sister. Moreover, the parents really appreciated being involved in this way. After some initial doubts most of the teachers noted improvements in the children's attitude to reading and the amount which they read. They also found that the project led to better general relations with the children and their parents.

Hannon and some colleagues also examined comments on the 10 000 reading cards which had been generated by the seventy-six children who had completed three years in the project (Hannon *et al.*, 1986). It was clear that both teachers and parents had made extensive use of the reading cards, especially for the younger children and poorer readers. Particularly interesting was the large number of comments which were directly about teaching points: for instance a teacher might suggest to a parent that the child read more slowly or be helped to make a certain sound. In some cases, teacher and parent had entered into a friendly dialogue about methodology. On the whole the teachers viewed the use of the reading cards positively; most had not found completing them burdensome, and were encouraged particularly when parents replied to their suggestions. One teacher said:

> It was good for having feedback with parents you don't see, and excellent for encouraging the children. There's nothing nicer than saying to children you're going to write on the card saying how well they've done − and when they come bounding into the room saying, 'look what my mum's written'. (p.273)

As Hannon and his colleagues (p.279) comment, 'The system of cards was itself a communication in which the school effectively said to the parent, "We recognise you as your child's teacher too".'

A detailed analysis of tape-recordings of children reading at home and school

(Hannon, Jackson and Weinberger, 1986) threw up a number of points about the strategies used by parents and teachers. In many respects each partner operated in much the same way, indicating mistakes, providing words which the children did not know, or helping them to infer meaning from the text. This certainly belied the notion that working-class parents lack the necessary skills to help teach their children to read. There were, however, some differences in approach. In particular, whereas parents tended to avoid intervening until the child had made a mistake or had hesitated, the teachers took initiatives at other points particularly to remind children that the point of reading was to gain meaning from the text.

In spite of the many good things which emerged from the Belfield Project, the results were disappointing in terms of improvement in reading levels. A comparison between the scores of pre-project and project children in two reading tests (NFER Test A and Young) did show gains in favour of the latter group, but these were small and statistically insignificant (Hannon, 1987). The fact that the findings are at variance with the Haringey results by no means implies that the Belfield Project was unsuccessful. Apart from the fact that, as we have seen, there were many other kinds of benefits gained in terms of children's positive motivation and increased parental interest, one must beware of assuming that standardised reading tests give an indication of all one wants to know about a child's reading progress. For instance, they do not measure attitude or enjoyment. Further, the degree to which children understand a text which they are asked to read for assessment depends not only on their reading ability but also on their past experiences and cultural background, which in turn affects their test scores (Hannon and McNally, 1986).

Hannon (1987) also suggests that there may have been less scope for improvement at Belfield compared with Haringey. For one thing, the Belfield area had a stronger tradition of parental involvement, not least in hearing children read on a regular basis. For another, Haringey contained many families for whom English was a second language. Another possibility is that the Haringey project benefited from greater resources which enabled a more structured programme of home visiting by outside researchers (Hannon and Jackson, 1987b).

The Pitfield Project, PACT and Caper

In 1980 Alex Griffiths, an Educational Psychologist, and Dorothy Hamilton, an Advisory Teacher, initiated a home–school reading programme at a Junior school in the Hackney division of the Inner London Education Authority. Like the Haringey and Belfield enterprises, the Pitfield Project was set up in an area of social disadvantage, with high levels of unemployment and many children in care. It was guided by a committee consisting of heads, an inspector, a children's librarian, community relations workers, representatives of adult education, and parents. The success of the project led to the development of similar schemes in many other schools.

The movement which developed from the original project is called

PACT – Parents, Children and Teachers – an acronym which emphasises the three-way partnership. The enthusiastic response to the early meetings once again exposed the myth that working-class parents are apathetic about their children's education. It seems that parents will relinquish their suspicions, fears or even hostility about approaching teachers when they are taken into the school's confidence and invited to work as partners in their children's education.

Griffiths and Hamilton (1984) see the successful operation of a PACT scheme centering around three essential principles. The first concerns the forum for launching the project. The usual procedure is to call parents to a meeting, which can be at school or class level. The success of this depends on how effectively the school staff can present a programme which is purposeful and helpful whilst also getting across the message that the parents will have a major say about the way the scheme develops. The project must be seen as a *dialogue* with parents, not something which the school is imposing.

The second principle put forward by Griffiths and Hamilton is to have a set of simple, well thought-out guidelines for parents. These could be given orally at the first meeting, but would normally be supplemented in booklet form. At PACT meetings a video is often used to demonstrate how and how not to hear your child read.

The third principle is to keep in regular touch with the parents in order to maintain the necessary dialogue. Central to the communication is a record card on the lines of the Haringey and Belfield projects. This gives space to indicate what reading has to be done and for teachers and parents to make comments (see Figure 9.1). Direct communication, however, is also important to deal more

Book	Date	Page	Comments
Journey to a New Earth	15/10/81	pg 16	Good few mistakes. 15 minutes reading
" "	18/10/81	Completed	Jason can do with a slightly more advanced reading book. I agree – hope this one will be more of a challenge for him!
Jackanory			
"	20/10/81	Pg 15	Twenty minutes reading fair
	1/11/81	Completed	Reading is improving looses concentration + becomes restless
Fairy Tales of China	19/11/81		Pages are not numbered Jason becomes bored with reading. Appears tired. We talked to Jason about the tiredness, and we agreed that it would help if he read for no more than 10 minutes at a time, and if you "agree" him the difficult words, the next important thing is for him to enjoy reading with you. + I think these two things will help. Let me know if not.
"	6/12/81	completed	Reading very jerkily. I hope you will be able to hear Jason read something in the holidays.
Jackanory	5/1/82	pg 27	Not interested in reading during the holidays
Hercules	11/2/82	pg 28	Jason enjoyed reading this book.
Sinbad the Sailor	18/3/82	completed	Was unable to hear Jason read he said he read it himself.

Figure 9.1 A home reading card using in the PACT scheme
Source: Griffiths and Hamilton (1984) *Parent, Teacher, Child* (p.42) Methuen & Co.

effectively with issues and problems which crop up during the reading sessions. Home visiting can be very helpful here, but in any event parents need to know how to get advice from teachers in the school.

PACT schemes offer a flexible framework in which teachers and parents can work as partners. However, no school is likely to set up a home-liaison programme without encountering problems, as Giffiths and Hamilton (1985) noted in their interviews with heads and teachers in Hackney. The main difficulty was finding enough time to talk to parents and to monitor children's progress, to provide for parents whose first language was not English, and to arrest the apathy of uninterested parents. Most of the teacher–parent contact was taking place with the infants, and only a small number of teachers were undertaking home visiting. Another problem was finding enough books and other resources. Nonetheless, all teachers who had used the scheme found it beneficial, often developing it for older children by setting more structured activities such as dictionary work or criticism. Factors which seem to affect the success of the scheme include the head's leadership, a member of staff to act as coordinator, a timetable arrangement which accommodates PACT activities, special strategies for dealing with uninterested parents or those whose first language is not English, and a school policy for involving parents in a range of ways, and not just reading.

In a recent literacy study in Hackney (ILEA, 1988), PACT was included as a possible factor associated with reading progress. Its effect was difficult to assess since almost all the sixteen primary schools in the survey claimed to have a home–school liaison programme. However, the researchers concluded that reading progress (as measured by the Hunter-Grundin test based on the clozed procedure) was less in the schools which had long-established PACT schemes and best in those which had introduced the scheme within the previous two or three years. This suggests that an initial favourable impact is not enough to guarantee long-term success, and that teachers need to make special efforts to keep interest alive and to appraise the scheme at regular intervals.

Similar schemes to PACT have been developed in other authorities. One such example is Caper (Children and Parents Enjoying Reading), originally devised for schools in West Glamorgan. Peter Branston and Mark Provis (1986) have described how daily contact between home and school is provided in this scheme through a Comment Booklet, while momentum is maintained through devices such as bookmarks which bear such reminders as 'Give plenty of praise' and a parent workshop each half term. Additionally, clinics are held where a parent can receive advice after the teacher has watched her read to the child. The scheme is kept under review through two evaluative measures consisting of an attitude scale for children and a questionnaire for parents.

Paired reading and shared reading

In the projects so far considered, although parents have been given general advice and a clear framework in which to help their children, no special training has been provided. By contrast, some other projects have involved training parents to use special strategies to help children read. One of these, the Derbyshire Project, used *paired reading*, a technique now practised in varying degrees in about half the local authorities in England and Wales (Jowett and Baginsky, 1988).

The paired reading approach was developed by Roger Morgan (1976) for children with reading difficulty. Although originally conceived as a device for use by professionals, the technique soon proved effective for parental use and also for use by other children. Parent and child begin by reading together from a book which, irrespective of its level of difficulty, is chosen by the child. It is important that the child sets the pace and does not 'shadow' the adult, and that every word is attempted, even if this amounts to only sounding the first letter or making a guess. When the child makes a mistake, the parent makes no adverse comment but supplies the right word which the child repeats before continuing. When the child wants to read aloud alone, he or she gives an agreed signal, such as a knock on the table, and the parent stops while the child carries on. As the child reads correctly, the parent reinforces correct reading by supplying plenty of praise and positive comment; when the child makes an error or cannot read a word, the parent stops and waits a few seconds for the child to try again before supplying the word, which the child repeats. The parent and child then start reading in synchrony once more.

The cycle continues in this way with the child signalling each time he or she wishes to read alone. Morgan (1976) claims that, through free choice of reading material, the strategy helps to provide intrinsic motivation for the child to read; through reading in tandem with the parent, the child benefits from a good model and is enabled to read fluently and for meaning; through independent reading and through praise without criticism, the child is given practice and reinforcement in a context free from anxiety. From the parent's point of view, the training, monitoring and structured technique reduces uncertainty and boosted confidence.

Paired reading is usually used for periods of two or three months rather than continuously. An example of its application is the Derbyshire Project, which operated in the early 1980s under the auspices of three educational psychologists, Andy Miller, David Robson and Roger Bushell. The main study involved thirty-three children and their parents (mainly mothers) in thirteen randomly-chosen schools, and focused on eight- to eleven-year-olds who were experiencing persistent difficulties in learning to read (Miller *et al.*, 1985). As in the previous projects we have considered, the children came from economically disadvantaged homes. To allay apprehension and to provide introductory training, parents were seen first in small groups. The researchers acted out a typical 'bad' reading session in which parent and child became increasingly tense and agitated. They then demonstrated the technique of paired reading, which the parents applied during daily twenty-minute reading sessions with their children over the course of six weeks. Further training was also provided through fortnightly home visits.

The experiment was evaluated by administering the Neale Analysis of Reading Ability before and after the project to children who had engaged in paired reading and also to controls. The results showed clear improvement in reading accuracy and comprehension, well above the normal rate of progress for children with similar reading problems (though only the accuracy gains reached statistical significance). Striking changes were also noted in the children's willingness to read and their confidence in doing so. Similar evidence has emerged from other evaluation reports. In a recent study by Morgan and Gavin (1988), the progress of fifteen nine- to eleven-year-olds, whose reading age was two or more months behind their chronological age, was carried out in three Cambridgeshire schools. Over a three-month period, the eight children who had used the paired reading method gained an average of 6.29 months for reading accuracy on the Neale test, whereas the control group of seven, improved by only two months; for comprehension the differences were even more striking, 9.29 months compared with −0.4 months.

In many local authorities paired reading is now an established practice. It has been popularised in particular through the work of Keith Topping, who claims that evidence from research in eighty schools in Kirklees shows progress in paired reading schemes to be about three times normal rates with respect to reading accuracy and about five times normal rates with respect to comprehension (Topping, 1987 and *The Times Educational Supplement*, 11.11.88). The strategy is said to work well because of the absence of any tension. The parent is encouraged to give frequent praise and to respond to errors by simply giving the correct word which the child repeats. There is no discussion or any attempt to get the child to analyse the word phonically. Also important is the ability of the parent to maintain fluency by sliding easily back into the simultaneous reading mode. The experience is also fun for the child who feels in charge of the situation, choosing his or her own book and controlling movements to independent reading.

The approach, however, is not without its critics, at least in terms of its suitability for general parental use. Greening and Spencer (1987), for instance, note that in spite of Morgan's claim that the parent pays no attention to the child's mistakes, the fact that corrections are made during the independent reading mode allows the child to experience failure and impedes fluency. Another major problem is the time and expertise required to train parents and to visit their homes. In response to these criticisms, a series of projects in Cleveland primary schools have used a strategy known as *shared reading*, devised in 1983 by L. Mottram of the county's Learning Support Service and D. Guy of the Psychological Service. Shared reading is an adaptation of the simultaneous reading mode used in paired reading and is essentially a modelling technique (though the term is sometimes used more loosely to describe any scheme in which the parent and child share a reading activity, as in a Hertfordshire scheme described by David and Stubbs (1988). Reading in tandem without being concerned about getting on to the independent reading mode and correcting mistakes allows the child to concentrate on the story without interruption, while benefiting from the parent's model pronunciation, intonation and rhythm.

In the Cleveland scheme, the parents are asked to read with their children for about ten minutes each night for six days of the week, using a book which the child has chosen and brought home from school. Because the teacher will have practised shared reading in the classroom, the child will already be familiar with the technique. The parent has no special training or visits to the home, but is shown a video at the initial meeting and can receive support from teachers by visiting the school.

After successful pilot trials, the Cleveland shared reading scheme was evaluated using the Salford Reading Test and comparing the pre-project scores of 107 children in nine schools with scores obtained after eight weeks (Greening and Spenceley, 1987). Some of the children were beginning readers while others had experienced poor reading attainment or severe reading difficulties. Although six children showed no improvement, one in five made reading gains of at least nine months. Furthermore, the children were, in general, more enthusiastic and discriminating in their choice of books and more confident about reading.

The Birmingham Study: 'Pause, Prompt and Praise'

As we have noted, a reason why some children experience reading failure is that their parents tend to focus most of their attention on the mistakes rather than on the successful aspects of reading. In these circumstances the child finds it almost impossible to read fluently and so fails to pick up contextual clues, such as the context of the story, language patterns, and letter and sound cues. The parent's good intentions are thus counterproductive: far from helping the child to read more accurately, the child's reading ability is held back. Like paired reading, the 'pause, prompt and praise' technique is a structured strategy which attempts to change such inappropriate parent behaviour and hence the child's response.

Following a successful project in New Zealand, Ted Glynn (1980) undertook a small-scale study in Birmingham involving the parents of four ten-year-old boys whose reading ages were between two years and two years ten months below their chronological age. The parents were given a sheet which explained the strategy in ten statements. These emphasised the importance of (*a*) pausing for the child to correct errors himself, (*b*) giving clues to meanings of words pronounced wrongly, for example by referring to the context of the story or by giving a hint, and (*c*) praising for correct reading, for self-corrected errors and for errors corrected following a prompt.

Training took place during twice-weekly visits to the children's homes. During one visit each week the parent would first be asked to recall as many of the ten 'should' statements as possible. The visitor gave reinforcement and set a model for the parent to copy by praising instances of correct recall, and then asked the parent to read out the remaining statements. The parent then tutored the child, trying to put the 'should statements' into practice, after which the visitor went over various points arising from his observation. The other visit was spent discussing tape-recordings of tutoring sessions which the parent had made while hearing the child read from a book of his or her choice. Additionally, once or twice a week the children read to their teacher in class from a graded text.

The results were as predicted. Comparisons with data collected before the project showed that over the course of three months the parents increased the amount of time they gave for self-corrections, offered more prompts, and praised more frequently. The children in turn were correcting themselves much more often and generally showing more independence and confidence in their reading, with gains of between four and eight months on the Neale test. In short, the children were learning to read more fluently through changes in the parents' reactive behaviour. Other evaluations have suggested that the 'pause, prompt and praise' technique is particularly effective with older primary children who have previously made poor progress (Wheldall *et al.*, 1987).

Other home-based reading programmes linked to behavioural strategies have used tangible rewards, systematic instruction to help the child to master a sequence of small steps in a learning hierarchy ('precision teaching'), and commercially produced packages based on direct instruction programmes which specify a series of objectives (see Topping and Wolfendale, 1985). All these techniques require careful training and systematic record-keeping to monitor progress. Whether these approaches will appeal to teachers will depend on their beliefs about the most appropriate ways to teach children to read, a topic which is beyond the scope of this book. However, certain aspects of behavioural approaches, such as an emphasis on praise and encouragement, are considered to be 'good practice' in all projects.

PROFESSIONAL ISSUES AND PRACTICAL PROBLEMS

In this part of the chapter we consider a number of questions which are often asked by teachers who are thinking about involving parents directly in teaching their children to read. Most of the issues have in fact been touched on in our review of some home–school reading projects, but here we deal more explicitly with the practical problems. Items in the suggestions for Further Reading at the end of the chapter will enable the reader to explore the issues more fully.

1 Getting started and ensuring success

(a) How do you get a home-reading scheme started?

No stage in the development of a home–school scheme is more important than the inception. It is vital for parents to know that they have a unique and valuable role to play. They must also feel that they are working within a purposeful structure in which they can be assured of advice and support. These considerations make it essential for the staff as a group to think out its reading and language policy and what needs to be done to involve parents, so that the philosophy of the school's approach and the practical implications of parental involvement are understood, with as many problems as possible forestalled.

The school's reading policy encompasses such matters as the concept of literacy, the place of reading schemes, and whether 'real' books should be colour-coded. The practical aspects include the wording of the invitations to parents, the form of the introductory meeting, the content of any demonstration video, the layout and wording of printed guidelines and the reading cards, arrangements for seeing parents, whether home visiting is to be included and, if so, how. It is prudent to anticipate the sorts of questions parents are likely to ask and how the staff can allay the anxieties which some parents will naturally have.

Thought will clearly need to be given to material resources, possible re-arrangement of the timetable to allow time for follow-up work with the children, funding, and record-keeping. Whether teachers will visit homes is another important matter to consider (see section 2 below). Psychological appeal factors should also be considered, for example whether the project should have a special name and logo, and whether the children might carry their materials in a special wallet or bag.

(b)   What kinds of things need to go in the printed guidelines?

Experience has shown that each of the following needs to be emphasised:

– the importance of making reading sessions enjoyable, relaxed, regular, and not too long. 'Little and often!' should be the rule – perhaps ten to fifteen minutes unless the child wants more;
– the importance of finding somewhere quiet and comfortable to read, without distraction from the radio or TV, and to share the book by sitting together;
– giving plenty of praise, whilst refraining from criticism or putting pressure on the child. The activity must enable the child to experience success;
– allowing the child time to attempt words and to self-correct
– knowing what procedure to follow if the child cannot read a word after trying (see question 3(d) below);
– before reading begins, spending some time talking about the book in general and discussing the pictures;
– talking about the material being read and relating it to the child's experiences;
– helping the child to read for meaning;
– the importance of reading to the child as well as hearing him or her read, particularly in the early stages. The aim should be to *share* reading, with the adult presenting a good literate model; and
– the importance of making reading a natural event in all kinds of contexts and not just for set times each day. In a study of six families containing successful readers, Denny Taylor (1983, p.92–3) noted how literacy was not 'some specific list of activities added to the family agenda to explicitly teach reading' but was 'deeply embedded in the social processes of family life'.

(c)   What are the administrative factors which enable a successful scheme to be maintained?

Mention was made earlier of evidence to suggest that a favourable initial impact is not enough to sustain a scheme long-term. The main factors which have been found to be important to keep interest alive are as follows:

– a teacher who acts as coordinator;
– reading cards or booklets for completion by parents and teachers. Parents should be encouraged to be free with the comments, suggestions and questions, and teachers should be sure to respond;
– clearly understood and convenient arrangements for meeting parents at school and/or in their homes;
– regular newsletters, preferably illustrated and humorous. Besides reinforcing the main guidelines, these can make suggestions for extending language opportunities through talking and listening to the child, using the local library, and buying books for presents. They can also encourage the children to write. Newsletters can even raise the possibility that the parent and child might make their own books;
– small group meetings for parents to share issues and problems and make views known to the school;
– careful monitoring of the scheme and a preparedness to alter arrangements if need be;
– displays of books and reading games which can be borrowed;
– liaison with the local library, school library service, and bookshop; and
– workshops in which parents can help prepare reading games and other materials

(d) With all their other commitments, how can teachers give the time to operate a scheme successfully?

Regular weekly time is certainly needed if the scheme is to operate smoothly, and clearly this must be built into the teacher's regular timetable and not regarded as an extra. Many schools have quiet activity periods during which the teacher can complete the comment cards. It is more difficult for a teacher to find time for home visits, particularly if the LEA cannot be persuaded to provide extra help (see question 2(*c*)).

(e) Can an individual teacher run a scheme without the rest of the school being involved?

Yes, many successful programmes have begun in this way, usually developing into whole-school enterprises. To avoid an unhealthy competitive spirit, however, it is important for teachers working with the same year group to organise the scheme collaboratively within a common framework of understanding.

2 Home visiting

(a) Is home visiting really necessary?

Home visiting as a strategy was discussed in the previous chapter (see pp.128–31). Some reading programmes have operated successfully without home visiting. Visits will no doubt be more important for some families than others, but they seem likely to be particularly productive in areas where the parents are reluctant to come to school, feel diffident about their personal competence, or cannot read English. If home visiting is not possible, then teachers need to give special attention to ways in which parental involvement can be sustained at school, for example through 'surgeries', group meetings, workshops, demonstrations.

Preliminary visits may help to enlist the cooperation of parents who do not come to an introductory meeting at school. Once the parent has agreed to participate, regular home visiting can be a positive experience for parent, teacher and child.

(b) Do parents welcome home visiting?

See pp.130–1.

(c) Isn't home visiting impossibly time-consuming?

Even if home visiting is seen as desirable, many schools will say that their teachers have no time to do it. In some of the projects reviewed earlier, researchers or educational psychologists did this work: but in regular circumstances outside assistance may not be feasible. Undoubtedly special arrangements need to be made. If home visiting is seen as a priority, then it is worth trying to see if it is possible to redeploy teachers within the school to allow time for home visiting. For instance, in the Belfield Project some teachers were freed to visit homes on a half-day or in the evening.

(d) When and how often should teachers visit homes?

If parents work during the day, the evening is the only time possible for visits, but daytimes are useful where possible since it is sometimes easier to talk to parents if the child is not there. On the other hand, the child's presence will obviously be necessary if the parent is to watch the visitor hear the child read. This will be necessary for some programmes which involve special training, but may in any case be helpful to allay the parent's anxiety or to demonstrate a point.

3 Books and teaching approaches

(a) Doesn't a home–school programme involve extra book resources?

Given that reading for enjoyment is the basic principle of home reading schemes, a wide selection and plentiful supply of fiction and non-fiction is needed. The school must therefore determine its priorities in the way the funds are allocated. However, the schools library service can usually help, and parents should be encouraged to take their children to the public library.

(b) Don't books taken home get lost?

In general, this does not seem to be a problem. Special carrier folders and careful monitoring should ensure that children get into the habit of taking books back and forth from school.

(c) Should the school send home 'real' books or those from a graded scheme?

Whether graded schemes or 'real' books should be used in teaching children to read is a controversy beyond the scope of this book. Many schools do use published schemes for home reading, if only because parents sometimes request this, but ordinary books are used as well. Given that a main purpose of home–school projects is to help children to develop a love for reading as well as to acquire reading skills, a plentiful supply of good-quality 'real' books is essential. The Caper scheme suggest at least fifty books per class per half term. Books need to reflect different ethnic groups and social classes and avoid the stereotyping of gender roles. Some schools colour code 'real' books to ensure that children do not perpetually choose material which is too easy or too difficult.

(d) What should parents be advised to do when children miscue or cannot read a word?

In the early stages the parent can just supply the correct word; but as the child begins to make progress the parent should pause and allow time for the child to make an attempt or to self-correct. When the child is 'stuck', the parent might prompt or refer to contextual information. Some schools may also feel that parents could, on occasion, help the child to sound out words phonically: however, care needs to be taken that enjoyment is not sacrificed. Whatever the procedure, schools need to remind parents not to criticise or become impatient since the whole object of the exercise is to help children enjoy the experience of reading.

(e) What about children with reading difficulties?

Many projects have shown how poor readers have the most to gain from their parents' help, while the paired reading and other structured techniques were specially developed for children with reading difficulties. Of course, there is the danger that parental pressure and anxiety will simply make things worse, so it is especially important in these cases to encourage parents to praise frequently and generally to make reading sessions enjoyable occasions. Reading games can also be sent home. Some children can benefit from specially produced books written in local dialects.

4 Parents' attitudes and skills

(a) What about uninterested parents?

Some schools see little point in starting a scheme which involves parents who have never or seldom come to school and seem uninterested in their children's education. As far as reading programmes are concerned, experience suggests that even in schools which have had a poor record of parental involvement, most parents do want to take part. It seems that, given the opportunity to be *directly and responsibly* involved in their children's learning, almost all parents take it.

Parents who will not come to large, introductory meetings, may respond to a personal letter or a phone call. As previously noted, visiting the child's home, while time-consuming, is often productive and helps the teacher to gain a new perspective on the situation. In the last analysis, however, schools have no powers to demand parental involvement in reading programmes. In any case, it would be counter-productive to make parents join against their will. If all attempts to enlist the parent's cooperation fail, a parent–helper in school might be used to hear the children read.

(b) What about parents who do not read English or who are illiterate?

Even if a parent cannot read English, he or she can make a good listener and provide encouragement. Clearly the child must be able to manage the book unaided, but the parent can always talk to the child about the pictures and what has been read. The child may be able to read to another adult relation, an older brother or sister, or a neighbour who reads English. The school's printed guidelines will need to be translated for ethnic minority parents who do not read English. Sometimes non-English reading parents learn to read alongside the child.

Particular sensitivity will be needed in dealing with parents who cannot read at all since they will probably be embarrassed and may feel they cannot possibly help. Yet they can, and the substance of the above comments apply to illiterate parents as well. Such parents might also be encouraged to attend an adult literacy class.

(c) What about children with 'difficult' parents?

There may be a few 'pushy' parents who do not make easy partners in a home–school programme. Because they have unrealistic expectations, these parents will subject their children to undue pressure. For these, the school has a special responsibility to try to ensure that the school's guidelines are followed (see question 1(b) above) – particularly the items which emphasise the importance of being patient, giving praise and enjoying reading – and to provide continuing support. With parents who seem hostile to their children, it sometimes happens that the experience of sitting down with the child helps to create a better relationship.

(d) Doesn't a home–school reading project reduce the professional significance of the teacher?

No. What teachers or other professionals are doing is making their expertise available to parents and giving guidance (and, for the structured schemes, training). Equally, they use their professional expertise in monitoring and evaluating the scheme, in assessing children's progress and knowing how to extend reading and language skills in class by more sophisticated strategies. It is also part of being a professional to recognise the value of other sources of help and to make effective use of these.

SUMMARY AND CONCLUSIONS

This chapter has reviewed a selection of partnership projects in reading and has considered various practical and professional issues. No one scheme is clearly superior to another. The success of the projects is likely to be due less to the features of the strategies and more to the fact that they all involve parents. The power of home–school reading schemes to secure significant improvement in reading levels was seen to be controversial – though certainly many projects have claimed such success. It would, however, be a mistake to evaluate the programmes simply in terms of performance gains as measured by conventional reading tests. As Hannon (1989) has pointed out, evaluation needs to take account of the scale and permanence of parental involvement, the advantages which parents have over teachers when they hear children read, the effects of parental involvement in terms of classroom practice and relationships between child, parent and teacher, and parents' and teachers' views about a scheme's value.

The following are important benefits that have been widely reported:

1 Parents can substantially boost the time which children spend reading to adults. Tizard (1987) found that in top infant classes children spent only 2 or 3 per cent of the school day in any kind of reading activity, while in a survey of first and second year junior classes, Southgate *et al.* (1981) found that teachers gave an average of only two to three minutes per child per day. Parental involvement should not mean that teachers spend less time on reading, but rather that they use their time more effectively, perhaps developing more sophisticated approaches.
2 Children's interest in reading is likely to increase, as is the range and quantity of reading matter attempted.
3 Children are also likely to be more highly motivated towards school learning in general and behaviour is consequently better.
4 Relationships between parents and teachers are enhanced, and parents who formerly had remained distant from the school's effort to involve them usually take the opportunity to become more directly involved in their children's learning.
5 Parents and children develop closer relationships as the parents become more knowledgeable about their children's reading progress and more interested generally in their children's education, while children benefit from their parents' undivided attention for a short period each day.

It is important to remember, however, that home–school reading projects in which children read to or with their parents are not a substitute for parents reading stories to their children. Rather, they should be regarded as facilitating the transition from listening to a story to reading independently.

Needless to say, success is dependent upon the efforts of teachers to give professional support to parents, to provide a good range of quality books, and to monitor the scheme carefully. But with careful attention to the programme's sequencing and arrangements, most schools – and not least those in economically disadvantaged areas and with poor readers – should see benefits. The involvement of parents in children's reading is no substitute for the work of the teacher, but nor is it a cosmetic 'extra': it makes an invaluable contribution to the child's learning and to mutual understanding between home and school.

Further Reading

The PACT scheme is clearly described in *Parent, Teacher, Child: Working Together in Children's Learning* by Alex Griffiths and Dorothy Hamilton (Methuen, 1984), who discuss all kinds of issues and provide many suggestions. A wealth of practical ideas (e.g. for introducing a scheme, running workshops, and evaluating progress) is contained in *Children and Parents Enjoying Reading by Peter Branston and Mark Provis (Hodder and Stoughton, 1986)*, in *Reading: Involving Parents*, (Community Education Development Centre, 1984) and in *Word Play: Language Activities for Young Children and their Parents* by Sheila Wolfendale and Trevor Bryans (NARE Publications, 2 Lichfield Road, Stafford, 1986). In *Shared Reading in Practice* (Open University Press, 1988), two teachers, Chris Davis and Rosemary Stubbs, use transcripts of conversations with parents, teachers and children to show the value of parental involvement and some of the key features which make a scheme successful.

The Reading and Language Information Centre at the University of Reading publish an excellent booklet called *Working Together: Parents, Teachers and Children* (1987). This includes four case studies, an account of paired reading, and a list of videos to support parental programmes.

A general overview with a strong practical element is provided by Wendy Bloom in *Partnership with Parents in Reading* (Hodder and Stoughton, 1987). A twenty-three-minute video *Partners in Reading* is available from Chiltern Consortium, Wall Hall, Aldenham, Watford WD2 8AZ.

For a very useful collection of articles which discuss a wide range of issues and give reports on many different kinds of projects (including structured techniques and working with children who have special needs) see *Involvement in Children's Reading* edited by Keith Topping and Sheila Wolfendale (Croom Helm, 1985).

For those interested in the paired reading technique, Roger Morgan's handbook *Helping Children Read* (Methuen, 1986) will prove invaluable, as will the *Paired Reading Training Pack* available from the Paired Reading Project, Kirklees Psychological Service, Oldgate House, Huddersfield, HD1 6QU. The article by Greening and Spenceley on the Cleveland shared reading scheme is reprinted in A. Cohen (ed.) *Early Education: the Parents' Role* (Paul Chapman, 1988).

10 | PARTNERSHIP PROJECTS IN WRITING AND MATHEMATICS

Although the majority of home–school learning schemes have focused on children's reading, projects have also been developed in other curriculum areas. A very important aspect of these initiatives is the contribution they make to the *parents'* education as well as the children's. This chapter is concerned with ways in which teachers and parents can work together to improve the parents' understanding of writing and mathematics and help them to become further involved as educators of their own children.

WRITING PROJECTS

In their recent study of inner-city nursery and infant schools, Tizard *et al.* (1988) found that the great majority of parents interviewed were encouraging their children in writing activities, such as stories, letters, and captions for pictures. By contrast, few teachers had developed policies for involving parents in this aspect of the curriculum. A comparable finding emerged in a recent survey by the National Writing Project: of the 426 parents of children aged between three and six, mostly in 'disadvantaged' areas, who replied to a questionnaire, 90 per cent said they helped their children with writing and would like to do more – though few knew anything about how it was taught in school (Hall, 1989). There thus seems to be a mismatch between what parents can and want to do and what teachers tend to expect of them.

Involving parents in their children's writing is not so straightforward as in reading. In the latter, the adult can quickly help the child to relate to the context which the author has created, but in the former the adult has to be sensitive to the context which the child has chosen. For learning to write involves more than the development of handwriting skills and knowing how to spell and punctuate. As Pam Czerniewska (1988), the Director of the National Writing Project explains, the process is a life-long one which entails:

> thinking through ideas; deciding what to say; working out how to say it best; physically putting the words down; revising; editing and eventually deciding whether to send, publish, file or even throw away the end product.

The range of activities involved in the process of writing was recognised in the attainment targets recommended for primary schools by the Cox Report on English in the National Curriculum (NCEWG, 1988).

Nonetheless, although the task is more demanding than in reading, there are many ways in which parents can be valuable facilitators of their children's writing, supplementing and contributing to the activities provided in school. Children are more likely to want to write if they are asked to do so for a particular purpose, and the home provides an excellent context for this. Examples are shopping lists, a message to a neighbour, invitations to a party, a thank you letter to a relation, a story which will amuse the family, a poem which shows how the child feels about an aspect of family life. Parents can provide encouragement not only in what they say and in providing materials, but in arranging for the child's work to be read by others (sisters and brothers, grandparents, friends) and kept in albums or exhibited on the kitchen notice board.

In the early stages, parents might be encouraged to invite their children to tell them stories and then write down for them what they say. Most children get a thrill when they can read their stories and poems to members of their family and to friends. It is also important for children to experience writing as a means of two-way communication and as a collaborative exercise. Parents might therefore write *to* their children and compile stories with them. Parents can also act as good writing models by sharing their own writing (e.g. shopping lists, notes and letters) with their children. This will help to get over what writing involves – including getting into a mess and starting again – so that the child does not feel that attempts must be perfect first time. The role of the teacher, therefore, is not only to suggest ideas for parents to follow up but to encourage them to make the activities an occasion for conversation with the child and to treat the child's efforts, however simple, with respect. Above all, the child must regard the activities as a source of pleasure.

Unfortunately, there is evidence to suggest that many teachers give the impression that successful writing is essentially an exercise in conforming to technical criteria rather than a pleasurable experience in communicating. In their study of the classroom learning experiences of six- to seven-year-old children, Bennett *et al.* (1984) found that in three-quarters of the writing tasks observed, the teachers laid emphasis on quantity of output, neatness and punctuation. Furthermore, conversations with the children revealed that they even interpreted the instruction to 'write me an exciting story' in these terms, for they knew the criteria on which their work would in fact be judged! Hence before teachers involve parents in writing, they may need to think carefully about their own aims.

Some parents, as well as some teachers, will be tempted to focus unduly on accurate spelling and neatness, which may have a dampening effect on the child's progress. The technical aspects of writing are, of course, very important, not least because they help to ensure successful communication. At the same time, as the Cox Report recognised, 'Teachers provide the greatest encouragement for children to communicate in writing when they respond more to the content of what is written . . . and when they share a child's writing with other children' (NCEWG, 1989, para. 17.12). The parent's role can be significant in these respects, helping the child to feel that his or her writing is valued as a medium of communication and entertainment. For as Gordon Wells (1980) has emphasised:

> Learning one's native language is not simply a matter of learning vocabulary and grammar, but rather of learning to construct shared meanings as part of collaborative activities in which words and sentences both refer to the shared situation and reflect a particular orientation to it. (p.133)

The impact of parental involvement in young children's writing was demonstrated in a recent American study (Green, 1987). Half of the sixty-four kindergarten children who participated formed the experimental group, the rest the control group. In a series of workshops, teachers showed three informal ways in which the parents of the experimental group could help their children with writing. One way was to 'be a secretary' by taking dictation. The idea behind this was that the children would understand the connections between speech, reading and writing. The second way was by writing to their children (e.g. notes in their lunch boxes, silly rhymes, invitations to go on a picnic). Here the point was that communication in writing would stimulate the child to respond in writing. Thirdly, the parents were invited to encourage their children to engage independently in various types of writing – notes and letters, lists, signs and labels, captions for pictures, calendars, stories – and examples were shown of each. The parents were also given a booklet to reinforce the workshop information and were asked to complete weekly response sheets. On two days each week, the children spent some time reading their writing to others in the class or asking the teacher to do so. The experiment was evaluated by comparing the progress in writing made by the experimental and control groups.

The results showed that the children in the experimental group had made significantly greater gains in their understanding of print, writing fluency and composing development. The parent response sheets revealed that most parents and other members of the family were willing to write with the children, who responded positively to the activities. Overall, the findings indicated that parents can play an important role in helping their children to write freely, with confidence and enjoyment.

Bringing children and parents together in writing partnerships is a key feature of the National Writing Project, which has been initiating local projects all over the country since 1983. The value of the activities, which have involved thousands of parents and teachers in England and Wales, can be seen from contributions to the project's newsletters *About Writing*. One aim in this enterprise is to give children the experience of writing for a purpose. For example, the children in one primary school class wrote to their parents to explain why they had selected a particular piece of their language work for a parents' evening. The parents were then invited to respond to their child's letter, and most did so. Besides helping the children to see the value and demands of writing for a purpose and to reflect critically on their work, the results increased the parents' understanding of the complexities of the writing process and stimulated discussion between child and parent about their learning.

Other primary schools involved in the project have devised opportunities in which children can see their parents as writing models and be involved in determining the content and format of their parents' writing. For example, parents who had helped to build a school pond wrote with their children about the work as it progressed. This collaborative enterprise enabled both the children and their parents to appreciate the need for drafts and editing, and with the teacher's assistance books were produced both by individual families and collaboratively. Nor is work with adults outside the school confined to parents. One school operated a successful project with senior citizens. Called 'Grab a Gran', the children visited a local club for old people, whose memories of their childhood, songs they had sung and stories they had been told were recorded in writing – sometimes collaboratively with the pensioners themselves.

In short, parental involvement in children's writing gives greater opportunity for varied writing activities than a teacher could ever provide alone. More evaluation needs to be carried out on this aspect of working with parents, but it is likely that children do more than learn to enjoy writing and improve their writing skills. The social experience of writing for a purpose and successfully engaging the attention of a listener is likely to make the children more socially confident and to improve their self-esteem.

MATHEMATICS

The Cockcroft Report (1982) on the teaching of mathematics, although recognising the importance of schools explaining their approaches to the subject and discussing children's progress with parents, did not address the possibility of projects which would help parents to become more directly involved. Moreover, many teachers seem reluctant to involve parents in mathematics. Tizard *et al.* (1988) found that the same teachers who were happy for parents to hear their children read were hesitant about involving them in mathematics. Yet over 90 per cent of the parents themselves were already teaching their children to count, to recognise numbers and learn number series, whilst over two-thirds were teaching adding, and two-fifths subtraction. The researchers conclude: 'Rather than resisting parental involvement, teachers might do better to acknowledge the help that parents are already giving children with maths, and seek to work with, rather than against, parents' (p.79).

It is understandable, however, that teachers should be unsure about involving parents in mathematics. As the PrIME project (Primary Initiatives in Mathematics Education) acknowledges, 'Parents . . . may have negative attitudes to mathematics, or old-fashioned ideas which only value the ability to do pencil and paper calculations. These are easily passed on to children' (*PrIME Newsletter* 3). However, as teachers concerned with this project point out, it is the very danger that some parents will communicate their own fears and invalid preconceptions of mathematics to their children that constitutes the reason for involving them:

. . . parents anxieties are real; it is thus better to have them out in the open and discuss them;

children whose parents are fully involved and informed are more likely to succeed at school;

any project which enables parents, children and teachers to work together promotes an increased trust between parents and school.
(Report of PrIME Conference, Dec. 1986, *Newsletter* 3)

Of course, a prerequisite for success here is that the teachers themselves are clear about the goals which they are hoping to achieve and why they are adopting one approach rather than another.

Given the fact that many parents have negative feelings about their experiences of mathematics when they were at school, and that most will not be acquainted with new developments in primary school mathematics, how can teachers go about organising partnership schemes? In addition to school-based events discussed in the last chapter, two main sorts of strategies are currently being tried out with parents and children at home. One involves engaging parents and their children in playing games. The other strategy, as used in the IMPACT project, involves constructing special materials involving not only games but also data collection and investigations. Each of these will now be described.

Mathematical games for parents and children

The M.A.T.H.S project (Multiply Attainments Through Home Support), organised by Kirklees Psychological Service, advocates the use of games as the ideal medium for parents and children working together. Like paired reading, which the same authority recommends, games can provide a relaxed, enjoyable and non-threatening learning experience. The 'paired number' projects, which are run with infants and first year juniors, have been described by Tiny Arora and Judy Bamford (1986; 1988), who maintain that playing mathematical games have important features apart from enjoyment. In particular, they provide opportunities for discussion and stimulate the use of mathematical language. Other advantages include the following:

−games are already part of normal home experience;
−games are highly motivating because the child is actively participating and is in control, whilst there is immediate feedback and an element of competition;
−games have well-defined limits and directions;
−games are meaningful experiences, somewhere in between reality and the abstract world. (Arora and Bamford, 1988, p.18)

Each project lasts from six to eight weeks. At the start, the parents attend a meeting at school when they are shown how to play the maths games. They then agree to play a game with their child for ten to twenty minutes on six days each week, coming into school every week to help their child choose a new game. This exchange meeting provides an opportunity for talking about the value of the experiences and the merits of different games. Each game is designed to teach a particular mathematical concept (counting, conservation, pattern, ordering, matching and shape) and the parents complete a record card which also lists the key terms to use with the game. For instance, the words for the game which focuses on 'Conservation' are: 'long', 'short', 'too many', 'too few', 'more', 'same', 'exactly', 'longer', 'less' and 'different'. The parents are asked to talk to the child about what they are doing during the game and to include the listed words in the conversation. Clearly it is necessary for the school to acquire a stock of the games, and the handbook gives full particulars (see Further Reading).

Evaluation is carried out by means of a questionnaire to parents, conversations with them at the end of the project, interviews with the children before and after the project using diagnostic materials, and feedback from class teachers. Reports so far indicate positive responses from children, parents and teachers and a significantly greater improvement in understanding the mathematical concepts involved compared with controls (Arora and Bamford, 1988).

Another scheme based on games, but one involving parents with children who have special educational needs, has been developed by Perry and Simmons (1987) with children from several primary schools. In the game 'Battleships', for example, the parent and child 'hide' toy battleships and other craft on a grid. They then try to find each other's vessels by asking if anything is hidden in positions which they name by referring to the axes, the player who finds all the opponent's ships first being the winner. As in other home–school pojects, informal discussion with the parents emphasises that the activities should be fun, that there should be plenty of talking and working together, and that the children should not be pushed but given plenty of praise. Using an NFER mathematics test as a criterion for progress, most of the children in the nine to ten week experiment showed gains in understanding which were greater than would have been expected in the ordinary way. Further, according to feedback from parents, the children's attitude towards mathematics greatly improved, as did their confidence in handling mathematical concepts.

IMPACT

The IMPACT project (ILEA Maths for Parents and Children and Teachers), was developed in London and Oxfordshire primary schools by Ruth Merttens and Jeffrey Vass (1987). Like the reading scheme PACT, described in the last chapter, IMPACT involves parents in a structured way. But whereas PACT relies on published books, IMPACT is based on specially made materials to encourage an investigative approach to learning maths and to ensure that parents and teachers are working within a common framework. Whereas in reading projects the parents (with some exceptions) are not themselves learning to read, by using mathematics materials the parents as well as the children are acquiring new knowledge.

The IMPACT scheme works like this. At regular intervals, the researchers discuss the mathematics curriculum with each of the class teachers, and particular activities are identified as lending themselves to home–school cooperation. Ideas arising from classroom activities are discussed with the teachers who then construct materials for children to take home at each weekend. The activities could involve the collection of data for use in class, making simple things to display in class and use in discussion, or undertaking simple, structured activities related to everyday pursuits. Examples of two such activities can be seen in Figures 10.1 and 10.2.

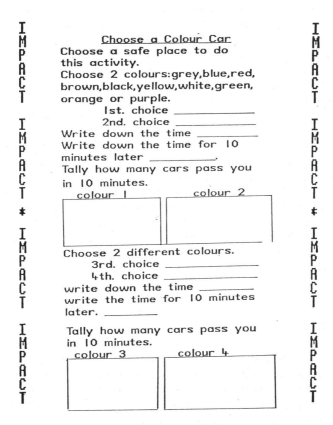

IMPACT IMPACT IMPACT IMPACT IMPACT

Choose a Colour Car
Choose a safe place to do this activity.
Choose 2 colours:grey,blue,red, brown,black,yellow,white,green, orange or purple.
    1st. choice _____
    2nd. choice _____
Write down the time _____
Write down the time for 10 minutes later _____.
Tally how many cars pass you in 10 minutes.
    colour 1   colour 2

Choose 2 different colours.
    3rd. choice _____
    4th. choice _____
write down the time _____
write the time for 10 minutes later. _____

Tally how many cars pass you in 10 minutes.
    colour 3   colour 4

IMPACT IMPACT IMPACT IMPACT IMPACT

Figure 10.1 Example of IMPACT activity sheet

The work is followed up in class the week after, using the children's and parents' responses. About once a month, the parents come to school to discuss the activities

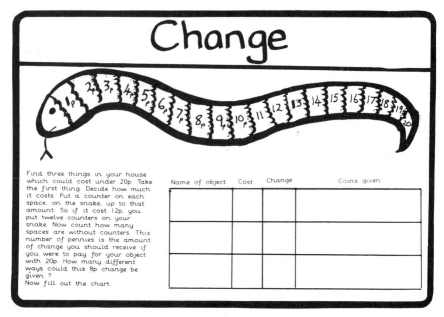

Figure 10.2 Example of IMPACT activity sheet

and any difficulties which were encountered. Parent education is therefore an important function of these meetings, and concepts (e.g. Venn diagrams) with which many parents will be unfamiliar can be explained. Evaluation is provided through weekly response sheets completed by the parents, children and teachers, plus interviews with parents; in some classes, video and audio tapes have been analysed as well. The report for 1987/88 showed that an average of 86 per cent of parents were participating each week and that responses from each partner were positive; furthermore, teachers were becoming less dependent on the INSET worker and more successfully integrating IMPACT work into classroom activities (Merttens and Vass, 1988).

Merttens and Vass (1987) argue that this kind of parental involvement subtly alters those adverse attitudes to mathematics which are held not only by some parents and children but also by some teachers. Questions concerning 'What is the point of doing . . .?' become irrelevant as parents come to see the value of the activities in familiar everyday situations. The researchers also report that many children for whom mathematics was an unpleasant subject, even one to avoid, have grown not only in understanding but in enthusiasm. Further, the emphasis on cooperative investigative work allows them to transfer skills to new situations more easily than hitherto. For the teacher, IMPACT provides a constructive context for in-service training: because the focus is on parents working with their children rather than teachers in the classroom, the training is less threatening and encourages teachers to change their practices more quickly than is usually possible.

A starter-pack of fifty activities has been produced for schools to use, and further projects in other authorities are being planned within the framework of the National Curriculum.

Other approaches to parental involvement with mathematics include displays, videos and family workshops in community centres and local libraries. Because these are available for the general public as well as parents of school children, they help to increase general community awareness of primary school practice, and hopefully to correct wrong impressions about children 'just playing games all day' instead of doing 'serious work'.

SUMMARY AND CONCLUSIONS

The successful development of partnership projects in writing and mathematics means that parental involvement in all the three Rs is now a realistic possibility for primary schools. There is no reason why the principles of the approaches outlined in this chapter and the last should not be extended to other areas of school learning such as health education, history, environmental studies, and craft, design and technology. As Tizard and Hughes (1984) point out, mothers are particularly well placed to play an important teaching role because they share the child's world more intimately. The problem is not one of finding suitable curriculum contexts but of teachers finding time to organise schemes and of parents finding time to participate.

The main potential advantages of these collaborative approaches would seem to be that they:

- develop mutual understanding between home and school by providing a purposeful context for curriculum debate;
- improve relationships between parents, teacher and child by providing enjoyable activities which the three partners can share and through which the child can experience success and feelings of achievement;
- provide more time than the teacher would normally have in class to help children acquire skills and understanding; and
- tap the expertise of parents to complement that of the teacher.

At the same time, it needs to be appreciated that the success of home–school curriculum projects depends not only upon the enthusiasm and energy of teachers but also upon their attitude towards parents in engaging them as educators of their own children. Far from bringing teachers and parents closer together, relationships could deteriorate if teachers regard themselves as experts whose job it is to tell the mums and dads 'how it ought to be done', for this emphasises the parents' dependency on the teacher. Certainly school staff must be clear about their beliefs concerning the purposes of teaching children the curriculum area in question, and certainly they must offer a carefully structured support system for parents. All the same, the teacher's job is not to 'present' a pre-packaged scheme with instructions for parents to 'follow', like painting by numbers. Rather it is to engage the interest of the parents, to help them acquire the requisite skills and understanding, to respond sympathetically and positively to their anxieties, and generally help them gain knowledge and confidence so that they can take initiatives themselves. As McConkey (1985) has importantly emphasised the teacher's job is not to make parents *into* teachers, which they are already, but to help them become *better* teachers.

Further reading

Some of the main respects in which young children learn in the home from almost every occasion are described, with extracts from conversations, by Barabara Tizard and Martin Hughes in *Young Children Learning: Talking and Thinking at Home and at School* (Fontana, 1984).

Although written for parents, *Learning at Home* by Alex Griffiths and Dorothy Hamilton (Methuen, 1987) is a very useful source of ideas for teachers who wish to involve parents in curriculum activities. The Home and School Council publishes several inexpensive booklets about involving parents in the curriculum.

Books with many practical suggestions which teachers might like to recommend to parents are: *Be Your Child's Natural Teacher* (Penguin, 1987), and *Children Can Enjoy Writing Stories* (Home and School Council Publications, 1988), both by Geraldine Taylor; and *Help Your Child with Maths* (BBC Books, 1988), edited by Angela Walsh.

The National Writing Project newsletters *About Writing* (SCDC Publications) and *Gnosis* no. 13 include contributions about ways in which schools involve parents in their children's writing. The newsletters and project materials are now published by Nelson; back issues are obtainable from the National Curriculum Council.

The MATHS project handbook by Tiny Arora and Judy Bamford (1988) is available from Kirklees Psychological Service, Oastler Centre, 103 New Street, Huddersfield HD1 2DU.

11 | PARENTS AND OTHER ADULTS IN SCHOOL

Most primary schools invite parents to help in various ways such as preparing materials, running clubs, assisting with school productions and sports, undertaking clerical duties, supervising the lunchroom and playground, decorating the building, repairing equipment, raising funds at fetes and looking after children on visits and outings. Increasingly, however, parents now assist teachers in classroom curriculum work. This chapter is concerned with this latter category of activities, in which parental involvement is not just 'support' but is directly associated with the children's learning. Unlike the home–school schemes discussed in the last two chapters, these usually involve parents working with other people's children, often in groups as well as individually, and sometimes delivering talks to the whole class. As we shall see later, there is more controversy surrounding the involvement of parents in classroom activities than in teaching their children at home because of the professional, political and practical problems raised.

WHY USE PARENT HELPERS?

A recent survey in Oxfordshire revealed that in 87 per cent of primary classes parents were involved in classroom activities on some occasion each week, typically for one or two hours at a time (Thomas, 1987). This level of participation is probably exceptional since Oxfordshire LEA places special emphasis on parental involvement and the integration of children with special needs into mainstream schooling. However the NFER survey (Jowett and Baginsky, 1988) showed that primary schools in at least a quarter of local authorities involve parents as 'extra hands' in the classroom, particularly with the younger age groups; and Steirer's (1985) survey of 500 primary heads across England revealed that 53 per cent enlisted the help of parents and other volunteers in children's reading. A recent enquiry conducted for the Professional Association of Teachers revealed similar levels of parental involvement, one school in Birmingham even asking candidates at interview to commit themselves to parent participation before they accept the post (McQuillan, 1987).

There is a wide range of curriculum activities in which parents can be involved. The most usual appears to be hearing children read, though often with the average and above-average readers only (Stierer, 1985; McQuillan, 1987). Other activities include: reading stories to children, helping them select books, and talking to them about books; teaching children about traditions in minority cultures; helping with special needs; supervising language and number games; computer work; assisting with practical activities such as art, model-making, needlework and cookery; lending a hand with swimming, games and the Duke of Edinburgh scheme; and participating in school assemblies.

Whether this involvement amounts to 'teaching' is a moot point. The teachers would probably prefer to think of the parents' contribution in terms of 'helping', 'supervising' and 'guiding'. Yet the responses which are likely to be made by a parent–helper who is hearing a child read (being encouraging, helping to choose the book, giving praise, asking questions, drawing attention to the context, helping with words) are clearly part of the teaching process. The teaching role is even more obvious when parents come in to talk about their experiences, demonstrate a special skill or explain their occupation. Nonetheless, although the parent can be said to be involved in the process of teaching, she (or very occasionally he) remains under the supervision of the classroom teacher, who is responsible for what is done and not done.

Parental involvement in the classroom can be justified on two main counts: those which accrue from the presence of any extra hands and those which relate to the fact that the assistance is provided by parents specifically.

As regards the former, schools that have worked successful schemes with parents argue that the pupils receive more individual help and are provided with a greater range of experiences than could otherwise be realistically envisaged, even if classes were smaller. Stierer (1985) found that, although 'extra reading practice' was the main benefit mentioned by heads, about a third also mentioned the fact that the teacher was relieved to undertake more specialised work with those pupils who have reading difficulties. Other advantages include the facility for basic concepts to be reinforced through parents playing word and number games with pupils and supervising small group investigative activities (e.g. using reference books or a simple science experiment) which have been set up by the teacher (Bailey *et al.*, 1982).

Apart from the parents who wish and are able to help on a regular basis, others may be willing to come in occasionally. It is not just that parents can talk about their jobs (and perhaps arrange to visit the place of work) and their special interests; some are able to contribute to a better understanding of other regions and cultures by talking about other parts of the country or other countries from which they come. The teacher can also utilise the special skills of some parents, for example in crafts, hobbies, the performing arts, or sports. The pupils therefore have access to a greater variety of experiences and skills than all the teachers together could possibly provide.

From the parents' perspective, a major benefit is the greater insight gained into classroom practices and the way the school functions. From their interviews with parents, Becher *et al.* (1981) record how:

. . . mothers in Sussex who had helped in one way or another within the classroom had often changed their opinions about school quite radically, and described how they had come to understand the work of the school through having had the chance to see at first hand what it was all about . . .' I didn't think much of teachers before I began this work . . . but now I appreciate her problems. I think she's a real brick.'

Parents also find it personally satisfying to work in the school community: they enjoy the company of the pupils and feel reassured to be responding to their learning needs.

At the same time teachers must not be fooled into thinking that parents necessarily pick up the rationale of classroom learning activities simply by helping the teacher. Explanation is also needed. As Tizard *et al.*, (1981) point out, the teacher may understand that the purpose of using play materials is to help children acquire scientific concepts, but parents may think that they are just to keep the children amused.

PROFESSIONAL ISSUES AND PRACTICAL PROBLEMS

From the account so far, it seems that parents, teachers and children have much to gain from parental involvement in curriculum activities. Nonetheless, a number of problems have to be faced. In spite of the claimed advantages of having parents in the classroom, some teachers have reservations about the desirability of involving parents, either on grounds of principles related to professional boundaries and/or because of practical problems.

As regards the *principle* of parental involvement in classroom learning, some teachers argue that it is professionally wrong for parents to encroach upon territory traditionally regarded as the reserve of those who have had special training and possess relevant formal qualifications. In particular, it is feared that children with learning difficulties will be subjected to undue pressure and an inappropriate style of instruction.

Pollard (1986) quotes from a letter, written in 1970, in which the branch secretary of a teacher union reprimanded an infant head for bringing mothers into the classroom to hear children read. The official wrote: 'The union takes the view that listening to children read is a teaching operation . . . and it is professionally unacceptable by the NUT for unqualified persons to carry out this task'. More recently, Bennett (1985) quoted one primary head as saying: 'I've changed things a lot since I took over. The mothers used to have to wait at the gate in all weathers. Now I let them into the entrance hall . . . they help put the children's coats and shoes on. But I won't let them any further.'

Parents themselves are not always happy at the prospect of their children being helped by other parents who have no qualifications to teach. One parent was so incensed that she published a newspaper article in which she described parent–helpers as 'jumped-up, self-styled educators, whose only qualification for the job seems to be the rather arbitrary one of parenthood' (Grassie, 1987).

These objections would obviously have force if it was clear that the pupils' learning and motivation were suffering because of the parents' presence. Although, as we saw in Chapter 8, research has been conducted on the effectiveness of parents teaching their children to read at home, data on the impact of parent–helpers in the classroom is lacking. However, most teachers who use parent helpers maintain that their contribution is valuable (Stierer, 1985). If they are right, schools would be professionally irresponsible *not* to involve parents. It should also be noted that the teacher remains fully in charge, and there should be no question of her leaving parents to their own devices. Parents should be encouraged to discuss classroom procedures and to contribute ideas; but it is the teacher who, in the last analysis, evaluates the appropriateness of their suggestions.

A second professional issue concerns the fact that, because parents constitute a body of unpaid helpers, they provide a disincentive for the authorities to provide more teachers and smaller classes. Schools are thus presented with a professional dilemma: they value parent–helpers but fear the authorities will use this goodwill as a reason for not improving staffing levels. Some heads therefore refuse to use voluntary help, or only for activities which do not involve teaching, such as clerical work, preparing materials, or supervising children in the school library.

In spite of these professional difficulties, some of the teacher unions have recently developed constructive policies for involving parents in classroom activities. The Professional Association of Teachers, for instance, has published a useful guide (McQuillan, 1987); and the National Union of Teachers, whilst insisting that no teacher should be forced to use parent helpers and that, where they do, 'the parents' role is to benefit pupils, not to provide free labour and resources', recognises that 'parents . . . often have talents and expertise which the teacher may not have' and draws attention to the fact that 'teachers will be aware that they are using helpers as a valuable educational resource' (NUT, 1987).

Additionally, there are *practical* problems which need to be faced. One of these does not relate to parents specifically but to any team teaching situation, even if the other adults are trained teachers. Thomas (1987) notes the decline of experiments in team teaching which were pioneered in the 1960s in the UK and USA. He also points to research into the effects of paid ancillary help which suggests that some teachers find they are spending less rather than more time with individuals because they are preoccupied with problems of organisation. As Thomas suggests, part of the difficulty is that teachers are typically not trained to work as the coordinator of a team in the classroom, a role which requires special skills in organising, directing, and relating to other adults. Given the burgeoning interest in involving parents and other adults in school, it is essential for initial training and in-service courses to include work on skills required for the constructive deployment and management of parents in the classroom. Without such support, some teachers may feel unsure about their capabilities in this respect – though by starting with just one or two the task is more manageable.

Certainly, involving parents will mean that the teacher's style of working will change, and this may raise new issues about his or her role. Some of these will be logistical: how to deploy parents to the best advantage; how to fit helpers into the space available; what arrangements should be made at breaktime if the staffroom cannot accommodate all the teachers and helpers. Other issues, however, will take the form of teaching dilemmas. For instance, a teacher may wish to take advantage of the freedom to give more specialised help to less-able or more-able children, yet fear that concentration on these children all the time could carry counterproductive 'labelling' messages for both the class and the parent–helpers about who needs help and who doesn't.

The teacher needs to give guidance to parent–helpers so that they are clear about their role. These include:

−how the class is organised;
−classroom rules, for example about what children must have permission to do;
−which children the parents should work with, on what task and for how long;
−what is the purpose of the activity (workshops for parents help here − see pp.125–6);
−what level of achievement to expect;
−how much help the children should be given;
−what to do if children make mistakes;
−where children can find materials and reference books; and
−where parents are to work (there may not be room in the classroom).

Some teachers may claim that they are too busy to undertake so much work in organising and supporting parents and explaining practices; and certainly they will find there is more rather than less work at the start. The test is whether the resulting benefits make the time spent on initial preparation worth the effort.

A second practical problem concerns enlisting parent help and dealing with possible conflicts in relationships. Most schools use parents' meetings or specific invitations to draw up a rota of volunteers, and suggest that interested parents might like to come in one afternoon to observe and discuss the matter with the class teacher before deciding whether they wish to commit themselves. In the event, some parents may turn out to be unsuitable. They may be unreliable or bossy, breach confidentiality by gossiping about individual children, or spend too much time with their own child.

Fortunately, problems do not appear to loom large among the schools which use parents. Stierer (1985) found that at least one-third of head teachers experienced no problems at all, and the most frequently cited difficulties were mentioned by no more than one in ten heads. Nonetheless, in any collaborative work, there is the risk that tensions will be created which were not present before. The question is whether the danger of such a possibility outweighs the likely benefits of parental involvement. The risk can be reduced by establishing certain rules in meetings at the outset (perhaps supported by written explanations and guidelines) and in ongoing discussion. Steps should be taken to ensure that parents are given activities which are suitable for them. Screening parents for general suitability would be divisive and likely to create friction in the parent community; indeed some schools like to involve 'difficult' parents in the belief that their involvement will lead to greater mutual understanding.

Friction is less likely to occur when parents feel that what they are doing is useful and valued by the teacher. While some parents may prefer to contribute to classroom work by helping to prepare teaching materials, those who have expressed an interest in working with pupils are not likely to feel fulfilled if they are simply invited to 'see who needs help'. It is more rewarding to be given specific tasks which, though straightforward, engage the interest of the parent and allow interaction with a particular child or small group of children.

OTHER ADULTS IN SCHOOL

In his Oxfordshire primary schools survey, Thomas (1987) found that many categories of adults besides parents were working with teachers in curriculum activities. Apart from students training to be teachers, these were general ancillaries, welfare assistants, special needs support staff, nursery nurses, and peripatetic specialists such as teachers of English as a second language and speech therapists. There were also young people on government training schemes, students other than those in teacher-training, and voluntary workers. The main reason for involving these extra people in school appeared to be to provide support for children with special educational needs.

A particular interesting development in using adults outside the parent body is the involvement of elderly voluntary helpers. In September 1985 the project 'Open Doors' was set up in Newcastle upon Tyne by Community Service Volunteers 'to recruit and support elderly people in voluntary work in primary schools' (Parker and Davis, 1987). The aims are not just to provide extra pairs of hands but to develop a two-way partnership between the school and the volunteers as a contribution to community education. For the first two years, the participating schools worked closely with CSV, but they are now responsible themselves.

This work is seen as firmly rooted within the primary school curriculum, with the elderly helpers seeing themselves as a natural and integral part of the educational process. Volunteers are located through the social services, voluntary organisations such as Age Concern and Friends to the Elderly, clubs and churches. Besides activities such as story-telling and hearing children read, the helpers are often able to offer a range of skills including those in traditional and dying crafts. They can also make a unique contribution to the children's understanding of the past, as the following example illustrates:

> The explicit aim of one teacher was to teach children how to become historians and not merely to learn facts in chronological order . . . Children were led to books, pictures and museum articles through the recollection of volunteers. They were able to recognise history as an inquiry, not an already established narrative. (Parker and Davis, 1987, p.15)

The children's social education also benefits from their interactions with the volunteers: their perceptions of old age and their feelings and understanding of the needs of the elderly are developed and refined. For the volunteers themselves, physical and mental health is enhanced from being given a sense of purpose: they know they have something to offer and have not become so incapable that they are just a burden on the community. They also enjoy being among children in a warm and friendly environment which helps to close the generation gap between the old and young.

Of course, the school needs to give more support for this group of volunteers than for parents. Some elderly people will be nervous and most will be unfamiliar with current primary practices. The CSV handbook (see Further Reading) therefore emphasises that schools undertaking such work must have a genuine interest in working with elderly people. Given this prerequisite, the potential social and educational benefits for both the children and the old people are undoubtedly considerable.

SUMMARY AND CONCLUSIONS

More and more, teachers are using parents and other volunteers to support curriculum activities in school. It is clear that many teachers and the helpers themselves value the opportunities which such collaboration makes possible: in particular, the pupils are given more individual attention and have access to a range of skills and interests which go beyond what teachers could otherwise provide. Of course, because only certain parents take on this work, it cannot be said to constitute a major contribution to parent–teacher collaboration. Nonetheless, for those assisting, the activities are personally rewarding and helpful in increasing understanding of the school.

Innovatory projects involving elderly people in the classroom represent an important extension of voluntary help in schools. They contribute to pupils' affective education and allow them access to new kinds of learning opportunities whilst providing benefits for elderly people in terms of mental and physical well-being.

It must be borne in mind, however, that voluntary help in school requires managerial skills which not all teachers possess and for which few have received any training. Nor has there been any research to show the extent to which children make greater progress in schoolwork as a result. Given that voluntary help is now taken for granted in so many primary schools, there is a clear need for research on its effectiveness and for formal induction schemes at pre-service and in-service levels.

Further reading

The booklet *Parents in the Classroom* by Gerry Bailey and others (Community Education Development Centre, Coventry, 1982) contains much useful advice for setting up schemes for classroom helpers. A pamphlet of the same title by Renee McQuillan is available from the Professional Association of Teachers.

For an examination of implications arising from the evidence on parent helpers for reading, see the article by Barry Stierer, 'A symbolic challenge: reading helpers in school' in M. and C. Mills (eds) *Language and Literacy in the Primary School* (Falmer Press, 1988).

For specific suggestions on mathematical activities, see *Sharing Mathematics with Parents* (Mathematical Association and Stanley Thornes, 1987.)

Schools wishing to involve elderly people in the classroom should first read *Open Doors* by C. Parker and P. Davis, an illustrated practical guide published by the Health Education Authority and CSV Tyne and Wear, 1987. It is obtainable from CSV, 3rd floor, Exchange Buildings, Quayside, Newcastle upon Tyne NE1 3AQ.

12 | HOME–SCHOOL LIAISON AND PUPIL BEHAVIOUR

HOME BACKGROUND AND PARENT INFLUENCES

Ask any teacher what is the most important influence on children's behaviour and the response in all probability will be 'the home'. In a study of perceptions held by 428 junior school heads and teachers, deficiencies in the child's home circumstances or parenting styles were used to explain two out of every three children who had behavioural, emotional or discipline problems (Croll and Moses, 1985). Similar findings have been reported by Dawson (1987), following a survey of perceptions among teachers in Barnsley.

The recent inquiry into school discipline chaired by Lord Elton (DES, 1989a) also found that teachers were quick to cite the home as a principal source of behaviour problems in school:

> The majority of individual teachers who wrote to us suggested that the attitudes and behaviour of some parents were major causes of bad behaviour by their children in school. We were told that the factors involved ranged from family instability, conflict and poverty to parental indifference or hostility to school. (para.141)

Undoubtedly there is much truth in the general proposition that home influences are of the greatest importance in children's behavioural development (for a brief review, see Docking, 1987). However, the general statement that the home is important in relation to school behaviour needs to be qualified in a number of important respects.

First of all, although pupil behaviour is related to social class, the same does not apply to motivation and attitude to school. The Junior School Project, based on 2000 children in fifty London schools, showed that, according to teachers' assessments, children from semi- and unskilled manual backgrounds had greater behavioural problems in school; on the other hand there was little difference between social classes as regards attendance, attitudes towards school or self-concept (Mortimore et al., 1988; Sammons and Mortimore, 1989). Again, recent evidence from the ORACLE research on 489 pupils in fifty-eight primary and primary/middle schools in the Midlands, showed that while pupils from middle-class backgrounds had higher levels of academic achievements, pupils from different social backgrounds had very similar levels of motivation to work, attitude to school, and involvement in classroom tasks (Croll, 1981).

Secondly, it is important to correct the prevailing view that children from one-parent or black families are more difficult to handle because of those particular background factors, for these are, in turn, associated with material domestic circumstances. Mortimore *et al.*, (1988) found that once economic circumstances had been taken into account, children from one-parent families were no more likely to present behaviour problems in school than those from two-parent families. In the Junior School Project, a higher incidence of behaviour difficulties in school was found among children of Caribbean origin. However, this apparent relationship was probably due to the fact that Caribbean children had underachieved in reading, which itself was significantly related to behaviour. Controlling for reading attainment removed the relationship between ethnicity and behaviour completely. As far as attendance was concerned, Caribbean children had a better record than white children. In all, these considerations suggest no evidence for believing that racial background as such is directly related to the higher incidence of behaviour problems found among black pupils.

Thirdly, it is misleading to think that home background factors are so important that school processes cannot make an impact. The Junior School Project found that striking differences in behavioural standards remained between schools *after* ratings had been adjusted to take account of a range of background factors. Lawrence and Steed (1986) found that among primary schools whose pupils at entry were described as 'difficult' by the local authorities, the proportion of pupils whom the heads perceived as 'disruptive or difficult' in school varied from half of one per cent to 40 per cent. It seems unlikely that a discrepancy of this magnitude was due simply to differences in tolerance levels, and more likely that they reflect different rates of success on the part of the schools. The incidence of bullying also varies considerably between schools, those experiencing the least trouble having clear policies about this problem (Stephenson and Smith, 1989).

Fourthly, it is one thing to acknowledge that parental practices influence children's behaviour in school and another to *blame* parents for unacceptable conduct at school. In some cases, of course, the root of the problem is to do with parents' irresponsible attitudes; but more often it seems to be associated with stress generated by social and economic pressures, poor understanding of parenting skills, and parents' ambivalent feelings about what values should be passed on to children today. While this does not absolve parents of their responsibilities, it does make it difficult for some to fulfil them (DES, 1989).

Lastly, it is important to understand that the better behaved children do not come from homes where they are punished more regularly. Of course, where parents are permissive, setting no clear limits on what will be tolerated or failing to signal pleasure and displeasure, they do nothing to help their children develop sensitivity to others' feelings and often seem to produce disagreeable and offensive children who lack feelings of security and self-worth. At the same time, control which relies on punishment is often counter-productive, not least because the feelings of hurt and humiliation produced prevent children attending to the reasons for the punishment and set up a model of aggression which the child subsequently imitates and views as socially acceptable.

A number of recent studies have indicated the kind of home environment which is conducive to emotional stability and most likely to produce pro-social behaviour and attitudes in children. For instance, the work of Sparkes *et al.* (1984) with three- to six-year-olds and of Hoffman (1970) with twelve-year-olds suggests that children who show concern for others tend to have parents who show the following characteristics:

–they express affection frequently and praise for good behaviour;
–they vary their means of control according to the situation;
–they suggest means of reparation whenever possible;
–they allow scope for genuine choices so that children gain experience in predicting the consequences of their actions;
–they can be assertive and express anger without resorting to physical punishment or making the child feel devalued as a person.

The Elton Committee was therefore right to suggest that parents should provide 'firm but affectionate guidance', 'set a good and consistent example by their own behaviour' and 'avoid permissive or harshly punitive responses to aggression' (DES, 1989, p.136). The Committee properly refrained from reproaching parents who failed to meet these criteria and instead insisted that the requisite skills can be learned through parent education and support by welfare agencies. Attributing all the fault to parents not only creates resentment but renders teachers powerless to effect change in the children's behaviour. A more positive approach involves the school setting up strategies for constructive two-way communication, helping both parents and teachers to manage their children more successfully without resort to regular punishment. The importance of this has been emphasised by David Winkley, who draws on his experience as a junior school head:

> In many cases the unhappy child is deprived of good parenting experiences . . . Any school response which fails to understand this and fails to engage the parents in the subsequent management and support of the child is forgetting a critical element in the jigsaw of the child's needs. It is presumptuous to suppose that the school can resolve issues of disaffection on its own. A first step in helping to make the child happier and more settled will be to enlist the support of parents, and to bring the family as far as possible into the business of managing the child in school. (Winkley, 1989, p.84)

 Home and school need to work together so that each understands the other's perspective and adopts practices which support those of the other in working towards a solution of the problem. The initiative, however, has to be taken by the school. We turn now, therefore, to consider a range of possible approaches.

THE ELTON INQUIRY RECOMMENDATIONS

Following reports of surveys from some of the teacher unions alleging that disruptive behaviour in primary and secondary schools was becoming more violent and prevalent, the Education Secretary in March 1988 set up an inquiry, chaired by Lord Elton, to consider what action should be taken by various parties to secure order in schools. Research commissioned by the Elton Committee and published as part of its report (Gray and Sime in DES, 1989) found the unions' claims exaggerated, but did conclude that in some schools there were frequent incidents of misbehaviour which, though not serious in themselves, cumulatively led to a lack of order and contributed to teacher stress. Of the Committee's many recommendations, we shall concentrate on those relating to home–school liaison.

The link between home–school liaison and standards of behaviour

A set of recommendations in the Elton Report are based on the belief that the level and pervasiveness of parental involvement in the school is related to standards of pupil behaviour. These recommendations reflect issues which have been addressed in the last five chapters of this book, and suggest that good behaviour is better in schools which keep parents informed and develop pro-active home–school liaison policies. More specifically, the Elton Committee advises schools to:

–ensure that their schools provide a welcoming environment for parents;
–encourage parental involvement in the classroom and in home learning schemes;
–produce written communications to parents in a simple, friendly style, with translations for parents whose first language is not English;
–organise effective induction arrangements for parents of new pupils;
–make time available for home visits in liaison with the education welfare service and other agencies; and
–ensure that parent–teacher association activities are accessible and rewarding to as many parents as possible and not just the more articulate.

(Based on recommendations 58–63, 66, 67 and 72)

It will be noted that the above recommendations are about *general* aspects of home–school liaison rather than behaviour policies specifically. The recommendations are consistent with research findings which we have noted earlier, that schools differ in their general 'ethos' and that pupil behaviour is better among those schools which have developed well thought-out policies for developing relationships with parents.

In this context it is worth recalling one particular outcome of partnership schemes in reading, discussed in Chapter 9, that improvement occurred in children's motivation towards learning in general, and not just to reading alone. Involving parents in curriculum activities seems to increase children's interest and confidence in basic school work, and therefore remove one source of poor self-esteem and consequential behaviour problems in school. When parents demonstrate that they both enjoy and value the activity, the child is given a reason for liking schoolwork and taking it seriously. Further, for parents who find it difficult to relate to their children, engagement in a shared activity which both enjoy provides a suitable context for developing a relationship of mutual respect. The meetings which form part of the projects also provide a ready forum for discussing any behavioural problems with parents before they get out of control. In short, working collaboratively with parents in their children's learning facilitates a constructive triangular relationship between parents, teachers and children which has outcomes beyond the immediate objective.

Similar outcomes were noted in the previous chapter which discussed parental involvement in the classroom and other school activities. The presence of more than one adult in the classroom enables children to receive more individual attention and opportunities for immediate feedback and commendation than would otherwise be possible. Additionally, it encourages a greater sense of community and affords more opportunity for parents and teachers to understand each other and to work within a common framework.

Keeping parents informed

The Elton Committeee urged heads to 'ensure that their schools' behaviour policies are communicated fully and clearly to parents, who should be reminded of them regularly and informed of any major changes to them throughout their child's career' (recommendation 64). Another recommendation concerned letters home. Schools often write to parents when a pupil's behaviour is a cause for concern, but rarely when behaviour is especially good. As the Elton Committee comments. 'This must mean that some parents get nothing but negative messages about their children from school . . . It seems likely that they will become hostile to the school rather than being prepared to work with teachers to improve matters' (p.125). The Committee noted a study by Wheldall and Merrett (1988) which had found that, among secondary pupils, a positive letter home was one of two rewards most valued. It therefore recommended 'that headteachers and teachers should ensure that parents receive positive and constructive comments on their children's work and behaviour as a matter of course' (recommendation 57).

Since younger children have a more unilateral respect for adults, it is likely that positive letters home would be especially productive in terms of primary school behaviour. An experiment in an American school with a multiracial class of eight- to nine-year-olds suggests that this is so, at least in the short term. The teachers sent a note to parents whenever a child had observed the classroom rules for a full day, and the parents responded by praising or rewarding the child. Violation of rules was reduced by 80 per cent, increasing somewhat as the notes were phased out but still well below the original level after several weeks (Taylor *et al.*, 1984).

The Elton Committee also noted that schools too often involve parents only as a last resort in behaviour problems, and it advised schools to involve parents at an early stage (recommendation 58). One of the findings of the Junior School Project was that behaviour was better in schools where the head was available at regular times each week to see parents without appointment (Mortimore *et al.*, 1988). This strategy presumably created the opportunity for conduct problems to be discussed before they became serious, as well as facilitating home–school relationships in general. As was noted in Chapter 8, evidence suggests that many parents do not get to hear of their children's bad behaviour at school at an early stage: this is partly because some schools rely on parents using their own initiative to visit teachers, partly because some teachers are hesitant about mentioning behaviour problems lest this be taken as an adverse reflection on their professional competence, and partly because teachers fear that the parents might overreact by punishing their children severely. However, children who are badly behaved at school are not necessarily badly behaved at home, and vice versa (McGee *et al.*, 1984), so that unless parents are informed about disciplinary matters at school they may remain ignorant about them. The risk of parents 'taking it out' on their children is reduced by talking about the reasons for the problem (which might reflect difficulties at school), listening to what parents say about their children while not assuming that they are to blame, and working out an agreed approach. Some ideas presented later in this chapter could help in this respect.

Parental accountability

The Elton Committee noted that, because the minimum age of criminal responsibility is ten, most primary pupils cannot be prosecuted for criminal offences such as attacks on school staff or damage to school property. Although there is no minimum age of civil responsibility, a young child who is successfully sued for damages will not normally have to pay and nor will the parents since (with the exception of employers) a person cannot be held liable for a civil wrong committed by another. The Committee therefore recommended 'that the Government should explore the possibilities for imposing on parents civil liability for their children's acts in school' (recommendation 74).

Whether this strategy would be productive depends on the attitude taken by the courts. Where the parents are negligent, the children in some cases might benefit from legal action which is designed to increase the parental accountability; however, as Elton recognised, it could be more beneficial in appropriate cases if the courts were to arrange family counselling rather than inflict punishment inflexibly. Punitive measures are unlikely to be relevant in cases where parents are under stress or need help in managing their children more effectively.

Liaison with support services

The Elton Inquiry considered the possibility of home visiting, the usefulness of which we discussed in Chapter 8 (see pp.128–31). However, although many teachers have found home visiting useful in developing constructive home–school relationships and in increasing parents' understanding of school processes, their training does not equip them to deal with those parents who neglect or reject their children; and even if they do possess skills of this kind, they have not sufficient time to deal with such cases. Teachers need, therefore, to act in liaison with support services, such as educational welfare officers and psychologists. The Elton Committee noted that many EWOs have excessive case loads and recommended that these should be eased in order that pupils 'at risk' are identified at the earliest possible stage (recommendations 104 and 122). The Committee also suggested that, where possible, EWOs should serve clusters of secondary and related primary schools, thus ensuring continuous contact with families through the children's school careers – though this is not easy in those areas where secondary schools have numerous feeder schools.

To develop a spirit of partnership, it is important that the EWO does not just function as a messenger, explaining the school's position to the parents and relaying information about the home to the teachers. Ideally, the EWO should act as a catalyst in setting up a dialogue between parents and teachers. Some primary schools might find it useful to adopt a strategy employed in the secondary schools of one authority where the EWO, a senior teacher and form tutor meet the parents of new entrants to discuss their roles and the problems which children might meet (Bowdler and Johns, 1982).

Contracts and undertakings

The National Association of Head Teachers had pressed the Elton Committee to recommend the use of home–school 'contracts', which some schools already employ on a voluntary basis. When the child enters school, the parents and head sign a document which sets out what the school will provide for the pupil and parent and what behaviour and effort on the part of the pupil the school requires in return. The Committee, however, rejected the notion of a contract which could be enforced in civil law because it foresaw legal complications: for instance schools would have to prove 'damages' and they would be subject to litigation by parents claiming that teachers had not honoured their side of the contract. Nor was it thought appropriate to recommend that parents be required, as a condition of the entry, to sign a simple undertaking to ensure the child behaved in accordance with the school's policy. Complications were foreseen if a parent refused to sign, and no penalties beyond those already available could be imposed if the undertaking was breached. On the other hand, the Committee did recognise that where a child had been excluded from school, it would be appropriate to make such an undertaking a condition of re-entry (recommendation 65).

FURTHER APPROACHES TO IMPROVING HOME–SCHOOL LIAISON

The ideas presented in the previous section were based on recommendations in the Elton Report, but there are other possibilities too. These can be divided into three categories:

1 Those aimed at improving parenting skills and understanding.
2 Those which involve parents reinforcing the child's efforts to behave well in school.
3 Those in which parents and teachers collaborate in decision-making about strategies to improve children's behaviour.

Some of the illustrations which follow relate only to parents whose children are presenting behaviour problems, while others are about preventive strategies aimed at pupils in general.

Improving parenting skills and understanding

This category includes workshops for parents and teachers, possibly using video feedback and role play, to improve skills in managing children. Wheldall *et al.* (1983) has supplied a colourful booklet for parents which could be used to support such a venture. The booklet explains a series of tactics such as praise, rewards and the modelling of good behaviour in older siblings and friends.

Another possibility is to organise mutual problem-solving groups for parents of children in trouble with their teacher. Coulby and Harper (1985) have shown how these have worked in some primary schools in Tower Hamlets. Meeting weekly, or each day in a single week for more intensive work, the parents were assisted by a teacher, an EWO, and a member of a peripatetic team which had been set up primarily to support teachers experiencing discipline problems. The parents discussed solutions to everyday behaviour difficulties, agreed to try out new responses or make changes to the family routine, and reported how things went to the next meeting. Although there was no formal evaluation, the parents seemed to find the meetings beneficial, partly no doubt because the ideas tried out arose from self-perceived needs in the context of mutual support, and partly because feedback was so immediate. Lickona (1988) has similarly described how some American schools have organised small parent support groups which meet in school or in a parent's home to discuss violence on television, drug abuse and other matters of common concern.

Home–school reinforcement schedules

Home–school reinforcement schedules are used in some local authorities in cases of referals for disruptive behaviour. These schedules are based on behavioural strategies in which conduct is shaped through the setting of clearly defined targets and the systematic use of praise and rewards. In the scheme developed by Martyn Long and others of the West Norfolk School Psychological Service, the procedure in primary schools is along the following lines.

When a child is referred to the Behaviour Support Service, a worker from the service, the class teacher and the parent(s) meet to identify the facts of the situation in a non-judgemental atmosphere. The parents are then invited to support a report system, whereby the school gives daily ratings for the child's behaviour according to agreed, short-term targets. The child monitors his or her own progress in reaching the targets by completing specially illustrated record sheets which have been drawn up to tap the child's interests. For instance, for a child keen on motor-racing, the record sheet might depict a race track, for another who liked animals the sheet might contain a drawing of a zoo: as each stage of the task is successfully completed, the boy or girl colours points on the race track or animals in the zoo. On this basis, the child receives a total score for target achievement each day.

The parents use the daily scores to vary a system of rewards which reflect the child's favourite activities at home, for example watching television or riding a bike: the higher the daily number of points, the greater the reward. The support services also maintain weekly contact with the parent, teacher and child. As the behaviour improves, the scheme is gradually phased out by progressively increasing the time in which targets are to be achieved. The scheme is said to be successful in improving children's on-task behaviour, and parents readily cooperate. It is also more cost-effective than referring children to special units.

In a scheme described by Jacquie and David Coulby (1989), the progress and behaviour of *every* child in the class is monitored by means of a 'Success Card' to which parent, teacher and child make their respective contributions. On the left-hand side of the card is listed the various curriculum activities in which the child is expected to engage, plus some social activities such as 'being friendly in the playground', 'arriving at school on time', 'looking after the classroom'. At the end of each week, the child draws by each item one of three symbols – a star for 'I have done really well', a smiley face for 'I have tried very hard', or a hand showing thumbs down for 'I could have done better'. On the right-hand side of the card there are sections to record the comments of the child, the teacher and the parents. Thus, through quite a simple strategy in which, importantly, the child's perspective is respected, the parent and teacher together monitor progress and provide support.

David Winkley (1989) describes a home-liaison reinforcement scheme which he has used in his Birmingham junior school. This scheme, however, is not directed at school behaviour but conduct at home. The parent and head teacher agree a particular behavioural target, such as going to bed at a reasonable time, with supporting sanctions and rewards. The parent or child completes a record card, which the head sees each morning, thereby supporting the parent by monitoring the child's home behaviour. The procedure also demonstrates to the child that the school and the parents are working systematically in the same direction.

Parent–teacher collaboration in developing behaviour policy

Parents and teachers can also work together in developing policy about school behaviour. A useful illustration comes from Laycock Primary School in Islington,

North London, where the staff were concerned about the extent of fighting, bullying and disobedience in the playground. In 1988 Chris Miles, the Acting Head, launched an experiment in school democracy with the help of two lecturers from the London Institute of Education. All the children from bottom infants to top juniors discussed their attitudes in the classroom, and parents were invited to watch the children act mini-dramas depicting playground behaviour problems such as bullying, swiping balls, and excluding other children from playing. The parents then discussed these incidents with the children, teachers, dinner-helpers and other non-teaching staff. A four-point playtime code was then drawn up by two teaching children from each class. This consisted of promises to be kind and considerate to everybody at playtime, keeping the playground clean, sharing space so that games other than football can be played, and stopping to listen to instructions from adults. The importance of the project is that it tackled a community problem by strategies which gave everyone involved a strong sense of community.

Some American schools have collaborated with parents in the development of personal and social education programmes (Lickona, 1988). In one elementary school parents and teachers jointly produced a 'Family Guide' which gave details of the lessons in a programme for social development, with suggestions for follow up at home. For example, after a lesson for five-year-olds on family responsibilities, the teacher would ask the children to suggest a job they could do to help at home and to draw their suggestions on prepared sheets which, for each day of the week, had spaces for parent and child to write a comment about the way the responsibility was carried out.

BULLYING

In contrast to the widespread concern expressed about pupils' classroom behaviour, remarkably little attention has been given by officials to physical and verbal violence directed by one child against another who is unable to put up an effective defence. Yet, judging from recent evidence, the incident of bullying in primary schools, at any rate among juniors, is worrying. In a sample of 700 eleven-year-olds, 26 per cent of mothers reported that their children were bullied at school and another 22 per cent said they were bullied in the street (Newson and Newson, 1984); and a recent survey among 1078 final year primary pupils in Cleveland revealed that almost a quarter were either bullies or victims of bullying or both, the incidence being higher among boys, and with marked differences between schools (Stephenson and Smith, 1989). In their report for the Elton Inquiry, Gray and Sime (1989) found that while only 1.6 per cent of primary teachers reported that pupil aggression had been directed towards them, 86 per cent reported incidents involving other pupils. Racial harassment is also a cause of concern, according to a recent study by the Commission for Racial Equality (1988).

Scandanavian studies (Roland, 1989) and the Cleveland investigation, reported above, suggest that school policies can be effective in discouraging the bully and helping the victim to be assertive – but only when there is high involvement among the staff. In this respect, it seems enlisting the cooperation of parents is very important. First of all, the school's policies should be drawn up collaboratively with parents. Tattum (1989) suggests that teachers should heighten parental awareness of the extent of bullying, both inside and outside school, by conducting their own surveys and discussing the findings with parents at class meetings (rather like the example given earlier to show the effectiveness of involving parents in reducing playground violence).

Secondly, the cooperation of parents is needed to arrest bullying tendencies in young children since the evidence suggests that these are otherwise likely to persist (Manning *et al.*, 1978; Stephenson and Smith, 1989). As we saw earlier, some parents need help in developing strategies which enable them to deal firmly and consistently with their children's anti-social behaviour. However, any parental involvement should discourage the use of physical and other forms of harsh punishment since the child might model the adult's aggressive behaviour, so exacerbating the problem. From the Cleveland survey, it would seem important to involve the psychological and welfare services where inappropriate parenting styles are seen to be at the root of the child's aggression towards other children.

Stephenson and Smith (1989) suggest that parents can help discourage the aggressive behaviour of bullies by adopting approaches which help both to control and prevent aggression. Aggressive behaviour might be discouraged through methods such as the loss of privileges, while non-aggressive behaviour might be encouraged by enabling the child to experience rewarding relationships through tutoring or caring for younger children. In the case of anxious bullies, who represent a minority of cases, it is suggested that the cooperation of parents can help in boosting self-confidence and social skills.

PUNISHMENT AND EXCLUSION

Corporal punishment

Apart from the work of the Society of Teachers Opposed to Physical Punishment (STOPP), it was pressure from parents which got the law on corporal punishment changed. At the European Court of Human Rights, parents challenged the right of schools in Britain to use physical punishment. The test case was Campbell and Cosans v. The United Kingdom, 1978, brought by two Scottish mothers, one of whom complained that the LEA refused to guarantee that her nine-year-old son would not receive the tawse. In 1982 the Court agreed that the authorities must heed the mothers' 'philosophical convictions'.

It was in response to this judgement that the Secretary of State for Scotland immediately asked local authorities north of the border to ban corporal punishment in their schools. For England and Wales the Government presented a Bill to the House of Commons in 1985. This would have preserved the right of schools to administer corporal punishment, but parents would have been allowed to choose whether their children should be subjected to it. Not surprisingly, a chorus of derision from the parent and teacher organisations greeted this compromise solution which would have involved dividing pupils into beatables and unbeatables! The House of Lords sensibly threw out the 1985 Bill, and during the passage of the 1986 Education Bill introduced a successful amendment to outlaw corporal punishment. The Commons passed this by only one vote – and might not have done that had Conservative members not missed the division bell because of the royal wedding traffic chaos in Parliament Square!

Under the 1986 Education (No. 2) Act (Sect.47) teachers in maintained schools in England, Wales and Scotland who use corporal punishment in any form (including slapping or throwing chalk or rough handling) render themselves open to civil proceedings for battery. Corporal punishment is still not a criminal offence, provided it is moderate and reasonable, but teachers can no longer appeal to the common law defence that they were acting *in loco parentis*. Physical force can be justifiably used in certain circumstances such as self-defence, to prevent a crime, or to break up a fight between pupils (DES Circular 7/87). The Act does not apply to children in private schools, however, except to those on the Assisted Places Scheme or at independent special schools, but it is likely that parental pressure through the European Court will force the Government to ban physical punishment in all schools. EPOCH (End Corporal Punishment of Children) was launched in 1989 to prohibit physical punishment of children in all circumstances, following the example of Sweden, Finland, Denmark, Norway and Austria.

Exclusion

All head teachers have to face the possibility that a pupil who causes serious disruption must be debarred from attending school. At best the process is 'a means of restoring peace, buying time, giving people the chance to say sorry, and signalling that a process of constructive talk begins'; at worst it is 'legalised truancy for the pupil who does not wish to be at school and an excessive punishment for one who does' (Sallis, 1989).

Exclusion involves suspension for a fixed period, indefinitely, or permanently. In the latter case, LEAs are legally bound under the 1944 Act to find the pupil alternative educational provision. The Elton Inquiry into school discipline (DES, 1989) considered indefinite suspension to be an unsatisfactory practice, however, and recommended that heads should require both parents and pupils to sign an agreement which specified the conditions under which an excluded pupil would be re-admitted. Failure to sign would lead to the exclusion being permanent.

The 1986 Education (No. 2) Act for the first time set out the procedures to be followed by all parties in exclusion cases, and it gave parents specific appeal rights (Sects 23–8). Until then parents could usually appeal only to the school governors, who often saw their role as supporting the head teacher. Some authorities had set up independent bodies, but many had no formal mechanism for appeals at all. Where they did, the object was often to censure pupils and parents rather than to reach an unbiased judgement (Ling, 1984).

The statutory procedures which all heads, governors and LEAs must now observe are complicated; but their purpose is to ensure that the power of the head is subjected to the rules of natural justice. First, the Act makes it a duty of the head teacher to inform the parents about their excluded child without delay, setting out the full reasons and stating how long the exclusion is for, or if it is indefinite or permanent. The head must also inform the governors and LEA in cases where the exclusion is more than a total of five days in a term or is permanent. (Ideally, though not required in law, heads should also tell the parent of sources of free independent advice, such as the Advisory Centre for Education or the Children's Legal Centre.)

Secondly, governors have the power to direct reinstatement, as does the LEA except in cases of permanent exclusion from aided schools. The Elton Committee, remembering the controversy surrounding a case in 1985 when pupils who had been excluded from Poundswick Secondary School in Manchester were ordered by the LEA to be reinstated, recognised that reinstatement against a school's will would have damaging effects on staff morale. It therefore recommended that in such cases the LEA/governors and head should each supply a report for the Secretary of State, who could intervene if necessary, using his powers under the 1944 Act.

Thirdly, in the case of a permanent exclusion which the LEA or governors refuse to overturn, the parent has the right of appeal to a local independent appeal committee which can direct a school to reinstate the pupil. Governors may also use this procedure in cases where the LEA orders reinstatement. Local appeal arrangements may also be made for cases of temporary or indefinite exclusions, and LEAs are also free to establish less formal conciliation arrangements.

Local authority associations have since drawn up a code of practice to govern exclusion appeals (Council of Tribunals, 1988). For instance, LEAs are urged to ensure that alternative educational arrangements are discussed with the parents of children permanently excluded, making clear that this does not prejudice rights of appeal. Authorities are also advised to make the atmosphere of appeal hearings informal, giving parents and other parties time to put their case.

The Advisory Centre for Education (1987b) has highlighted the way that suspensions are sometimes used to accelerate referal to special education. This constitutes malpractice. Special needs should be identified before a point of crisis is reached. As ACE points out, it is wrong that pupils should be punished because of their special needs. Nor does it further the cause of partnership between parents and professionals if parents feel pressurised by the educational psychologist into accepting assessment for special needs because their child has been suspended.

SUMMARY AND CONCLUSIONS

This chapter began by discussing the influence of the home on children's behaviour and noted the evidence which demonstrated that, while a child's behavioural patterns are certainly influenced by parenting styles and domestic circumstances, school factors are also of the greatest importance.

It was then argued that standards of behaviour both at home and school can be improved by parents and teachers working together, and various approaches were outlined, including those recommended in the Elton Report. Some of the strategies are essentially preventive and pro-active. These include those improving the quality of home–school relationships in general, informing parents about the school's behaviour expectations, increasing parents' understanding of behaviour issues and ways of managing their children's behaviour, enlisting the cooperation of parents in helping children to develop feelings of responsibility, and involving parents in the decision-making about behaviour matters and social education.

In addition to these strategies which concern *all* parents, it is necessary to have constructive home–school reactive strategies to help individual children who present behaviour problems. These, it was suggested, include: involving parents constructively at an *early* stage to minimise the risk of the problems escalating and becoming difficult to control in the later primary years or in secondary school; agreeing with parents a set of targets to which their child should work; developing a structure to allow the parent to monitor the child's progress and reinforce good behaviour; and liaising with support services. Finally, the legal position affecting home–school liaison in cases of exclusion was explained.

Of course, some parents will not wish to cooperate in schemes of the kind we have been describing; but the experience of those schools which have tried to develop home–school liaison programmes to promote better behaviour is that parents generally respond positively. In any case, as Lickona (1985) comments:

> . . . It doesn't take everybody to make an idea work; it takes only a critical mass . . . Many parents are willing to join forces with schools to help their children grow into good and decent people. That alliance offers the hope of a new and promising era in moral education. (p.38)

Further reading

Although there are now many books on behaviour in school, few of these attend to issues of home–school liaison. The Elton Committee report *Discipline in Schools* (HMSO, 1989), however, devotes a fair amount of space to this area; and Maurice Chazan *et al.*, in *Helping Young Children with Behaviour Difficulties* (Croom Helm, 1983) include clear advice for teachers talking to parents about their children's behaviour.

Penelope Leach (1989) has written a booklet *Smacking – A Short Cut to Nowhere*, arguing the case against the right of parents and others to smack children and suggesting a range of alternative and more effective strategies (EPOCH, PO Box 962, London N22 UX). These arguments are developed by Peter Newell in *Children are People Too: The Case Against Physical Punishment* (Bedford Square Press, 1989), who proposes changes in the law to prohibit parents hitting their children and steps to help parents adopt non-violent, positive methods of control. Positive strategies are also the subject of a colourful and amusingly illustrated booklet *Seven Supertactics for Superparents* by Kevin Wheldall *et al.* (NFER-Nelson, 1983). These publications would make stimulating source material for discussion between teachers and parents.

The Advisory Centre for Education publishes an information sheet *Exclusion for Schools*, and DES Circular 7/87 gives official guidance on corporal punishment and exclusion.

SOURCES OF INFORMATION

ORGANISATIONS FOR PARENTS

All London Parents' Action Group (ALPAG), 39 Dartmouth Road, London NW2 (01–450 1193) (see p.92).

Advisory Centre for Education (ACE), 18 Victoria Park Square, London E2 9PB (01–980 4597) (see p.88).

Campaign for Real Education (CRE), 18 Westlands Grove, Stockton Lane, York YO3 0EF (0904 424134) (see p.92).

Campaign for the Advancement of State Education (CASE), The Grove, High Street, Sawston, Cambridge CB2 4HJ (0223 833179) (see p.86).

Education Alert, PO Box 255, Aberdeen AB9 8EG (see p.90).

Education Otherwise, 25 Common Lane, Hemingford Abbots, Cambridge PE18 9AN (0480 63130) (see p.38).

European Parents' Association, 51 Rue de la Concorde, B–1050 Brussels, Belgium (see p.93).

Home and School Council, 81 Rustlings Road, Sheffield S11 7AB (0742 662467) (see p.84).

Lothian Federation of Parent and Parent Teacher Associations, 35 Dudley Avenue, Edinburgh EH4 6PL (031–554 2076).

National Confederation of Parent Teacher Associations (NCPTA), 2 Ebbsfleet Industrial Estate, Stonebridge Road, Northfleet, Gravesend, Kent DA11 9DS (0474 560618) (see p.84).

Parental Alliance for Choice in Education (PACE), 2 Kingsdown House, Kingsdown, Corsham, Wilts SN14 9AX (0225 742219) (see p.91).

Parents in Partnership (PIP), 2 Woodnook Road, London SW16 6TZ (01–789 4944) (see p.91).

Parent Teacher Association of Wales, Talgoed, Pen y Lon, Mynydd Isa, Yr Wyddgrug, Clwyd CH7 6YG (0352 4652).

Scottish Parent Teacher Association. 30 Rutland Square, Edinburgh EH1 2BW (031–229 2433) (see p.86).

81 Action, 52 Magnaville Road, Bishop's Stortford, Herts CM23 4DW (0279 503244) (see p.91).

COMMUNITY/PARENTS' CENTRES

Community Education Development Centre (CEDC), Briton Road, Coventry CV2 4LF (0203 440814).

Newham Parents' Centre, 743–7 Barking Road, Plaistow, London E13 9ER (01–472 2000).

Partnership in Education, 179 Muirshiel Crescent, Priesthill, Glasgow G53 6PS (041–880 6786).

Parents Support Programme, Department of Education, University of Liverpool, 19 Abercromby Square, PO Box 147, Liverpool L69 3BX (051–709 7312).

ORGANISATIONS FOR GOVERNORS

Action for Governors' Information and Training (AGIT), c/o CEDC, Briton Road, Coventry CV2 4LF (0203 440814).

National Association of Governors and Managers (NAGM), 81 Rustlings Road, Sheffield S11 7AB (0742 662467).

OTHER USEFUL ADDRESSES

Board of Deputies of British Jews Education Department, Woburn House, Tavistock Square, London WC1H 0EP (01–387 3952).

Centre for Studies on Integration in Education (CSIE), 840 Brighton Road, Purley, Surrey CR2 2BH (01–660 8552).

Children's Legal Centre, 20 Compton Terrace, London N1 2UN (01–359 6251).

National Association for Gifted Children, 1 South Audley Street, London W1Y 5DQ (01–499 1188).

Muslim Educational Trust, 130 Stroud Green Road, London N4 3R (01–272 8502).

(**Note**: Some other addresses are given under 'Further Reading' at the end of relevant chapters. The *Parents' Directory* by Fiona Macdonald (Bedford Square Press, 1989) gives details of 800 voluntary organisations which can give help to parents.)

REFERENCES

NB Additional items are given under 'Further Reading' at the end of each chapter.

ADAM SMITH INSTITUTE (1984) *The Omega File: Education Policy 1983–84*. London : Adam Smith Institute.

ADVISORY CENTRE FOR EDUCATION (1987a) The governors' report – a first step. *ACE Bulletin*, 17, 3.

ADVISORY CENTRE FOR EDUCATION (1987b) Suspension: guidance for parents. *ACE Bulletin*, 16, 6–8, 15.

ADVISORY CENTRE FOR EDUCATION (1988) Submission on 'The Regulations on the Keeping and Disclosure of Pupil Records'. London: ACE.

AHLBERG, G. and AHLBERG, A (1988) *Starting School*. London: Viking Kestrel.

ALLEN, L. (1986) Who couldn't care less? *ACE Bulletin*, 14, 8 and 14.

APLING, G. and PUGH. G. (eds) (1983) *Perspectives on Pre-School Home-Visiting*. London: National Children's Bureau.

ARORA, C.M.J. and BAMFORD, J. (1986) Multiply attainments through home support: piloting 'paired number' in an infant school. *Educational and Child Psychology*, 3, 68–74.

ARORA, C.M.J. and BAMFORD, J. (1988) *M.A.T.H.S. Project Handbook*. Huddersfield: Kirklees Psychological Service.

ASHRAF, S.A. (1986) Forward to HALSTEAD, J.M. *The Case for Muslim Voluntary-Aided Schools*. Cambridge: The Islamic Academy.

ASSISTANT MASTERS AND MISTRESSES ASSOCIATION (1988) *Learning to Read – Reading to Learn*. London: AMMA.

ATKIN, J. and BASTIANI, J. (1986) Are they teaching? An alternative perspective on parents as educators. *Education 3–13*, 14, 18–22.

ATKIN, J., BASTIANI, J. with GOODE, J. (1988) *Listening to Parents: An Approach to the Improvement of Home-School Relations*. Beckenham: Croom Helm.

BACON, W. (1978) *Public Accountability and the Schooling System*. London: Harper and Row.

BAILEY, G., BULL, T., FEELEY, G. and WILSON, I. (1982) *Parents in the Classroom*. Coventry: Community Education Development Centre.

BASTIANI, J. (1986) 'Going up to the big school: parents' experience of the transition from primary to secondary schooling' in YOUNGMAN, M.B. (ed.) *Mid-Schooling Transfer: Problems and Proposals*. Windsor: NFER-Nelson.

BASTIANI. J. (1988) 'How many parents did you see last night? A critical look at some of the problems of evaluating home/school practice' in BASTIANI, J. (ed.) (1988) *Parents and Teachers. 2: From Policy to Practice*. Windsor: NFER-Nelson.

BEATTIE, N. (1985) *Professional Parents*. Lewes: Falmer Press.

BECHER, T., ERAUT, M., BOOTH, J., CANNING, T. and KNIGHT, J. (1979) *Accountability in the Middle Years of Schooling*. Final report to the Social Science Research Council.

BECHER, T., ERAULT, M. and KNIGHT, J. (1981) *Policies for Educational Accountability*. London: Heinemann.

BENNETT, A. (1985) Partnership and choice. *Times Educational Supplement*, 1 February.

BENNETT, N., DESFORGES, G., COCKBURN, A. and WILKINSON, B. (1984). *The Quality of Pupil Learning Experiences*. Hillsdale, N.J.: Erlbaum.

BHACHU, P. (1985) Parental Educational Strategies: The Case of Punjabi Sikhs in Britain. Coventry: Centre for Research in Ethnic Relations, University of Warwick.

BIRD, J. and CROSON, B. (1988) 'Involving parents and the wider community', in BASTIANI, J. (ed.) (1988) *Parents and Teachers. 2: From Policy to Practice*. Windsor: NFER-Nelson.

BLATCHFORD, P., BATTLE, S. and MAYS, J. (1982) *The First Transition: Home to Pre-School*. Windsor: NFER-Nelson.

BOARD OF EDUCATION (1931) *Report of the Consultative Committee on the Primary School* (Hadow Report). London: HMSO.

BOWDLER, D. and JOHNS, P. (1982) Non-attendance at school: three approaches, *AEP Journal*, 5, 8.

BRANSTON, P. and PROVIS, M. (1986) *Children and Parents Enjoying Reading: A Handbook for Teachers*. London: Hodder and Stoughton.

BRUNT, M.P. (1987) 'Marketing schools,' in CRAIG, I. (ed.) *Primary School Management in Action*. London: Longman.

CALLAN, E. (1985) McLaughlin on parental rights. *Journal of Philosophy of Education*, 19, 111–27.

CENTRAL ADVISORY COMMITTEE FOR EDUCATION (ENGLAND) (1967) *Children and their Primary Schools* (Plowden Report). London: HMSO.

CENTRAL STATISTICAL OFFICE (1988) *Social Trends 19*. London: HMSO.

CHAPLIN, J. (1987) The power and the product, *Times Educational Supplement*, 4 December.

CHARTERED INSTITUTE OF PUBLIC FINANCE AND ACCOUNTANCY (1988) *Performance Indicators for Schools*. London: CIPFA.

CHAUDBURY, A. (1986) *Annual Report*. London: Advisory Centre for Education.

CLOVER, J. and GILBERT, S. (1981) Parental involvement in the development of language. *Multiethnic Education Review*, London: Inner London Education Authority.

COCKCROFT REPORT (1982) *Mathematics Counts: Report of the Inquiry into the Teaching of Mathematics in Schools*. London: HMSO.

COMBES, G. and CRAFT, A. (1987) *Parents, Schools and Community: Working Together in Health Education*. London: Health Education Council.

COMMISSION FOR LOCAL ADMINISTRATION IN ENGLAND (1988) Report by the Local Ombudsman on an Investigation into Complaint No. 87/C/0779 against Stockport Metropolitan Council.

COMMISSION FOR RACIAL EQUALITY (1987) *Response to the Government's Consultative Paper 'Admission of Pupils to Maintained Schools'*. London: CRE.

COMMISSION FOR RACIAL EQUALITY (1988) *Learning in Terror! A Survey of Racial Harassment in Schools and Colleges*. London: CRE.

COMMITTEE ON CHILD HEALTH SERVICES (1976) *Fit for the Future* (Court Report). London: HMSO.

COMMUNITY EDUCATION DEVELOPMENT CENTRE (1984) *Reading: Involving Parents*. Coventry: CEDC.

COOPERS AND LYBRAND (1988) *Local Management of Schools*.

COULBY, D. and HARPER, T. (1985) *Preventing Classroom Disruption*. Beckenham: Croom Helm.

COULBY, J. and COULBY, D. (1989) 'Intervening in junior classrooms,' in DOCKING, J.W.

(ed.) *Education and Alienation in the Junior School*. Lewes: Falmer Press.

COUNCIL OF TRIBUNALS (1988) *Code of Practice on Schools Exclusion Appeals*. London: Council of Tribunals.

CRAFT, M., RAYNOR, J. and COHEN, L. (eds) (1980) *Linking Home and School*, 3rd edition. London: Harper and Row.

CROLL, P. (1981) Social class, pupil achievement and classroom interaction, in SIMON, B. and WILLCOCKS, J. (eds) *Research and Practice in the Primary Classroom*. London: Routledge and Kegan Paul.

CROLL, P. and MOSES, D. (1985) *One in Five*. London: Routledge and Kegan Paul.

CULLINGFORD, C. (1984) The battle for schools: attitudes of parents and teachers towards education. *Educational Studies*, 10, 113–19.

CUNNINGHAM, C.C. (1983) 'Early support in intervention: the HARC Infant Project,' in MITTLER, P. and McCONACHIE, H. (eds) *Parents, Professionals and Mentally Handicapped People: Approaches to Partnership*. Beckenham: Croom Helm.

CZERNIEWSKA, P. (1988) Parents and writing. *ACE Bulletin*, 25, 7–10.

DARLING, J. (1986) Parents, teachers and the messages of the experts, *Universities Quarterly*, 40, 21–30.

DAVIE, C.E., HUTT, S.J., VINCENT, E. and MASON, M. (1988) *The Young Child at Home*. Windsor: NFER-Nelson.

DAVIS, C. and STUBBS, R. (1988) *Shared Reading in Practice*. Milton Keynes: Open University Press.

DAVIS, J. (1988) Evaluating an LEA approach: the Liverpool Parent Support Programme, in BASTIANI, J. (ed.) (1988) *Parents and Teachers. 2: From Policy to Practice*. Windsor: NFER-Nelson.

DAWSON, R. (1987) 'What concerns pupils about their teachers', in HASTINGS, N. and SCHWIESO, J. (eds) *New Directions in Educational Psychology: 2 – Behaviour and Motivation in the Classroom*. Lewes: Falmer Press.

DAWSON, R. and KIERNEY, J. (1988) A survey of parents' views, *British Journal of Special Education*, 15, 123–5.

DEPARTMENT OF EDUCATION AND SCIENCE (1975) *A Language for Life* (Bullock Report). London: HMSO.

DEPARTMENT OF EDUCATION AND SCIENCE (1977) *A New Partnership for Our Schools* (Taylor Report). London: HMSO.

DEPARTMENT OF EDUCATION AND SCIENCE (1978) *Special Educational Needs* (Warnock Report). London: HMSO.

DEPARTMENT OF EDUCATION AND SCIENCE (1984) *Parental Influence at School: A New Framework for School Government in England and Wales* (Cmnd 9242). London: HMSO.

DEPARTMENT OF EDUCATION AND SCIENCE (1985a) *Better Schools* (Cmnd 9469). London: HMSO.

DEPARTMENT OF EDUCATION AND SCIENCE (1985b) Homework: Note by the DES.

DEPARTMENT OF EDUCATION AND SCIENCE (1988a) *National Curriculum: Task Group on Assessment and Testing: A Report*. London: HMSO.

DEPARTMENT OF EDUCATION AND SCIENCE (1988b) *National Curriculum: Task Group on Assessment and Testing: Three Supplementary Reports*. London: HMSO.

DEPARTMENT OF EDUCATION AND SCIENCE (1989) *Discipline in Schools* (Elton Report). London: HMSO.

DEUTSCH, D. (1987) Kids don't have to go to school, ACE Bulletin, 18, 6–8.

DOCKING, J.W. (1987) *Control and Discipline in Schools: Perspectives and Approaches*. London: Harper and Row/Paul Chapman Publishing.

DOWLING, E. (1985) 'Theoretical framework – a joint systems approach to educational problems with children' in DOWLING, E. and OSBORNE, E. *The Family and the School: A Joint Systems Approach to Problems with Children.* London: Routledge and Kegan Paul.

DYE, S. (1989) Parental involvement in curriculum matters. *Educational Research*, 31, 20–35.

DYSON, S. (1987) 'Reasons for assessment: rhetoric in the assessment of children with disabilities' in BOOTH, T. and SWANN, W. (eds) *Including Pupils with Disabilities.* Milton Keynes: Open University Press.

EARLEY, P. (ed.) (1988) *Governors' Reports and Annual Parents' Meetings: the 1986 Act and Beyond.* Slough: NFER.

ELLIOT, J. (1981) 'How do parents choose and judge secondary schools?' in ELLIOTT, J., BRIDGES, D., EBUTT, D., GIBSON, R. and NIAS, J. *School Accountability: the SSRC Cambridge Accountability Project.* London: Grant McIntyre.

FLETCHER, M. (1989) Resolving to do better. *Times Educational Supplement*, 25 January.

FLEW, A. (1987) *Power to Parents: Reversing Educational Decline.* London: Sherwood Press.

FORBAT, G. (1988) Winning friends and influencing people. *Times Educational Supplement*, 16 December.

GARDNER, P. (1988) Religious upbringing and the liberal ideal of religious autonomy. *Journal of Philosophy of Education*, 22, 89–106.

GAY, J.D. (1988) *Opting Out: Grant-Maintained Primary Schools.* Abingdon: Culham Educational Foundation.

GINSBURG, H. (1972) *The Myth of the Deprived Child.* New Jersey: Prentice Hall.

GLIEDMAN, J. and ROTH, W. (1981) 'Parents and professionals' in SWANN, W. (ed.) *The Practice of Special Education.* Oxford: Basil Blackwell/Open University.

GLYNN, T. (1980) 'Parent-child interaction in remedial teaching at home,' in CLARK, M.M. and GLYNN, T. (eds) *Reading and Writing for the Child with Difficulties.* Birmingham: University of Birmingham Faculty of Education.

GOACHER, B., EVANS, J., WELTON, J. and WEDELL, K. (1988) *Policy and Provision for Special Educational Needs: Implementing the 1981 Education Act.* London: Cassell.

GOACHER, B. and REID, M.I. (1983) *School Reports to Parents.* Windsor: NFER-Nelson.

GOLBY, M. and LANE, B. (1988) *The New School Governors.* Tiverton, Devon: Fair Way Publications.

GOLDSTEIN, H. and CUTTANCE, P. (1988) A note on national assessments and school comparisons. *Journal of Educational Policy*, 3, 197–202.

GRASSIE, M. (1987) Parents should keep out of the classroom. *Sunday Times*, 7 June.

GRAY, J. and SIME, N. (1989) 'Findings from the National Survey of Teachers in England and Wales,' in DEPARTMENT OF EDUCATION AND SCIENCE (1989) *Discipline in Schools* (Elton Report). London: HMSO.

GREEN, C. (1987) Parental facilitation of young children's writing. *Early Child Development and Care*, 28. 129–36.

GREENING, M. and SPENCELY, J. (1987) Shared reading: support for inexperienced readers. *Educational Psychology in Practice*, 3. 31–7.

GRIFFITHS, A. and HAMILTON, D. (1984) *Parent, Teacher, Child: Working Together in Childen's Learning.* London: Methuen.

GRIFFITHS, A. and HAMILTON, D. (1985) Parent-teacher cooperation over reading in a junior school. *Early Child Development and Care*, 20, 5–16.

HALL, N. (1989) *Parental Views on Writing and the Teaching of Writing.* Didsbury: Department of Educational Studies, Manchester Polytechnic.

HALSTEAD, J.M. (1986) *The Case for Muslim Voluntary-Aided Schools: Some Philosophical*

Reflections. Cambridge: The Islamic Academy.

HAMMOND, J. (1989) Beating opting out. *Forum*, 36–7.

HANCOCK, R. (1987) *Parental Involvement in Children's Reading: Results of a Survey of Brent Primary School Headteachers*. London: Brent Learning Resources Services.

HANNON, P. (1986) Teachers' and parents' experiences of parental involvement in the teaching of reading. *Cambridge Journal of Education*, 16, 28–36.

HANNON, P. (1987) Parental involvement – a no-score draw? *Times Educational Supplement*, 3 April.

HANNON, P. (1989) How should parental involvement in the teaching of reading be evaluated? *British Education Research Journal*, 15, 33–40.

HANNON, P. and JACKSON, A. (1987a) *The Belfield Reading Project: Final Report*. London: National Children's Bureau.

HANNON, P. and JACKSON, A. (1987b) Educational home visiting and the teaching of reading. *Educational Research*, 29, 182–91.

HANNON, P., JACKSON, A. and WEINBEGER, J. (1986) Parents' and teachers' strategies in teaching young children to read. *Research Papers in Education*, 1, 6–25.

HANNON, P. and McNALLY, J. (1986) Children's understanding and cultural factors in reading test performance. *Educational Review*, 38, 237–46.

HANNON, P., WEINBERGER, J., PAGE, B. and JACKSON, A. (1986) Home-school communication by means of reading cards. *British Journal of Research Education*, 12, 269–80.

HAVILAND, J. (ed.) (1988) *Take Care, Mr Baker!* London: Fourth Estate.

HER MAJESTY'S INSPECTORATE FOR SCHOOL (1985) *Report by Her Majesty's Inspectors on the Effects of Local Authority Expenditure Policies on Education Provision in England, 1984*. London: DES.

HER MAJESTY'S INSPECTORATE FOR SCHOOL (1987) *Education Observed 4: Homework*. London: DES.

HEWISON, J. (1988) The long-term effectiveness of parental involvement in reading: a follow-up to the Haringey reading project. *British Journal of Educational Psychology*, 58, 184–90.

HEWISON, J. and TIZARD, J. (1980) Parental involvement and reading attainment. *British Journal of Educational Psychology*, 50, 209–15.

HEYNES, B. and CATSAMBIS, S. (1986) Mothers' employment and children's achievement: a critique. *Sociology of Education*, 59, 140–51.

HILLGATE GROUP (1986) *Whose Schools? A Radical Manifesto*. London: Hillgate Group.

HIRST, P.H. (1985) 'Education and the diversity of belief,' in FELDERHOF, M.C. (ed.) *Religious Education in a Pluralist Society*. London: Hodder and Stoughton.

HISKETT, M. (1989) *Schooling for British Muslims: Integrated, Opt Out or Denominational?* London: Social Affairs Unit.

HODDMAN, M.L. (1970) Conscience, personality and socialization. *Human Development*, 13, 90–126.

HOUSE OF COMMONS (1987) *Implementation of the Education Act 1981 – 3rd Report from the Education, Science and Arts Committee*. London: HMSO.

HOWARD, S. and HOLLINGSWORTH, A. (1985) Linking home and school in theory and practice. *Journal of Community Education*, 4, 12–17.

HUGHES, M. (1986) Early education and the community (1). *Scottish Educational Review*, 18, 31–67.

INNER LONDON EDUCATION AUTHORITY (1984) *Improving Secondary Schools* (Hargreaves Report). London: ILEA.

INNER LONDON EDUCATION AUTHORITY (1985a) *Improving Primary Schools* (Thomas Report). London: ILEA.

INNER LONDON EDUCATION AUTHORITY (1985b) *Parents and Primary Schools* (RS987/85). London: ILEA Research and Statistics Branch.

INNER LONDON EDUCATION AUTHORITY (1985c) *Educational Opportunities for All?* (Fish Report). London: ILEA.

INNER LONDON EDUCATION AUTHORITY (1985d) *Secondary Transfer Project: Bulletin No. 3 – The Views of Parents before Transfer* (RS990/85). London: ILEA Research and Statistics Branch.

INNER LONDON EDUCATION AUTHORITY (1988) *The Hackney Literacy Study* (RS1175/88). London: Research and Statistics Branch, ILEA.

INSTITUTE OF ECONOMIC AFFAIRS EDUCATION UNIT (1989) *Opting to Grant-Maintained Status*. London: IEA.

JEFFRIES, G. and STREATFIELD, D. (1989) *Reconstitution of School Governing Bodies*. Slough: National Foundation of Educational Research.

JOHNSON, D. (1987) *Private Schools and State Schools: Two Systems or One?* Milton Keynes: Open University Press.

JOHNSON, D. and RANSOM, E. (1980) 'Parents' perceptions of secondary schools,' in CRAFT, M., RAYNOR, J. and COHEN, L. (eds) *Linking Home and School: A New Review*. London: Harper and Row.

JOWETT, S. and BAGINSKY, M. (1988) Parents and education: a survey of their involvement and a discussion of some issues. *Educational Research*, 30, 36–45.

KOGAN, M. (1984) Over the top. *Times Educational Supplement*, 8 June.

KOGAN, M., JOHNSON, D., PACKWOOD, T. and WHITAKER, T. (1984) *School Governing Bodies*. London: Heinemann.

LABOUR PARTY (1988) *Parents in Partnership*. London: Labour Party.

LAWLOR, S. (1988) *Opting Out: A Guide to How and Why*. London: Centre of Policy Studies.

LAWRENCE, J and STEED, D. (1986) Primary school perceptions of disruptive behaviour. *Educational Studies*, 12, 147–57.

LICKONA, T. (1988) How parents and schools can work together to raise moral children. *Educational Leadership*, May, 36–8.

LING, R. (1984) 'A suspended sentence: the role of the LEA in the removal of disruptive pupils from school', in SCHOSTAK, J.F. and LOGAN, T. (eds) *Pupil Experience*. Beckenham: Croom Helm.

MACLEOD, F. (1985) *Parents in Partnership: Involving Muslim Parents in their Children's Education*. Coventry: Community Education Development Council.

MACLURE, S. (1988) *Education Re-formed: A Guide to the Education Reform Act 1988*. London: Hodder and Stoughton.

MAHONEY, T. (1988) *Governors, Accountability and Parents: A Report based on a Sample of Governors' Experiences in Leicestershire and Derbyshire in 1987*. Nottingham: Workers' Educational Association.

MANCHESTER CITY COUNCIL (1988) *Profiling for Children of Primary School Age*.

MANNING, N., HERON, J., and MARSHALL, T. (1978) 'Styles of hostility and social interactions at nursery, at school and at home,' in HERSOV, L.A. and BERGER, M. (eds) *Aggression and Anti-Social Behaviour in Childhood and Adolescence*. Oxford: Pergamon Press.

MARLAND, M. (1984) Could do better: how schools liaise with parents. *Westminster Studies in Education*, 7, 45–55.

MASON, S.C.W. (1986) Islamic separatism? *British Journal of Religious Education*, 8, 109–12.

McCAIL, G. (1981) *Mother Start*. Edinburgh: Scottish Council for Research in Education.

McGEE, R., SILVA, P.A. and WILLIAMS, S. (1984) Behaviour problems in a population of seven-year-old children: prevalence, stability and types of disorder – a research report. *Journal of Child Psychology and Psychiatry*, 25, 251–9.

McGEENEY, P. (1969) *Parents are Welcome*. London: Longman.

McLAUGHLIN, T.H. (1984) Parental rights and the religious upbringing of children. *Journal of Philosophy of Education*, 18, 75–84.

McLAUGHLIN, T.H. (1985) Religion, upbringing and liberal values: a rejoinder to Eamonn Callan. *Journal of Philosophy of Education*, 19, 119–27.

McQUILLAN, R. (1987) *Parents in the Classroom*. Derby: Professional Association of Teachers.

MEIGHAN, R. (1981) A new teaching force? Some issues raised by seeing parents as educators and the implications for teacher education. *Educational Review*, 33, 133–42.

MERTTENS, R. and VASS, J. (1987) Parents in school: raising money or raising standards? *Education 3–13*, 15(2), 23–7.

MERTTENS, R. and VASS, J. (1988) *The IMPACT project and the National Curriculum*. London: Polytechnic of North London.

MIDWINTER, E. (1984) The 24 hour service. *Times Educational Supplement*, 12 October.

MILLER, A., ROBSON, D. and BUSHELL, R. (1985) 'The development of paired reading in Derbyshire,' in TOPPING, K. and WOLFENDALE, S. (1985) *Parental Involvement in Children's Reading*. Beckenham: Croom Helm.

MILNE, A., MYERS, D., ROSENTHAL, A. and GINSBURG, A. (1986) Single parents, working mothers, and the educational achievement of school children, *Sociology of Education*, 59, 125–39.

MITTLER, P. and BEASLEY, D. (1982) *A Multi-National Family Training Workshop*. Brussels: International League of Societies for Persons with Mental Handicap.

MITTLER, P. and McCONACHIE, H. (eds) (1983) *Parents, Professionals and Mentally Handicapped People*. Beckenham: Croom Helm.

MORE, T.W. (1966) Difficulties of the ordinary child in adjusting to primary school. *Journal of Child Psychology and Psychiatry*, 7, 17–38.

MORGAN, R.T.T. (1976) Paired reading tuition: a preliminary report on a technique for cases of reading deficit. *Child-Care Health and Development*, 2, 13–28.

MORGAN, R. and GAVIN, P. (1987) Paired reading: evaluation and progress. *Support for Learning*, 3, 201–6.

MORTIMORE, P., SAMMONS, P., STOLL, L., LEWIS, D. and ECOB, R. (1988) *School Matters: The Junior Years* Wells: Open Books.

MOSES, D. and CROLL, P. (1987) Parents as partners or problems. *Disability, Handicap and Society*, 2., 75–84.

MUNN, P. (1985) Accountability and parent-teacher communication. *British Education Research Journal*, 11, 105–11.

NATIONAL ASSOCIATION OF GOVERNORS AND MANAGERS (1975) *School Managers: Some Facts and Figures*. London: NAGM.

NATIONAL ASSOCIATION OF GOVERNORS AND MANAGERS (1989) *Survey on LEA Provision for Governors' Training*. London: NAGM.

NATIONAL ASSOCIATION OF HEAD TEACHERS (1978) *The NAHT's Commentary on the Taylor Report*. Haywards Heath: NAHT.

NATIONAL ASSOCIATION OF HEAD TEACHERS (1988) *Home-School Contract of Partnership: A Discussion Paper*. Haywards Heath: NAHT.

NATIONAL CONFEDERATION OF PARENT-TEACHER ASSOCIATIONS (1985) *The State of Schools in England and Wales*. Gravesend: NCPTA.

NATIONAL CONFEDERATION OF PARENT-TEACHER ASSOCIATIONS (1986) *Parent-Partners in a Shared Task of Education*. Gravesend: NCPTA.

NATIONAL CONSUMER COUNCIL (1986) *The Missing Link between Home and School: A Consumer View*. London: NCC.

NATIONAL CURRICULUM ENGLISH WORKING GROUP (1989) *English for Ages 5 to 16*. London: DES/Welsh Office.

NATIONAL SOCIETY (1988) *Grant-Maintained Status and the Church School*. London: National Society.

NATIONAL UNION OF TEACHERS (1987) *Pupils, Teachers and Parents*. London: NUT.

NAYBOUR, S. (1985) The changing role of home-school associations. *Parents and Schools*, 43, 3.

NEWELL, P. (1983) 1981 Act: no parents' charter on choice appeals. *Where*, 185, 4–5.

NEWSON, J. and NEWSON, E. (1984) Parents' perspectives on children's behaviour in school, in FRUDE, N. and GAULT, G. (eds) *Disruptive Behaviour in Schools*. Chichester: John Wiley.

NIAS, J. (1981) 'The nature of trust' in ELLIOTT, J., BRIDGES, D., EBUTT, D., GIBSON, R. and NIAS, J. *School Accountability: the SSRC Cambridge Accountability Project*. London: Grant McIntyre.

OLAFSON, F.A. (1973) 'Rights and duties in education' in DOYLE, J.F. (ed.) *Educational Judgements*. London: Routledge and Kegan Paul.

PAIRED READING PROJECT (1987) *Paired Reading Training Pack*. Huddersfield: Kirklees Psychological Services.

PARKER, C. and DAVIS, P. (1987) *Open Doors: Elderly People as Volunteers in Primary Schools*. Newcastle-Upon-Tyne: Health Education Authority and Community Service Volunteers.

PEACH, R. (1987) Ending monopoly master plans. *Times Educational Supplement*, 6 November.

PERRY, J. and SIMMONS, K. (1987) 'Shared maths': a successful home-school project. *Support for Learning*, 2, 9–12.

PETCH, A. (1986) Parental choice at entry to primary school. *Research Papers in Education*, 1, 26–47.

POLLARD, M. (1986) A parent's place. *Junior Education*, February, 8–9.

PRYKE, J. (1989) Slow off the mark. *Times Educational Supplement*, 12 May.

PUGH, G. (1983) *Perspectives on Pre-School Home Visiting*. London: National Children's Bureau and Coventry Community Education Centre.

PUGH, G. (1985) 'Parents and professionals in partnership: issues and implications,' in PUGH, G. (ed.) *Parental Involvement: What does it mean and how do we achieve it?* Partnership Paper No. 2. London: National Children's Bureau

PUGH, G., APLIN, G., DE'ATH, E. and MOXON, M. (1987) *Partnership in Action: Working with Parents in Pre-School Centres*. London: National Children's Bureau.

RAAB, G.M. and ADLER, M. (1987) A tale of two cities: the impact of parent choice on admissions to primary schools in Edinburgh and Dundee. *Research Papers in Education*, 2, 157–76.

RAMPTON REPORT (1981) *West Indian Children in Our Schools*. London: HMSO.

RANSON, S., HANNON, V. and GRAY, J. (1987) 'Citizens or consumers: policies for school accountability', in WALKER, S. and BARTON, L. (eds) *Changing Policies, Changing Teachers: New Directions for Schooling?* Milton Keynes: Open University Press.

RAVEN, J. (1980) *Parents, Teachers and Children: A Study of an Educational Home Visiting Scheme*. London: Hodder and Stoughton.

REEVES, F. and CHEVANNE, M. (1983) The ideological construction of black underachievement. *Multiracial Education*, 12, 22–41.

REHAL, A. (1989) Involving Asian parents in the statementing procedure: the way forward. *Educational Psychology in Practice*, 4, 189–97.

REID, J. (1987) A problem in the family: explanations under strain, in BOOTH, T. and COULBY, D. (eds) *Producing and Reducing Disaffection*. Milton Keynes: Open University Press.

RENNIE, J. (1985) Community primary schools: their origins and development, in RENNIE, J. (ed.) *British Community Primary Schools*. Lewes: Falmer Press.

REX, J. and TOMLINSON, S. (1979) *Colonial Immigrants in a British City: A Class Analysis*. London: Routledge and Kegan Paul.

ROBERTS, B., BAKER, L. and GRIFFITHS, J. (1988) *School Governor Training: A Report to the Department of Education and Science*. Slough: National Foundation for Educational Research.

ROLAND, E. (1989) *Bullying in Schools: An International Perspective*. London: David Fulton.

RUNDALL, R.D. and SMITH, S.L. (1982) 'Working with difficult parents,' in BRIGHAM YOUNG UNIVERSITY PRESS (ed.) *How to Involve Parents in Early Education*. Provo, Utah: Brigham Young University Press.

RUSSELL, P. (1983) The Education Act 1981, *Concern*, 49, 6–13.

SALLIS, J. (1982) 'Beyond the market place: a parent's view,' in McCORMICK, R. (ed.) *Calling Education to Account*. London: Heinemann/Open University Press.

SALLIS, J. (1988) *Schools, Parents and Governors: A New Approach to Accountability*. London: Routledge and Kegan Paul.

SALLIS, J. (1989) Wrong to exclude. *Times Educational Supplement*, 9 June.

SAMMONS, P. and MORTIMORE, P. (1989) 'Pupil achievement and pupil alienation in the junior school,' in DOCKING, J. (ed.) (1989) *Education and Alienation in the Junior School*. Lewes: Falmer Press.

SARWAR, G. (1988) *What Can Muslims Do?* London: The Muslim Educational Trust.

SCOTTISH EDUCATION DEPARTMENT (1987) *School Management and the Role of Parents: Consultation Paper*. Edinburgh: SED.

SCRUTON, R. (1980) *The Meaning of Conservatism*. Harmondsworth: Penguin.

SELDON, A. (1986) *The Riddle of the Voucher*. London: Institute of Economic Affairs.

SELLICK, M.D.L. (1985) Parents' organisations and the articulation of wishes for secondary schooling. *Comparative Education*, 21, 47–65.

SEXTON, S. (1987) *Our Schools: A Radical Policy*. London: Institute of Economic Affairs.

SHARPE, L. (1980) Parent-school relations: a reconceptualization. Ph.D thesis, University of Sussex.

SKELTON, M. (1987) Parent power. *Times Educational Supplement*, 6 March.

SOUTHGATE, V., ARNOLD, A. and JOHNSON, S. (1981) *Extending Beginning Reading*. London: Heinemann.

SPARKS, A.D., THORNBURG, K.R., IPSA, J.M. and GRAY, M.M. (1984) Pro-social behaviours of young children related to parental childrearing attitudes. *Early Child Development and Care*, 15, 291–8.

STEPHENSON, P. and SMITH, D. (1989) 'Bullying in the junior school,' in TATTUM, D. and LANE, D. (eds) *Bullying in Schools*. Stoke-on-Trent: Trentham Books.

STEVENS, C. (1984) 'All parents as a resource for education,' in HARBER, C., MEIGHAN, R. and ROBERTS, B. (eds) *Alternative Educational Futures*. London: Holt, Rinehart and Winston.

STEIRER, B. (1985) School reading volunteers: results of a postal survey of primary school headteachers in England. *Journal of Research in Reading*, 8, 21–31.

STIERER, B. (1988) A symbolic challenge: reading helpers in school, in MILLS, M. and MILLS, C. (eds) *Language and Literacy in the Primary School*. Lewes: Falmer Press.

STILLMAN, A. (1986) Preference or choice? Parents, LEAs and the Education Act 1980. *Educational Research*, 28, 3–13.

STILLMAN, A. (1988) Parents and politics: choice and education, in BASTIANI, J. (ed.) *Parents and Teachers. 2: From Policy to Practice*. Windsor: NFER-Nelson.

SUTCLIFFE, J. (1986) Report calls for appointment of parent advisers. *Times Educational Supplement*, 31 October.

SUTTON CAMPAIGN FOR STATE EDUCATION (1989) *The Primary School Guide*. Sutton, Surrey: Sutton CASE.

SWANN REPORT (1985) *Education For All* (Report of the Committee of Enquiry into the Education of Children from Ethnic Minority Groups). London: HMSO.

TATTUM, D. (1989) Violence and aggression in schools, in TATTUM, D. and LANE, D. (eds) *Bullying in Schools*. Stoke-on-Trent: Trentham Books.

TAYLOR, D. (1983) *Family Literacy: Young Children Learning to Read and Write*. London: Heinemann Educational.

TAYLOR, M.J. (1981) *Caught Between: A Review of Research into the Education of Pupils of West Indian Origin*. Windsor: NFER-Nelson.

TAYLOR, M.J. (1986) *Chinese Pupils in Britain*. Windsor: NFER-Nelson.

TAYLOR, M.J. (1988) *Worlds Apart? A Review of Research into the Education of Pupils of Cypriot, Italian, Ukranian and Vietnamese Origin, Liverpool Blacks and Gypsies*. Windsor: NFER-Nelson.

TAYLOR, M.J. and HEGARTY, S. (1985) *The Best of Both Worlds . . .? A Review of Research into the Education of Pupils of South Asian Origin*. Windsor: NFER-Nelson.

TAYLOR, V.L., DEBORAH, D.C. and RILEY, M.T. (1984) Home-based contingency management programs that teachers can use. *Psychology in the Schools*, 21, 368–74.

THOMAS, G. (1987) Extra people in the classroom. *Educational Research*, 29, 173–81.

TIZARD, B. (1987) Parent involvement – a no-score draw? *Times Educational Supplement*, 3 April.

TIZARD, B., BLATCHFORD, P., BURKE, J., FARQUHAR, C. and PLEWIS, I. (1988) *Young Children and School in the Inner City*. Hove: Lawrence Erlbaum.

TIZARD, B. and HUGHES, M. (1984) *Young Children's Learning*. London: Fontana.

TIZARD, B. and MORTIMORE, J. and BURCHELL, B. (1981) *Involving Parents in Nursery and Infant Schools*. London: Grant McIntyre.

TIZARD, J. SCHOFIELD, W.N. and HEWISON, J. (1982) Collaboration between teachers and parents in assisting children's reading. *British Journal of Educational Psychology*, 52, 1–15.

TOMLINSON, J. (Chairman) (1987) *Informing Education: Report of the Committee of Inquiry into Freedom of Information*. London: ILEA.

TOMLINSON, S. (1984) *Home and School in Multicultural Britain*. London: Batsford.

TOPPING, K. (1987) Paired reading: a powerful technique for parent use. *The Reading Teacher*, 40, 608–15.

TOPPING, K. and WOLFENDALE, S. (eds) (1985) *Parental Involvement in Children's Reading*. Beckenham: Croom Helm.

TRAVERS, T. (1988) Who raises the dough? *Times Educational Supplement*, 15 July.

USHER, R. (1985) 'The public school' in BLATCHFORD, R. (ed.) *Managing the Secondary School*. London: Bell and Hyman.

VAUGHAN, M. (1989) Fish in troubled waters. *Times Educational Supplement*, 10 March.

WALLER, W. (1932) *The Sociology of Teaching*. New York: John Wiley.

WARNOCK, M. (1985) Teacher teach thyself. *The Listener*, 28 March.

WEEKS, A. (1987) School information brochures: a primary school survey, *Cambridge Journal of Education*, 17, 61–2.

WELLS, G. (1980) 'Talking with children: the complementary roles of parents and teachers', in REEDY, S. and WOODHEAD, M. (eds) *Family, Work and Education*. London: Hodder and Stoughton.

WELLS, G. (1984) *Language Development in the Pre-School Years*. Cambridge: Cambridge University Press.

WHELDALL, K. and MERRETT, F. (1988) Discipline: rewarding work. *Teachers' Weekly*, 16 May, 25–7.

WHELDALL, K., MERRETT, F. and COLMAS, S. (1987) 'Pause, prompt and praise' for parents and peers: effective tutoring of low progress readers. *Support for Learning*, 2, 5–12.

WHELDALL, K., WHELDALL, D. and WINTER, S. (1983) *Seven Supertactics for Superparents*. Windsor: NFER-Nelson.

WHITE, J. (1976) Teacher accountability and school autonomy, in FINCH, A. and SCRIMSHAW, P. (eds) *Standards, Schooling and Education*. London: Hodder and Stoughton.

WHITE, J. (1982) *The Aims of Education Restated*. London: Routledge and Kegan Paul.

WHITE, J. (1988) An unconstitutional national curriculum, in LAWTON, D. and CHITTY, C. (eds) *The National Curriculum*. Bedford Way Paper 33. London: University of London Institute of Education.

WHITE, P. (1983) *Beyond Domination*. London: Routledge and Kegan Paul.

WHITEHEAD, J. and AGGLETON, P. (1986) Participation and popular control on school governing bodies: the case of the Taylor Report and its aftermath. *British Journal of Sociology of Education*, 7, 433-49.

WIDLAKE, P. (1986) *Reducing Educational Disadvantage*. Milton Keynes: Open University Press.

WINKLEY, D. (1989) 'The management of children's emotional needs in the primary school' in DOCKING, J.W. (ed.) *Education and Alienation in the Junior School*. Lewes: Falmer Press.

WOLFENDALE, S. (1988) *The Parents' Contribution: Issues in Statementing Children with Emotional and Behavioural Problems – A Multi-Disciplinary Approach*. Windsor: NFER-Nelson.

WOODS, P. (1984) *Parents and Schools: A Report for Discussion on Liaison between Parents and Secondary Schools in Wales*. London: Schools Council Publications.

WOODS, P. (1988) A strategic view of parent participation. *Journal of Education Policy*, 3, 323–34.

WORSLEY, M. (1986) Parental reactions to an induction programme, in YOUNGMAN, M.B. (ed.) *Mid-Schooling Transfer: Problems and Proposals*. Windsor: NFER-Nelson.

WRAGG, T. (1988) *Education in the Market Place: The Ideology Behind the 1988 Education Bill*. London: National Union of Teachers.

INDEX